Finally, here it is! Garry Poole has captured everything you need to know to implement one of the most powerful and effective tools in evangelism. *Seeker Small Groups* describes a ground-breaking, step-by-step approach anyone can use. And it couldn't come at a better time—this ingenious strategy is perfect for reaching today's seekers. I encourage Christians everywhere to study these principles—and then put them into action!

**Lee Strobel,** *The Case for Christ* and *The Case for Faith*

For more than ten years we have seen Garry use his gifts, experience, and passion to pioneer and refine an approach that has revolutionized the way we do evangelism through small groups. I'm convinced that this simple, biblical strategy of building small groups for spiritual seekers is one of the greatest evangelistic discoveries at Willow Creek in the last decade—and this book, *Seeker Small Groups,* is the blueprint for that revolution.

**Bill Hybels,** Senior Pastor, Willow Creek Community Church

When it comes to seeker small groups, Garry Poole has a level of passion and a breadth of experience that I think are simply unequaled. You will be so inspired by what you read on these pages, that people in your life who right now do not know Jesus Christ will one day become his followers, his servants, and his friends.

**John Ortberg,** *The Life You've Always Wanted*

One of the most effective means for reaching out to spiritual seekers is through small groups where there is love, trust, safety, sincerity, and acceptance. *Seeker Small Groups* is an outstanding blueprint on how to build bridges to others so that they can experience God's bridge to them. This is a must read for serious-minded Christians.

**Luis Palau,** International Evangelist

Garry Poole's compassion for souls is contagious. He presents with great enthusiasm a simple and effective way to share the beautiful truth of Jesus Christ with neighbors, colleagues, and friends.

**Chuck Colson,** Founder and President, Prison Fellowship

In this excellent new book, Garry Poole passes on the practical wisdom he has gained from more than twenty-five years of experience leading small groups in an evangelistic setting. I learned a great deal from *Seeker Small Groups* and recommend it to others interested in this exciting ministry.

**Nicky Gumbel,** Founder and Director, The Alpha Course

Garry Poole hits the mark! In *Seeker Small Groups,* Garry has shaped a groundbreaking evangelism resource that is exceptionally practical, brilliant in thought, and written with phenomenal clarity and passion. This powerful book will open your eyes to your potential as a "living apologetic."

**Josh D. McDowell,** *Evidence That Demands a Verdict* and *More Than a Carpenter*

*Seeker Small Groups* is timely and urgent! Garry Poole presents a paradigm shift that moves us beyond the traditional view of reserving small groups exclusively for Christians to an incredible context in which to introduce seekers to the Redeemer. Here's an effective action plan for reaching seekers through small groups—a forum that inspires a natural, fresh, and authentic faith—which reminds me of how Jesus engaged spiritual seekers.

**Dr. Henry Cloud,** *Boundaries* and *Changes That Heal*

*Seeker Small Groups* is a huge step toward the church becoming the safest place on earth for people to ask the most important question they'll ever ask.

**Larry Crabb,** Ph.D., *Connecting* and *Inside Out*

As I read *Seeker Small Groups,* the word "masterpiece" kept coming to mind. Garry weaves inspiring, real-life stories with practical guidelines born of experience—all infused with his sincere enthusiasm and passion. He avoids formulas and manipulation, and promotes genuine relationships on every page. Thousands of seekers will be impacted because people like you read this book and put it into practice.

**Brian McLaren,** *More Ready Than You Realize*

Garry Poole has synthesized his rich experience in creating small groups that are winsome and free of the typical obstacles that prevent seekers from participating. In these effective outreach groups, the emotional, intellectual, and volitional barriers are overcome through relational integrity, reasoned answers, and reliance upon the work of the Holy Spirit.

**Kenneth Boa,** *Faith Has Its Reasons* and *I'm Glad You Asked*

*Seeker Small Groups,* written out of a wealth of wisdom and insight, will launch readers into the most significant venture of their lives.

**Jim Petersen,** *Living Proof*

This is one of those rare books that is certain to become a standard text for years. Garry's writing is engaging, readable, interspersed with captivating stories, and consistently practical. Reading *Seeker Small Groups* is like walking alongside and being coached by a seasoned pro.

**Gary R. Collins,** The Bridge Institute

If you are really serious about seeing the lost become the saved, read this book. You will discover one of the most dynamic tools in evangelism today.

**Dr. Thom Rainer,** Dean, Billy Graham School of Missions, Evangelism, and Church Growth

If you want to get on the boat with what God is doing, jump on board with this powerful concept.

**Steve Sjogren,** *Conspiracy of Kindness*

Garry has woven together a passion for seekers, experiences inspired by the Holy Spirit, and strategic thinking to present an outstanding blueprint for reaching people through small groups.

**Cliffe Knechtle,** *Give Me a Reason* and *Help Me Believe*

*Seeker Small Groups* is a winner—I can't imagine someone writing a better book. It's all here.

**Scot McKnight,** Karl A. Olsson Professor in Religious Studies, North Park University

God is using Garry Poole to open a window of unlimited evangelistic opportunity for every Christian—and every church—who takes *Seeker Small Groups* seriously.

**Mark Mittelberg,** *Building a Contagious Church* and *Becoming a Contagious Christian*

There is no better way to serve seekers today in their spiritual journey than through seeker small groups, and Garry's book is an invaluable resource for learning how to launch and lead them.

**Rick Richardson,** Associate Director of Evangelism, InterVarsity Christian Fellowship/USA

Christians everywhere—including those involved in the Lighthouse Movement—who read and apply *Seeker Small Groups* will be wonderfully inspired and equipped to impact seekers for Christ.

**Paul Cedar,** Chairman, Mission America Coalition

Garry Poole had me from his first line — expressing a passionate commitment to reach those without Christ. Two of the most important dynamics in a prevailing church are community and evangelism. This book brings the two together.

**Erwin McManus,** *Seizing Your Divine Moment*

# SEEKER SMALL GROUPS

## Engaging Spiritual Seekers in Life-Changing Discussions

## GARRY POOLE

*forewords by* **Bill Hybels & John Ortberg**

**ZONDERVAN®**

GRAND RAPIDS, MICHIGAN 49530 USA

**WILLOW**
Willow Creek Resources

ZONDERVAN.COM/
AUTHORTRACKER

We want to hear from you. Please send your comments about this book to us in care of zreview@zondervan.com. Thank you.

# ZONDERVAN®

*Seeker Small Groups*
Copyright © 2003 by Willow Creek Association

Requests for information should be addressed to:
Zondervan, *Grand Rapids, Michigan 49530*

**Library of Congress Cataloging-in-Publication Data**

Poole, Garry.
    Seeker small groups : engaging spiritual seekers in life-changing discussions / Garry Poole ; forewords by Bill Hybels and John Ortberg.—1st ed.
      p. cm.
     ISBN-10: 0-310-24233-9
     ISBN-13: 978-0-310-24233-8
     1. Evangelistic work.   2. Non-church-affiliated people.   3. Small groups—Religious aspects—Christianity.   I. Title.
    BV3793.P575 2003
    269'.2—dc21

                                          2003008407

*Interior design by Tracey Moran*

*Printed in the United States of America*

06 07 08 09 10 • 10 9 8 7 6

To the greatest seeker small group leaders
anyone could ever hope to have
*David and Barbara Poole*
who instilled in their son a lifetime
of wisdom and passion for evangelism

# Contents

*Foreword by Bill Hybels*. . . . . . . . . . . . . . . . . . . . . . . . . . . . . . . 9

*Foreword by John Ortberg*. . . . . . . . . . . . . . . . . . . . . . . . . . . . . 11

*Introduction*. . . . . . . . . . . . . . . . . . . . . . . . . . . . . . . . . . . . . . . . 13

### Part 1

## LAUNCHING SEEKER SMALL GROUPS

1. Catch the Vision . . . . . . . . . . . . . . . . . . . . . . . . . . . . . . . . 25

2. Build Strong Bridges. . . . . . . . . . . . . . . . . . . . . . . . . . . . 54

### Part 2

## ATTRACTING SEEKERS TO SMALL GROUPS

3. Extend Irresistible Invitations . . . . . . . . . . . . . . . . . . . . 79

4. Conduct the All-Important First Meeting . . . . . . . . . . . 98

Part 3

# LEADING SEEKER SMALL GROUP DISCUSSIONS

5. Ask Great Questions . . . . . . . . . . . . . . . . . . . . . . . . . . . 119

6. Listen Well . . . . . . . . . . . . . . . . . . . . . . . . . . . . . . . . . . . 143

7. Facilitate Captivating Interactions . . . . . . . . . . . . . . . . 168

Part 4

# REACHING SEEKERS THROUGH SMALL GROUPS

8. Maximize the Impact . . . . . . . . . . . . . . . . . . . . . . . . . . 203

9. Cultivate Contagious Small Groups . . . . . . . . . . . . . . . 228

10. Seize the Adventure . . . . . . . . . . . . . . . . . . . . . . . . . . . 248

Epilogue . . . . . . . . . . . . . . . . . . . . . . . . . . . . . . . . . . . . . . . . 278

Appendixes A–I . . . . . . . . . . . . . . . . . . . . . . . . . . . . . . . . . . 291

Notes . . . . . . . . . . . . . . . . . . . . . . . . . . . . . . . . . . . . . . . . . . 312

Recommended Resources . . . . . . . . . . . . . . . . . . . . . . . . . . 315

Acknowledgments . . . . . . . . . . . . . . . . . . . . . . . . . . . . . . . . 317

# Foreword by Bill Hybels

✦

Throughout the history of Willow Creek, I've never gotten over the breath-taking reality that God calls ordinary Christians like you and me to be his divine agents of reconciliation. It's amazing to me that the Holy Spirit can use our words and actions to influence the spiritual trajectory of others and, ultimately, their eternal destiny. I've become convinced that the greatest gift we can give another human being is an introduction to the One who can redeem them.

Willow Creek has long been associated with creative strategies to evangelize. However, I have been especially gratified to watch one approach — and the leader who set it in motion — thrive beyond our wildest dreams. I'm talking about seeker small groups under the gifted leadership of our evangelism director, Garry Poole.

As a rule, we don't launch ministries around here until God raises up the leadership. So for many years, when it came to the concept of reaching seekers in small group settings, we had no strategy and no point person to envision and train leaders to experiment with this cutting-edge idea. But when Garry came on the scene, it quickly became clear to me that he was God's man to crack the code for advancing seeker small groups here at Willow Creek. His heart for people far from God, in addition to his passion for relational evangelism, made him a natural leader in this arena.

For more than ten years we have seen Garry use his gifts, experience, and passion to pioneer and refine an approach that has revolutionized the way we do evangelism through small groups. Garry, who embodies the values of seeker small groups more than anyone I know, has managed to equip and empower hundreds of our leaders to launch this new species of small groups that currently enfold over a thousand people. And it's in these seeker groups that the most radical sort of life change takes place: *People give their lives to Christ.*

I observed this firsthand as I began to build friendships with a colorful group of non-Christian guys who would become my sailboat racing crew. As our relationships deepened, conversations often drifted from the superficial to the personal and spiritual. I soon began to see how a few friends who trust and care about each other could open up and interact naturally about the spiritual side of their lives. In short, we were experiencing a seeker small group before any of us even knew what to call it!

I'll sum it up this way: The seeker small group strategy is one of the greatest evangelistic discoveries at Willow Creek in the last decade — and this book is the blueprint for that revolution. And here's the "main thing": *Everyday, ordinary Christians can lead these groups.* You — yes, you — can lead a high-impact seeker small group that God will use to reach people who have lost their way.

I am convinced that this simple, biblical strategy of building small groups for spiritual seekers is one of the most innovative and powerful concepts to mobilize all types of churches to reach their communities for Christ. And this book, *Seeker Small Groups,* will inspire and equip you and your church to take part in this evangelistic adventure. Read it carefully. Roll up your sleeves. Learn from Garry. Go over it with your teams. Apply its principles rigorously. Pray fervently. Take some relational risks and get a small group of seeking friends together ... then watch what God does through you — with eternal returns!

*Bill Hybels*
*Senior Pastor*
*Willow Creek Community Church*

# Foreword by John Ortberg

I met Garry Poole back in our college days, and our first conversation involved his passionate concern for the spiritual destiny of a mutual friend. I have worked alongside Garry now for the past eight-and-a-half years, and the time that has elapsed between that initial conversation and today has only deepened Garry's passion as he's gained skill and focus.

This landmark book is the product of years of thought and learning harvested from the experiences of seekers and leaders in hundreds of seeker small groups. I too have been one of the many seeker group leaders who serve in the area that Garry oversees, and I know firsthand the joys and challenges of that adventure. There is the excitement of knowing what's at stake; the sense of inadequacy at not being able to give the right answer (somehow explaining the idea of the Trinity to a questioning seeker is much more challenging than explaining it on a test in a seminary class); and there is the amazing joy when a seeker becomes a follower of Christ.

When I was growing up, my parents would often invite friends and neighbors over to our home for a kind of Bible study on Sunday nights. They didn't have a name for it back in those days, but those were seeker small groups. I got to watch them up close. But with very limited resources and insufficient coaching, there was not much help available for what they were trying to do.

*Now there is.*

Anyone who has ever led such a group knows how valuable resources and coaching can be. It requires enormous amounts of discernment to recognize, for example, whether a person's primary obstacle to faith lies in the intellectual challenges they're raising or in some much more personal or emotional issue. Learning how to listen well, how to know which questions to pose when, how to handle rabbit-trail followers — these take the wisdom of Solomon.

That's why I'm so grateful for what Garry has done in this book. When it comes to seeker small groups, Garry has a level of passion and a breadth of experience that I think are simply unequaled. His words contain a great deal of wisdom. But they are not just theory. They have been distilled from thousands of interactions around thousands of circles. *This stuff really works.*

This book will enhance your evangelistic efforts. It will stretch your vision and make leading a seeker small group a more joy-filled experience. But most of all, you will be so inspired by what you read on these pages, that people in your life who right now do not know Jesus Christ will one day become his followers, his servants, and his friends.

*John Ortberg*
*Teaching Pastor*
*Willow Creek Community Church*

# Introduction

*⁂*

*Lord, make me a crisis man. Let me not be a mile-post on a single road, but make me a fork that men must turn one way or another in facing Christ in me.*

JIM ELLIOT


*He has committed to us the message of reconcil-iation. We are therefore Christ's ambassadors, as though God were making his appeal through us. We implore you on Christ's behalf: Be reconciled to God. God made him who had no sin to be sin for us, so that in him we might become the righteousness of God.*

2 CORINTHIANS 5:19–21


Ever since I can remember, I've been passionate about reaching out to spiritual seekers. Raised in a Christian home, I discovered early on that lost people really matter, and I soon recognized the significance of inviting people into a meaningful relationship with God through Christ. I became convinced that nothing quite compares with cheering seekers on as they take steps in their spiritual journey.

As a kid, I fondly remember sitting with my dad to watch the Billy Graham telecasts. We'd listen intently as Billy preached about the incredible responsibility and privilege we all have as Christians to reach out to others with the gospel, inspiring me by his own example as well as with his powerful sermons. I distinctly remember the one about Jim Elliot, the great missionary, and his wife, Elizabeth Elliot, who became an outstanding author and speaker. Billy Graham's words rang with passion: "Jim Elliot, martyred at twenty-three by the Auca Indians in the jungles of South America, wrote this prayer at the age of twenty-one: 'Lord, make me a crisis man. Let me not be a milepost on a single road, but make me a fork that men must turn one way or another in facing Christ in me.'

13

A crisis man—isn't that a tremendous thought—that when a person meets you, they are faced with making a decision one way or the other concerning Christ in you? Jim Elliott was such a man!"

*Lord, make me a crisis man.* When I heard those words, I knew I too wanted to grow up to be such a man. I wanted to be a crisis man for Jesus Christ.

And so I have spent my whole life on the lookout to develop and implement the best ways to convey the compelling message of the gospel of Jesus Christ. Along the way, however, I've come to discover one of the greatest challenges within the evangelism process: to find and strike that important balance between presenting the truths of the Bible with boldness and clarity while, at the same time, keeping my treasured friendships with seekers safely intact. My hope and dream has always been to spiritually impact people in my sphere of influence in ways that communicate my genuine care and concern for those friends no matter how they respond. And still to this day, my aim is to initiate conversations about spiritual matters in such a way that my relationships flourish and thrive, not falter.

With this passion for evangelism burning white-hot in my heart, I left home for Wheaton College, a well-known Christian school just west of Chicago. Almost immediately I was invited to participate in a small group Bible study sponsored by the Navigators. At first I was hesitant to join. I had never been in a small group before, I wasn't quite sure what to expect, and frankly the whole concept sounded a little odd. But the leader of the group, Larry Jones, seemed like a decent, normal guy and he persisted. "Garry, you need to be a part of our group. It's a way to get some input for spiritual growth, and besides, it'll be a good time. And you're not going to want to miss out!" So I took him up on his challenge and, every week for nine months, joined nine other guys for intense spiritual discussions. During that year we systematically worked through the Navigators' *Design for Discipleship* curriculum. We studied the Bible in depth and memorized scores of verses. We prayed together, took our spiritual growth very seriously, and at the same time developed some significant friendships.

To my surprise, that small group experience made an enormous impact on my life. I was sold. I became absolutely convinced of the power of a small group to change lives — for one had greatly changed mine.

Later that year I enrolled in the small group leader's training course offered by the Navigators, thinking that one day I would lead a small group and make a spiritual impact on a few people — just as Larry Jones had done with me. I attended every training session available to learn all I could about the fundamentals for leading a small group.

Due to a variety of circumstances, the next fall I transferred to Indiana University in Bloomington, Indiana. Imagine the culture shock of leaving a small college of two thousand Christians to attend a huge secular university of over thirty-three thousand students! Most of my new collegiate friends didn't demonstrate much interest in spiritual things, so for the first time in my life I was faced with the need to explain and defend my faith. I was constantly challenged to provide good, solid reasons for why I believed the way I did. As a result, those years at Indiana University afforded me plenty of opportunities to develop and pursue my primary passion for evangelism. But that was only the beginning of this unexpected adventure.

With my newly instilled interest to start up and lead a small group for Christians, I began exploring my options. I sought out the Navigators first, but when I offered my services as a freshly trained small group leader, the staff member didn't seem too impressed. Because I was unknown, he wisely suggested that I become a member of a group first and then explore leading one the following year. "I understand. No problem," I responded while exiting. "I'll see you around." I took off to check out another Christian organization, Campus Crusade for Christ, only to experience the very same thing. They didn't know me well enough to let me lead a group — and I didn't blame them either. "Okay, fine," I replied and left to check out a third Christian campus group, InterVarsity Christian Fellowship.

At the gathering that Friday night, I asked InterVarsity staff member Jerry Frederick if he could use another small group leader. "Absolutely," he said optimistically. "That would be great." (Jerry later told me that he was only willing to take that risk because he planned to keep a sharp eye on me! He became a close friend and mentor during my college years.)

"Perfect!" I said. "Where do I start?"

"Well, there is a slight catch," Jerry explained. "We're a fairly small fellowship here and most everyone is already connected into a group. So if you'd like to lead a small group, you can. You'll just be on your own to find people to attend."

Then he added the words that proved to be pivotal: "Now, don't let this minor hurdle stop you. Who knows what God might do through you? Just give it your best shot."

With those words ringing in my ears, I prayed all the way back to my apartment. With resolve — mixed with a certain amount of trepidation — I pulled out poster board and markers and created four signs: "Anyone interested in joining a small group Bible study? Call Garry at 555–9869 immediately." I posted them next to the elevators in Willkie Dorm and Read Dorm and went home to wait for the phone to ring. To my amazement, twelve people called within one week, and to my further astonishment, nine of them showed up for our first meeting!

I remember that first gathering well. We met on a Sunday night in the Landis Wing second-floor lounge of Read Dorm, and I arrived early to arrange the chairs and go over my carefully prepared lesson plan. I was filled with anticipation as I wondered who, if anyone, would actually show up. But to my relief, one by one they trickled in, until nine in all were sitting in the circle. We started things out that night by sharing some basic information about ourselves — including our religious backgrounds. As one after another described themselves and their spiritual experiences, I started getting a sinking feeling. I soon realized that these people lacked an important feature — they were not even Christians. They were not looking for a group within which to grow their Christian faith. Rather they were college students unconvinced of the credibility of Christianity and full of all kinds of doubts and unanswered questions.

One girl admitted not having any religious background at all. The next person talked about not ever having gone to church. A guy said his family used to attend church services but that it was a thing of the past. Then another person said he had a Jewish background and had always wanted to learn about the Bible. Each person indicated that he or she was open and curious but not really sure what to believe. Here I was, all prepared to lead an in-depth Bible study for the already convinced, but these students were far from persuaded! I was expecting to gather a group of Christians to shepherd and disciple in following Christ, but instead found myself smack-dab in the middle of a small group filled with spiritual seekers.

I had to shift gears — and fast. I slid my lesson plan aside and looked at my watch; only fifteen minutes had gone by. I needed a Plan B — now. Off the top of my head I asked a couple more ice-breaker questions. And then it happened. Somehow we landed on a great question, to which everyone really opened up: "If you could ask God one question you knew he would answer right away, what would it be?"

The response was simply incredible. Their questions were authentic, deep, and enlightening.

"I'd ask God if he in fact really exists."
"Why doesn't God just show up at a football stadium filled to capacity and make himself known once and for all? Wouldn't that make things a whole lot simpler for us?"
"If God does exist, I'd ask him why he allows so much evil and suffering in the world."
"Why are there so many different religions?"
"Don't all religions teach basically the same thing anyway?"
"How do I know for sure I'm going to wind up in heaven when I die?"

On and on came the questions for God. But we didn't just stop there. We took things to the next level when I asked each person *why* they chose their particular question. What prompted the responses they gave? What were their motivations? Their answers were surprisingly honest and profound, and this follow-up question drew out the group members even more. I discovered that they loved talking about the emotions behind their intellectual questions.

I didn't spend any time that night trying to answer their questions — partly because I didn't really know the answers! But somehow I did have enough sense to know that at this point in the discourse, they didn't need quick, two-cent answers from me — they simply needed to be heard and understood. So instead I asked more questions that were relevant and specific — and learned all I could about what was going on behind their responses.

When I asked Bob what prompted him to ask why God allows suffering in the world, he shared somberly, "I have an aunt dying of cancer, and I think it's unfair that God would allow such a terrible thing to happen to someone like her. She's a good person. If he really loved her and really cared about me and my family, then how could he allow this kind of suffering to happen?" I invited Bob to share more about how this made him feel toward God and how we as a group could come alongside him during this difficult time. Admitting that we too had some of those same questions for God, the rest of us empathized with him, sharing words of encouragement and support.

As the others continued to convey the reasons behind their intellectual questions, the group seemed to turn a corner. We began to build some bridges of trust as we extended ourselves and became genuinely open and vulnerable with each other. I also think each person felt respected by me as the leader, in spite of the spiritual differences we discovered. Significant connections were established as we sincerely listened and demonstrated that we truly cared about each other. Somehow, in a very short amount of time, this small circle became a very safe place. Not only did we feel the freedom to voice our theological issues and questions, but the group also became a place to begin to share our very lives. Amazing.

As that first meeting came to a close, I asked everyone if they had any interest in meeting again. I suggested that each week we could meet to discuss a different question they had for God. Almost in one voice the group insisted we do exactly that. So we met week in and week out for the rest of that school year, discussing their particular questions and looking at what the Bible had to say about those issues.

Over the course of that year, I saw six people from that small group cross the line of faith and put their trust in Jesus Christ. Their lives were completely changed — and what a thrill that was to watch!

One of those group members was Dave Kiningham. Before he attended that first meeting, he was walking away from God. But when he came across a simple hand-printed poster announcing the formation of a small group, he decided to find out the details. He took the risky step and came to the first meeting, which sparked an increasing curiosity about the Bible and spiritual things. This eventually lead to the biggest decision of his life, when he received God's forgiveness and committed himself to following Jesus Christ. To this day he's walking in that newfound direction, following after God with everything in him.

Turns out that small group changed everything for Dave. Where might Dave have wound up without that little group, I wonder. What would the others have done were it not for that safe place for seekers to explore spiritual things?

As I look back now, I realize that this single small group became for me a fusion of two growing passions — small groups and evangelism. The experience of leading my new friends to Christ through this small group merged these two important concepts in a very cool way. I didn't know what to call it at the time, but that gathering was actually a *seeker small group!* And I got to watch God use that little group to powerfully impact the lives of those seekers connected to it. That seeker small group marked my own life as well, and I have never been the same — I have been leading seeker small groups ever since.

This book is the culmination of more than twenty-five years of discovering and developing principles behind effectively leading seeker small groups. The guidelines and ideas you will find on these pages will provide the tools and principles you will need to lead your very own seeker small group within your own setting — and in so doing, point people to Christ. Here you will acquire the nuts and bolts for launching seeker small groups, as well as the vision and values that drives them. My prayer is that you will read this book with your eyes and your heart, all the while looking and hoping for ways in which you might launch a seeker small group to reach those in your world who are spiritually searching.

# DAVE KININGHAM'S STORY

### Student Counselor
### Fort Wayne, Indiana

*I couldn't wait to get the summer behind me. All I could think about was leaving my hometown of Tell City, Indiana, for the freedom and excitement I'd find at Indiana University. To my surprise, though, the thrill of being on campus wore off quickly. After two or three weeks, I was just another lonely, homesick college freshman.*

*I was definitely in search mode when I spotted a hand-printed sign tacked up on a wall in my dormitory: "Bible study. Call Garry at 555–9869. Call immediately."*

*Each time I walked past that poster in Willkie Dorm I had a different thought running through my head. "Maybe this would be a good way for me to make connections. But who would ever go to such a thing? I've never really studied the Bible before; I should check this thing out — but I don't want to get too fanatical about it! Well, at the very least it would please my mother!" My eye caught the word "immediately" again, and I could not shake it out of my head. I decided I'd better call right away before I missed out on a chance of a lifetime.*

*Making that phone call did wind up becoming a turning point in my life. Garry invited me to come and check out the group just one time. If I didn't like what I experienced, he promised there would be no pressure to ever come back. I took him up on his offer, arranging to meet the very next Sunday night with Garry and a few other students for an hour-long group discussion. I was a trusting kid from a small town, and in retrospect I realize how fortunate I was that this wasn't a cult or something weird. I still would have shown up — though I think I would have recognized I was in the wrong place.*

*As it turned out, I was in exactly the right place. There were eight or nine of us at that first meeting, and we spent our time getting to know each other and discussing our reasons for responding to Garry's sign. I was quite comfortable because from the beginning Garry came across as a very genuine, caring person. Besides, I'd been in church all my life, so I considered myself one of the few Christians in the group.*

*I was right about the people — they became some of my closest friends. But I was wrong about my spiritual condition. I realized that I truly didn't have a connection with God the way the Bible describes it and that without him in my life, I was headed down a dead-end road. I had plenty of religion in my life, but a real relationship with God was missing. The spiritual discoveries I made during our on-going discussions brought about a lifetime impact and difference. I remember how Garry would read Scripture to us about how our sin had created a separation from God and how we needed Christ to bridge that gap. I had never considered that before and I struggled long and hard with the concept. Then one night — walking back to my dorm room — I made the decision. I went up to my room and prayed a prayer to invite Christ into my life.*

*Garry encouraged me to write the date down as a symbolic way to seal the deal. The members of our group celebrated my decision, and later Garry confided that I was the first person, in the context of a small group, whom he had helped to cross the line of faith. When I married Mary, a fellow Christian student, I expressed my appreciation by asking Garry to be my best man. I will be forever grateful that he was willing to launch a small group for someone like me.*

*Now, more than twenty-five years later, I'm back on a college campus, working as a Christian counselor with students at Huntington College. And as I meet with various students every day, I can't help but remember my own college days when I was lacking direction, purpose, and meaning in my life. But that group became the ideal safe place for me to take an honest look into spiritual matters and start to make sense out of things. For the first time, I felt free to open up about my questions and uncertainties. The discussions were intense and informative, but enjoyable because there was never any pressure or criticism. And that's exactly what I needed.*

*I imagine that taking a chance on starting a small group for the spiritually unconvinced is a big risk. But I'm so glad someone was willing to get out there and make the effort on my campus, because God did some amazing things in and through that small group — and the impact will last for all eternity.*

Part 1

# LAUNCHING
# SEEKER
# SMALL
# GROUPS

The impact seeker small groups can make in the lives of people far
from God is unmistakable — not only for college students but for
*anyone* of *any* age. Locally — here at Willow Creek Community
Church — we've seen hundreds of seekers find new life in Christ as a
result of their small group experiences. On a national level we're seeing a seeker small group movement take root in all kinds of churches
across a wide spectrum of styles and approaches. And more recently
we're starting to see this concept blow fresh wind into the evangelistic
sails of churches internationally.

Remarkably, we've discovered that these groups can be led effectively by Christians with or without the gift of evangelism, with or
without formal apologetics training, and with or without much small
group experience. It's not surprising that this model for outreach is
quickly being recognized as a highly transferable tool in a variety of
settings and scenarios.

It's important to realize, however, that some key principles need to
be fully grasped and implemented right from the start. From the outside it may appear that these groups happen effortlessly — requiring
little preparation or forethought. But without the solid launching pad
of a few core ideas, your group just won't get off the ground.

Chapters 1 and 2 outline in detail some very important concepts for leading seeker small groups. Chapter 1, Catch the Vision, examines the vision and values behind seeker groups and sets up a platform from which the rest of the book should be viewed. Chapter 2, Build Strong Bridges, explores the real reason why seekers even consider attending a seeker small group in the first place. Master these two chapters and watch what God will do through you.

# Chapter 1

# Catch the Vision

<sub>✦</sub>

*I will search for the lost and bring back the strays.*

Ezekiel 34:16

*You've never looked into the eyes of another human being who doesn't matter to God.*

Bill Hybels

I locked eyes with the guy walking toward me on the third floor of Indiana University's Read Dorm, reached out my hand, and greeted him cordially. The instant he introduced himself, I recognized his name. "No way. You're not *the* Steve, the one who wrote all those letters last year, are you?"

"Yep, that would be me — I'm *the* Steve."

"Really? Wow! It's awesome to finally meet you."

Steve Parker had spent the previous year as a foreign exchange student in Spain. Almost every month he had written long letters back to his friends in the dorm, graphically describing all his wild escapades. He spared no details. The arrival of his legendary letters turned into a little ritual; the guys would gather around and read every word out loud, then march out into the hallway to post them on the bulletin board for everyone else to enjoy. They'd shout, "Hey, everybody, look at what Steve's up to now!" His stories always made for a great laugh.

So, from a distance, I felt I had already gotten to know this guy named Steve. From his monthly updates I knew how wild and crazy he was and how easily he could turn any situation into a good time. He was quite the popular guy, and everybody eagerly anticipated his return.

This year Steve and I were living on the same dorm floor, enabling me to finally meet him in person. The guy I had read so much about was now standing right before me — and I was looking dead center into the eyes of someone who mattered deeply to God.

"Steve, do you have any idea what a hit your letters were last year? You certainly had a blast in Spain. You've got quite a reputation around here — everyone thinks you're some kind of a hero!" Then, to my surprise, I took a risk and heard myself say, "Steve, this might seem a little off the wall, but I'm starting up a Bible discussion group with some of the guys here on the floor. We're going to talk about what we think about God and Christianity and stuff like that, and I'd like you to come. What do you think? Would you be willing to check it out?"

"Did you not pay any attention to my letters?" Steve taunted. "I'm not interested in the Bible. I'm not interested in God. I'm not interested in Christianity. And I'm *definitely* not interested in your Bible study. Are you crazy?"

I half laughed and agreed that maybe it was a wild idea. But I wanted to leave the door open, so I assured him that the invitation was always there if he ever changed his mind. Secretly I prayed that maybe, just maybe, he would somehow give it a shot. "Forget about it; I won't be there," Steve assured me. His good-natured, though pointed, response didn't discourage me. In fact, I was determined to build a solid friendship with him anyway, just as I intended to do with some of the guys who had accepted my invitation.

The year before, I hadn't intentionally planned my first seeker small group experience — it just came together by accident. Nevertheless, God used it in the lives of some of the seekers there. This time, however, I purposefully set out to lead a small group of non-Christians. I didn't want this year's group to come together by chance; I wanted to make good and sure it happened.

So during the first week of the semester, I introduced myself to the guys on the floor and let them know I was going to start up a weekly Bible study to talk about spiritual things. I invited almost everyone I met, and most of them said, "No thanks; I'm not interested."

I dared them, anyway, to come just one time to check it out and see what they thought. Several expressed interest and said they'd drop in to give it a try, but only five or six guys actually showed up for the first meeting. To my surprise, though, more and more of them showed up in the coming weeks. And the group proved to be very popular, because we not only openly discussed questions and objections everyone had about Christianity and the Bible, but in the process we began to develop some deep and meaningful friendships.

Even though Steve didn't show any initial interest in joining us, he and I continued to hang out together and our friendship grew. And then he totally caught me off guard one day by announcing that he planned to check out the Bible study group after all. "You know, for the past month I've been hearing all about your group and everyone says it's a good time," he said. "So I'm going to come to your next meeting and experience it for myself."

I was thrilled, but I couldn't pass up the chance to use a little reverse psychology — and to give him a hard time. "No way, Steve," I said. "It's too late. You can't come to our group. You've been banned."

"No, really, I'm going to be there. The guys say it's fascinating because you're open to getting different points of view. So I'm bringing my perspective on things."

"Is that right? Okay, Steve, try and join us if you're that curious. Maybe, if you're lucky, we'll let you in."

The very next week he was there! Steve's energy infused new life into our group's discussion. He didn't hold anything back. He didn't hesitate for one minute in asking tough questions, voicing his opinions, or sharing his past experiences. He also added fuel to the fire by raising issues and questions that some of the others either hadn't thought of yet or didn't know exactly how to express. So when Steve expressed some opposing viewpoints, they'd say, "Yeah, that's a good one; what about that?" Sparks flew with Steve in the group, and I was glad to have him there.

It really didn't surprise me when Steve returned the next week for round two. But when he came back the following week and the one after that, I was astounded. Although he was there to contribute his perspective, he began to learn a few spiritual truths along the way. Eventually he bought himself a Bible and began reading it for the first time in his life!

I have lingering memories of Steve's growing spiritual hunger and his quest to satisfy it. He was fervently trying to figure out what the Bible was all about and what it could mean to know God in a deeper way. There's one particular image I have in my mind of Steve banging on my dorm room door at around midnight. Flicking the light on and off with one hand and holding his open Bible with the other, he barged in, yelling, "Hey, Garry, wake up, wake up. Look, I've been reading in the book of Genesis. These genealogies don't really add up right and it doesn't seem to make sense. How do you explain this?"

Half asleep, I muttered something like, "Steve, nothing adds up after midnight. Just go to bed and forget about it. Ask me again in the morning." (I had developed similar stalling techniques for occasions such as this. It got him out of my way just long enough so I could run over and flip through the commentaries in search of answers to his questions!) Steve was always raising spiritual questions, many of which I could not answer. That kept *both* of us in search mode. He continued reading the Bible and seeking the truth with intensity, and it was simply amazing to watch.

Steve expressed a concern that even though he had gone to church occasionally while growing up, he hadn't heard much of anything the Bible actually teaches. "I don't ever remember learning what it means to be a Christian," he admitted. "So," he formally announced one day, "I scheduled an appointment to meet with the minister of my former church, because I've got some hard questions for him." Then, elbowing me, he added, "But I promised him you would be there too!"

I wondered what in the world I was getting myself into as I went with Steve to meet with his former minister. Then I watched in awe as Steve quoted John 14:6. "Jesus said, 'I am the way, the truth, and the life. No one comes to the Father but by me.' Now please explain this verse to me," Steve pleaded. "Is Jesus the only way to get to God or not?" Steve challenged that minister with many difficult questions from the Bible that day. It was one of the most remarkable encounters I've ever witnessed — a non-Christian confronting a religious leader about not taking the Bible's claims seriously enough.

Then, a few months later, it happened. Another knock came on my dorm room door. And I will always remember this one. Steve walked in with a big announcement. "Garry, I've been reading the Bible now for some time. I've studied it and I've asked a lot of questions and I've even prayed. But I think it's finally time. I want to invite Jesus Christ into my life. I'd like to receive his forgiveness and I'd like to follow him as best I can."

"You're kidding. I can't believe it!" I replied. He then asked if I would pray with him to make that commitment. So right there in that dorm room we prayed together, and he invited Jesus Christ to be the forgiver and the leader of his life.

Have you ever had that kind of thing happen to you? I'll never forget that moment. It was the first time I ever had the chance to pray with someone to receive Christ — and it marked me forever. I'll never forget hearing Steve pray in his own way and in his own words, admitting that he was a sinner in need of a Savior and inviting Jesus into his life. It was a privilege to witness the transformation process right before my eyes. It was in that moment that I became sold on the concept of providing a small group safe enough for non-Christians to come and bring their objections, questions, and obstacles in order to discuss spiritual things on a regular basis.

From that moment on, the trajectory of Steve's life totally changed. He was the classic example of someone who was running away from God. But then he found a place safe enough to ask his questions and begin his investigation of Christianity. And now he had turned around and was running *toward* God, chasing after him with all his might and all his heart, trying to honor him in his life.

It blew me away how quickly Steve grew spiritually after that. He became even more intense about reading and studying the Bible. He joined a discipleship Bible study and started memorizing literally hundreds of verses.

On an early Saturday morning Steve was at my door again — it seemed he was always banging on that dorm room door. He shouted, "Garry, get up, get up, get up, we're late."

"What in the world are we late for?"

"There's an evangelism training course starting right about now in the student union building, and we shouldn't miss it! It's a class about how to effectively share your faith, and you need to be there — you need the help! So let's go; we're late."

The next thing I knew, we were running across campus to this evangelism class. I have this image seared in my mind: We're trying to get to the student union building on time and Steve's four or five paces ahead of me. I'm doing my best to keep up with him, but he's outrunning me. And I'm thinking to myself, *This guy is on fire! He's the one leading now — he's out ahead of me!* What an example and thrill to watch. It was awe-inspiring to observe Steve's growth up close like that.

I went on to graduate from Indiana and worked as a computer analyst for Andersen Consulting in Chicago, while Steve stayed at I.U. to get his master's degree in linguistics. A year or so later I received a phone call from him while I was in my office. "I need you to pray for me because I'm at a crossroads," he said. "I'm trying to figure out exactly what I'm going to do with my linguistics degree. I'm thinking about going with Wycliffe Bible Translators, but I have to decide between a short-term commitment and a lifetime commitment. It's one or the other, and I have to choose."

Six months later Steve called me with his decision. "I've made my commitment. I'm signed up with Wycliffe. It's what I want to do more than anything else. And that's not all. I decided to devote my whole life to serving Christ as a missionary with Wycliffe, translating the Bible into languages that aren't even written yet." Steve told me his initial assignment would take him into the jungles of Peru, South America.

In fact, Steve is still with Wycliffe, and to this day I receive monthly updates from him. Now, of course, these missionary reports are quite a bit different from the letters I used to read when I first heard about Steve. I can actually *print* these letters! Here's an excerpt from one of them.

> Back in Peru. By God's grace I returned to Peru safely on August 31. After spending a few days in Lima to visit friends and renew my passport and visa, I flew out to the jungle where I have once again gotten back into my work, carrying out linguistic research and analysis and publishing studies of many different Peruvian languages.

He continues in his form letter with a complete update on his efforts in Peru, which he sends to all of his supporters. But as usual, my letter has a handwritten note at the bottom of it. This one says,

Garry, it was good to see you recently in Indianapolis. I continue to pray for you daily. God bless you in your work and relationships.

*In Jesus,*
*Steve*

This became his pattern — the form letter with an encouraging handwritten note that always included the words *I continue to pray for you daily.* Finally I had to ask him about this. "Hey, Steve, I enjoy getting your monthly updates, but there's one question I have. You keep saying you're praying for me daily. What's up with that? You don't need to keep writing that, when you and I both know that's not really the case."

But Steve stopped me dead in my tracks. "Wait just a minute. Time out. You don't understand. I *do* pray for you every day. I pray for you *every single day.*"

I was silent.

He continued, "I'm praying for your walk with Christ. I am praying for your ministry efforts. I'm praying for your relationships." Then he added, "It's the least I can do. After all, you were the one who opened up your small group to me. You invited me in and made it a safe place for me to raise my objections and ask my questions. I discovered a true relationship with Christ through that group, and I sort of owe you. I just want to show my appreciation and thank you by keeping you in my prayers. You know, Garry, I consider you to be sort of like a spiritual father to me. So I really *am* praying for you every day. And besides — if anyone needs it, it's you!"

I tell Steve's story for two reasons.

First, his story is an example of the power of a seeker small group, and an illustration of how God uses this amazing tool to reach people for himself. I've been leading small groups for spiritual seekers now for the past twenty-five years, and I've seen God use this evangelism concept in incredible ways. I cannot get over the impact this kind of group can make in the lives of non-Christians. And Steve's story has served as a shining example that has energized me over the years to strive to motivate others to lead small groups designed specifically with seekers in mind. It's also exactly what drives me to write this book.

But there is another, even more important reason for telling Steve's story. I am convinced that there is a "Steve" somewhere in your life too. Someone in and around your world is lost, disillusioned, and outside the family of God. But because of your natural connection with this "Steve," you could begin to build a genuine friendship with this person. You could invite him or her into a small gathering that you start up — a group context that would provide a safe environment for your seeking friend to discuss spiritual things, raise objections, or voice concerns. And who knows, eventually you just might have one of those life-changing encounters you'll carry around with you the rest of *your* life. And when that happens — when you play a role in leading someone across the line of faith — two lives will be changed for all eternity. The life of the one who received Christ *and yours* — because you were there!

Right now there's someone in your circle of influence — and there's someone in my world too — who could positively respond to the gospel message through this kind of specialized discussion group. There are men and women who are far from God but are open to launching the search. What if you were to build some true, caring friendships with each of them? What if, over time, you developed the courage to provide and lead a safe forum to which these seekers could bring their toughest spiritual questions? What if you were to facilitate a fun, relaxed environment where these seekers could raise their questions about God and their concerns about Christianity? What if you offered a safe place for them to discuss their spiritual issues on a regular basis? Just imagine what might happen. They just might find what they're looking for. They just might find Jesus — the only hope of the world!

## Defining the Terms

To start us off on the same page, certain terms used throughout this book need to be clearly defined and understood. First, someone is considered to be a non-Christian — no matter how far along this person is in his or her spiritual journey — if he or she has not yet personally received Jesus Christ as forgiver and leader. In addition, the terms "seeker," "seeking friend," "spiritual seeker," and "non-Christian" are used interchangeably and are, for the purposes of this book, one and the same. These terms signify anyone who has not yet crossed the line of faith and accepted Jesus Christ into his or her life — regardless of whether or not the person is in the process of seeking God.

Of course, not all non-Christians are actually seeking; many are running away from God and purposely avoiding a relationship with him. (In fact, Romans 3:10–11 and John 6:44–45 teach that no one can truly seek God *without* his help.) And even those non-Christians who *are* prompted by the Holy Spirit to seek God are doing so at differing levels of intentionality and various degrees of intensity. For the sake of simplicity, though, I'll refer to every non-Christian as a "seeker." This term has a much more positive, hopeful feel to it than most other descriptors — and besides, it's a more seeker-friendly (or seeker-sensitive) word because non-Christians can readily identify with it. (It's certainly far better than using terms like "heathen," "pagan," "hell-bound sinner," or something worse!)

When it comes to evangelism, the Christian's goal is to understand a seeker's perspective and figure out the best ways to challenge that seeker about what it means to know God. And, then prayerfully attempt to give him or her opportunities to receive Jesus Christ as the only means of finding forgiveness and a true relationship with God. This is what we view as the evangelistic process.

A seeker small group, then, is defined as a community of roughly two to twelve seekers and one or two Christian leaders who gather on a regular basis, primarily to discuss spiritual matters. These groups consist of people from a whole range of ages and stages of life, including singles, men, women, couples, moms, or dads. Groups may be made up of one type or may be totally mixed. They meet at a wide variety of locations, from homes and offices to restaurants and churches to bookstores and park district picnic tables. A Christian organizes and leads the seeker small group and facilitates the discussions based on the seekers' spiritual concerns and issues. Usually, at least one apprentice (or coleader) who is also a Christian assists the group leader. The rest of the participants are predominately, if not all, non-Christians. (So maybe two or three people in the whole group are Christians, but all the others are non-Christians.) These non-Christians will outnumber the Christians — an important point to remember. As you will see later, this is a key component to the powerful impact potential in a seeker small group.

Obviously, another approach to small group evangelism is through small groups consisting of Christians. This is certainly a worthwhile option, where three to twelve Christians in the context of their own small group extend themselves to reach and assimilate non-Christians. This is often accomplished through inviting and enfolding one or two seekers right into the believers' existing small group meetings. In other cases, a small group of Christians may organize various activities or outreach events to which they can invite their seeking friends. Because this small group evangelism strategy is not tailored directly and entirely to the needs of seekers, it has not proved to be quite as effective in reaching them as are those groups specifically designed for seekers. Reaching seekers through believer small groups, although not the primary focus of this book, will be covered at length in chapter 9.

## Seekers Matter

The single greatest value behind the seeker small group strategy is this: Seekers matter. This is the foundation on which you will want to build your seeker small group. The phrase *Seekers matter to God; therefore they matter to us* is the premise behind every evangelistic endeavor at Willow Creek Community Church, and seeker small groups are no exception. All the principles and practical ideas and suggestions outlined in this book flow from this one value.

The Bible clearly illustrates this critical value in Matthew 9:10–12, 36–38 (MSG).

> When Jesus was eating supper at Matthew's house with his close followers, a lot of disreputable characters came and joined them. When the Pharisees saw him keeping this kind of company, they had a fit, and lit into Jesus' followers. "What kind of example is this from your Teacher, acting cozy with crooks and riff-raff?"
>
> Jesus, overhearing, shot back, "Who needs a doctor: the healthy or the sick? . . . I'm here to invite outsiders, not coddle insiders." . . .
>
> When he looked out over the crowds, his heart broke. So confused and aimless they were, like sheep with no shepherd. "What a huge harvest!" he said to his disciples. "How few workers! On your knees and pray for harvest hands!"

My heart stirs as I picture this scene in my mind. How vividly I can see Jesus hanging out and eating with the "sinners" — the very ones the religious leaders considered outcasts. Society's rejects. The lost ones. I can almost hear Jesus saying, "I've come to the sick because they are the ones with the real need, and I'm here to give them hope because they matter to me. They are like sheep without a shepherd; they're lost and confused and in need of guidance and direction. I care about them and I'm here for them. That's the reason I came into this world in the first place. Now, the question is this: who among you will go and work in my field? Look! The harvest is ready now and time is short. Who here will gather my treasured harvest?"

Such biblical images give us a picture of just how much non-believers matter to God. When Jesus looked at the crowds, he saw people from a spiritual perspective. He saw them as lost and downcast and distressed. His heart broke for them. He wept for lost people.

That's the heart of God toward those still outside his kingdom. And the question that needs to be raised before any consideration is given to launching a seeker small group is this: Do we view lost people in the same way God does? When seekers cross our paths, do our hearts break with compassion? When we encounter those outside God's family, do we think about their spiritual conditions? Do we recognize that they are like sheep without a shepherd and that they really matter to the Father? And do we truly believe that if they matter to him, they need to matter to us? If we sincerely have that kind of heart attitude toward seekers, it changes everything: our whole perspective about how we interact with them, how we treat each one, and how we organize small groups for them — including the way we lead and facilitate their small group discussions.

If you get nothing else from this chapter, get this: Seekers matter. Non-Christians matter. The question is, do they matter to *you*? Do they matter to *me*? Before we can go any further, we need to be very clear on this point. Some of us may need to do business with God and recalibrate ourselves so we're aligned with his priorities. We may need to get alone with God and pray, "Lord, give me a renewed passion for lost people. Give me a heart that breaks when I encounter non-Christians in the crowds. Give me the same compassion you have for them. Give me new eyes to see them as they really are — lost, separated from you, and distressed."

Once we allow God to reignite that fire for lost people in us, the rest flows more easily. Everything else about how to practically provide a small group in which seekers can safely search will become second nature, based on common sense. Give yourself fully to this premise, and you're halfway there.

## A Closer Look

If seekers really matter, it is important for us to make a serious attempt to understand who they are and where they're coming from as they take steps along their spiritual journey. We will want to know our seeking friends well, especially as we think about forming a small group specifically for them. We will want to focus on their needs and interests and to make sure the design and structure and climate of the group reflects an accurate understanding of these seekers in a number of ways.

### Past Religious Experiences

Consider the past religious experiences of non-Christians. Did they attend church services while growing up or not at all? What about now — is there any current church involvement? If so, to what extent? How have their religious views changed over the years? What religions have they explored and what religion would they most align themselves with now? And what have their interactions and encounters with religious people, including religious leaders, been like? Some people may have positive recollections, but many more may have negative memories of their religious experiences.

### Biblical Understanding

The seekers' level of biblical understanding needs to be taken into account. Have they ever read the Bible? What knowledge do they have of Scripture and to what extent do they understand biblical teachings? It is important for us to be sensitive to the fact that most non-Christians do not know what the Bible actually says, let alone believe it.

### Spiritual Issues and Questions

We need to be aware that seekers are likely to have a number of intellectual objections and questions. Typically, they have many unresolved issues and concerns about Christianity. Too many times, I'm afraid, Christians have the feeling that we desperately need to tell non-Christians the Good News *before* we even try to understand what objections they're raising. *And we end up answering questions they're not asking.* It is far wiser for us to first know what specific objections and questions are going through their minds — and even to take the time to understand *why* they have the questions they do — and then respond accordingly.

## Other Barriers and Breakthroughs

Equally important to knowing where seekers are coming from on a spiritual level is to understand where they're at on other levels in their lives. Over time it's important to allow seekers to feel the freedom and acceptance to disclose the emotional, physical, and mental barriers they're facing, along with any breakthroughs they've realized in those areas. And as leaders, we must be willing to develop a caring attitude for the whole person. That includes openly sharing what's going on in our own lives as well as drawing out issues on a variety of levels from our group members. One seeker in my group, distraught over the death of a loved one, was so angry with God that she was in no position to participate in our group's discussions until she addressed her frustrations. The group graciously gave her time to process her emotions. This is, in part, what it means to "be there" for those seekers who mean so much to us.

## Spiritual Darkness and Blindness

We need to remember that non-Christians live in spiritual darkness and blindness. The Bible clearly teaches that spiritual seekers — people without Christ — are alive physically but dead spiritually. They are spiritually blind. It is important for us to be patient and caring as we bear this truth in mind.

As group participants express their thoughts and ideas about spiritual issues, you will notice that their views are, at times, filled with poor theology and even biblical heresy. But as we recognize that our friends have spiritual blinders on, we will understand that they simply are not yet able to see the big picture clearly. This is explained more fully in 1 Corinthians 2:13–14: "This is what we speak, not in words taught us by human wisdom but in words taught by the Spirit, expressing spiritual truths in spiritual words. The man without the Spirit does not accept the things that come from the Spirit of God, for they are foolishness to him, and he cannot understand them, because they are spiritually discerned."

Once we understand that seekers are not going to be able to see some spiritual truths until they accept Christ into their lives, we're more likely to dispel our need to attack or correct their views. Instead we'll remind ourselves that it's not necessary to immediately correct every last one of their misconceptions; our job is to patiently invite seekers to discover spiritual truths over time along the way. Understanding where they're coming from and recognizing their spiritual condition takes some of the pressure off, and we can be more concerned with providing a safe place for them to ask their questions and make their observations about biblical truths without fear of condemnation or criticism.

## Five Phases of Spiritual Discovery

It is usually fairly easy to determine the intensity level of a non-Christian's spiritual quest. For example, there are cynical people who have spent a lifetime avoiding Christianity at all costs, and those who are somewhat less resistant but still quite skeptical. Some people are neutral about spiritual matters — simply spectators making observations from a safe distance. (In some ways apathy or indifference expresses more opposition than hostility does.) Even among those who are more deliberately seeking, there are differences. Some lack confidence and are unsure what they believe, while others assign a low priority to their search. And then, of course, there are those seekers who are seriously pursuing spiritual matters and sincerely looking for answers.

But as we interact with our seeking friends about spiritual matters, there is another factor to be aware of besides the *intensity* of their search — and that's the *stage* of their discovery process. After observing hundreds of non-Christians take steps of faith in all kinds of settings, I've concluded that seekers advance through five distinct phases of spiritual discovery — and it's one of the most critical realizations I've encountered. If we can carefully and adequately identify where our seeking friends are in their discovery process, we will gain a much better understanding of how to best support and encourage them in their search for truth.

*Phase 1: Identification.* Seekers identify what they believe.

This phase is where most seekers really begin their spiritual journey — by figuring out where they stand and exactly what they believe. Here, non-Christians identify just what it is they think about God, the meaning of life, death, the afterlife, and many other spiritual issues. Generally speaking, seekers have rarely come to grips with what they specifically believe about these important matters. So we serve our seeking friends well when we ask questions to prompt them (and assist us) to define what they believe. Some examples of Phase 1 questions include the following: What do you believe about God? Who do you think Jesus is? What do you suppose happens after we die? What's your assessment of the Bible?

*Phase 2: Clarification.* Seekers clarify why they believe what they do.

Next, non-Christians need to move one step beyond identifying *what* they believe to clarifying *why* they hold those beliefs. Few seekers have taken the time to establish solid reasons for what they believe — they are not naturally driven to defend their spiritual viewpoints. Again, we demonstrate respect toward our seeking friends and family members when we make the effort to genuinely understand the reasons behind their beliefs. Phase 2 questions can include: Why do you believe there is no God? Help me understand why you think there is no life after this one? Give me your reasons for believing that all roads lead to God.

*Phase 3: Exploration.* Seekers explore alternative truth options.

Once seekers have put forth the effort to determine what and why they believe, they often become dissatisfied with their current beliefs. This is an exciting step in their journeys because they are at a place where they are ready and willing to seek after the truth. However, this process can also be somewhat chaotic because at this juncture seekers are usually left with more questions than answers — and more doubts than certainties. This unsettling notion often causes an eye-opening awareness that there just might be more to life than what they have experienced — and that something is missing. It's at this stage that seekers become eager to explore other options, including biblical truth, and are most open and receptive to hearing a clear presentation of the gospel. We wouldn't want to miss this opportunity.

*Phase 4: Evaluation.* Seekers evaluate new discoveries.

At this point, seekers begin to earnestly assess the validity of their beliefs and wrestle with the tough questions and objections they have about the claims of Christianity as well as other faiths. More than at any other time, they are willing to make comparisons between what they believe and what the Bible teaches — and determine which makes more sense from an intellectual perspective. We should make ourselves available to join them in this process and gently guide them toward biblical truths.

*Phase 5: Decision.* Seekers decide what to believe.

This stage in the process is very significant for non-Christians, because these crucial decisions of acceptance and belief not only involve the mind, but also the heart and the will. This is why most seekers draw conclusions about spiritual matters incrementally. For example, after moving through each of the phases, a seeker may decide to accept the existence of a personal God but then turn around and go back through the various phases again before making other decisions about the authority of the Bible or the identity of Jesus. It may take a series of such decisions before he or she eventually makes a commitment to receive and follow Christ.

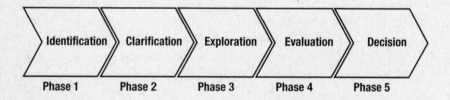

Seekers make spiritual discoveries in stages, and we must look for ways to honor this process as we reach out to them. For example, to more effectively share the gospel with our seeking friends (Phase 3), we must be willing to first take the time to genuinely understand what they believe (Phase 1) and why they believe it (Phase 2). And to someday earn the right to challenge our friends to make a solid decision for Christ (Phase 5), we must first engage them in ample dialogue about how to overcome their barriers to belief (Phase 4). We should be careful to resist the temptation to prematurely jump into Phase 3 and then skip over to Phase 5 without any regard to dealing with the spiritual issues related to the other phases. Otherwise we run the risk of unintentionally alienating our seeking friends.

Without a doubt, of course, the Holy Spirit can intercede at any moment in any phase and bring anyone to faith in Christ. But in general, our outreach efforts should demonstrate respect for this spiritual discovery process. And as you learn throughout the pages of this book, your seeker small group can provide a safe environment for seekers to progress through each phase — as many times as it takes — and make life-changing biblical discoveries along the way.

In my view, the most effective strategy to helping seekers advance through these phases and take steps of spiritual progress is something I've called "Empathic Evangelism." It's a simple outreach concept that can be summarized in one short statement: *Ask great questions and listen well.* This approach, outlined more thoroughly in chapters 5 and 6, has greatly served me in assisting seekers through the various spiritual discovery phases — especially within the context of a seeker small group setting. As we reach out to our seeking friends, we must take the time to ask great questions, listen well, and seek to fully understand the concerns of their minds and hearts. That will truly demonstrate the love of Christ and honor them in the process. And then, over time, we'll find ourselves with all kinds of opportunities to guide seekers to discover biblical truths for themselves.

In his book *Between the Words,* Norm Wakefield stresses the importance of honoring seekers in this way: "Frequently during my workshops and seminars on listening someone will say, 'You mean, all I can do is listen when I know the person is saying something wrong? That doesn't seem right. I need to straighten the person out. Isn't that an act of love?' If you are familiar with the Bible, you know that we *are* to offer counsel to the confused, correction to the erring, and even rebuke to the unrepentant sinner. The question is not whether or not such responses are appropriate — *it is a question of timing.*"[1]

### Trust Level

Finally, it is critical to ascertain the trust level of seekers concerning spiritual matters. In other words, how much trust will they place in a Christian friend or the Bible or a Christian church or God or Jesus Christ? People with a low level of spiritual trust usually are very cynical or skeptical about spiritual things, the Bible, or the church. And they certainly don't place their trust in God or in his Son, Jesus Christ. A really skeptical non-Christian will often question the agenda or motivation behind a Christian's efforts to befriend them, and thus try to avoid such interactions. Seekers who attend church usually have a somewhat higher trust level. It is important to figure out how much trust your seeking friends have or don't have in these spiritual areas and meet them where they are — and look for authentic ways to earn their trust and respect.

No two seekers are alike and, as with all healthy relationships, it requires sincere effort and patience to truly get to know someone. It's crucial to demonstrate your genuine care. The cliché is old but it's still true: *Seekers don't really care how much you know until they know how much you really care.* This is exactly why it's important to understand where your seeker friends are coming from and where they are in their spiritual journeys. And it's this depth of care, concern, and understanding toward your seeking friends that will shape the kind of small group you form.

Weigh these insights carefully before starting your seeker small group. They must drive everything you do. The rest of this book provides many practical ideas and suggestions for launching seeker small groups, and each and every one is based on our understanding that seekers matter. In reality, these groups are tailor-made for non-Christians — they're specifically designed from start to finish with the seekers' needs and concerns in the forefront of our thinking. When leaders put the needs and wants of seekers before their own, a seeker small group can be one of the most powerful evangelistic tools there is.

## Distinct Advantages

A seeker small group is a customized approach to reaching non-Christians. There are three distinct advantages to using this razor-sharp tool for reaching out to our friends and family for Christ.

### A Very Safe Place

The real beauty of a seeker small group is the remarkable extent to which seekers feel safe and secure. The first distinct advantage of a seeker small group is that it's a very safe place. Seekers can investigate the claims of Christianity at their own pace. They are accepted no matter where they are in their spiritual journeys. If they have little or no knowledge of the Bible, that's okay. If they are cynical or skeptical, they are welcomed anyway. There is no judgment, only a spirit of acceptance. ("What business is it of mine to judge those outside the church?" [1 Corinthians 5:12].) The goal of this safe place is to provide an invitation, opportunity, and environment for seekers to openly express their thoughts and feelings, to voice their observations and questions, and even to go so far as to assert their objections—all without inhibition or any fear of criticism. The hope is that they will get to the place where they look forward to sharing their issues and concerns about the Bible and its claims. It's been my experience that once they get to this point, they will enjoy even more the process of searching out the answers for themselves.

One of the components of the safety that unchurched people crave is having a place where they can connect with other seekers. There is definitely safety in numbers, and when the majority of participants are non-Christians, they can identify with each others' spiritual questions and concerns. Time and time again I've heard seekers say to another things like, "Oh, I can't believe you just said that! That's a good issue you just raised. I've had that same concern for a long time but thought I was the only one. Having some of the same questions as the rest of you makes me feel better." When seekers identify with one another, it legitimizes their questions and objections—and that's a great way to create a secure environment.

Seekers also feel safe when they are allowed to discover spiritual truths on their own. They're not coming to the group to hear a lecture or get talked at; instead leaders orchestrate a dynamic discussion in such a way that seekers have "aha moments" over and over again. The group provides the forum for an amazing process in which seekers investigate and learn on their own, in their own way, and at their own pace.

Safety, then, is the first distinct advantage of a seeker small group: a safe place for seekers to seek, a safe place to connect with other seekers, and a safe place for them to discover spiritual truths for themselves.

## A Highly Effective Tool for Evangelism

A second distinct advantage of a seeker small group is that it's a highly effective tool for evangelism. Over the years here at Willow Creek, we have seen scores and scores of non-Christians cross the line of faith within the context of seeker small groups. These groups have become one of the most effective evangelistic tools we have at our disposal. In fact, Bill Hybels, our senior pastor, recently told our congregation that he considers "seeker small groups to be one of the greatest discoveries we've made at Willow in the last several years."

But a word of caution is in order here. Some people have the mistaken belief that a seeker small group is a quick fix for instant evangelistic success, without any need for building solid friendships with seekers. They erroneously think it's a substitute for *personal* evangelism, and their hope is that the seeker group can become a magic formula for instant conversions in and of itself. In reality, though, quite the opposite is true; it's not a substitute, it's a *supplement* for evangelism. It's very important to understand that a seeker group cannot take the place of the leader's own personal relationships with non-Christians. It's only a tool — a means to an end — for effective evangelism, given the context of thriving friendships with seekers.

In large part that effectiveness depends on the leader's personal evangelistic efforts. Not that the leader needs to be an evangelism giant — in fact, as we shall see later, the leader doesn't need to have the spiritual gift of evangelism or be an expert on the subject or even be very experienced in efforts to bring people to Christ. But a leader of a seeker small group *must* be willing to get involved in the lives of the seekers in his or her care.

Once the seeker small group is viewed as a tool or supplement within the evangelistic process — an extension of the leader's personal evangelistic efforts — the leader can establish and maintain genuine friendships, build bridges of trust, and enter into occasional dialogues about Christianity with a few non-Christians. Then, as a supplement to the evangelistic process that has already been established, the leader can invite these individuals to visit the group as a way to continue the spiritual discussions with others who are also seeking.

Have you ever had the experience of using a few good illustrations to share your faith with someone and then having him or her say to you, "Well, that sounds fascinating. I never thought about things that way before. It seems like a nice idea — for you — but it's not really something I'm interested in right now." At that point the conversation comes to a screeching halt. You don't really know where to go from there, and the next time you see your friend, you're not sure how to come back around and pick up the conversation. You're just sort of stuck.

But while it's difficult to know how to reengage when a previous conversation has ended so abruptly, a seeker small group provides a built-in "excuse" for ongoing dialogue about spiritual matters. It's like having a set appointment every week with a group of non-Christians to talk about faith-related issues. It's far easier — both for the leader and the seeker — to strike up spiritual conversations on a regular basis when it's already scheduled. In fact, I've had seekers tell me they were working on a whole list of objections to Christianity and could hardly wait to bring it to the next group meeting to discuss. For them, the group became their own special opportunity to fully engage in the seeking process. It was something they really looked forward to!

In addition, what transpires during the seeker group can prompt conversations that take place outside the group. If the leader notes various individual responses, he or she can initiate a time to get together on a one-on-one basis and dig deeper into those particular issues. Group discussions provide easy avenues for the leader to meet with each group member individually, share meals, or hang out together and get to know each other better. The leader can ask to hear more about certain issues, inquire about what exactly the seeker meant by something he or she said, or simply ask how the group is meeting that person's needs. This is an excellent chance to help the seeker take one more step in his or her spiritual journey — and another example of how the group can become a vehicle for ongoing personal evangelism.

## An Easily Transferable Concept

The third distinct advantage of the seeker small group strategy is that it's easily transferable. Seeker groups work well in a wide variety of church and ministry settings, styles, and formats. And whether the church utilizes a traditional worship format, a seeker-sensitive or seeker-targeted approach, or anything in between, these small groups can flourish. No radical changes within your church or ministry structure are needed to launch these groups.

This evangelistic tool offers an excellent next step for seekers already attending a church or taking part in a ministry. Until we made seeker small groups available at Willow Creek, we did not have next steps for the seekers who came to our weekend services. We had lots of next steps for believers — Christians could get connected into small groups and find places to serve. Seekers, though, were at a loss as to what to do beyond attending our services on a regular basis. Now we have discovered the perfect outlet for them. Once we established a seeker small groups ministry, hundreds and hundreds of seekers stepped out and got connected into these groups, facilitating forward movement in their own spiritual journeys. And the missing next step for seekers attending our services had been found.

More recently, our seeker small groups have also become a springboard for unchurched seekers. Those not yet ready to attend services can find freedom and safety within a seeker small group to take steps along their spiritual paths. These groups meet in the neighborhoods and in the marketplace, and as group participants make progress in their spiritual journeys, they inevitably become interested in getting connected to a church where they can grow in their understanding and interest in spiritual things.

In summary, a seeker small group is a highly transferable concept. It is easily adaptable within any church or ministry setting. It is an excellent next step for seekers already attending church services, as well as a great springboard for seekers not yet ready for church.

## A Challenge

As you read this book, I want to extend this challenge to you. From this point on, read with the mind-set that you will indeed launch your own seeker small group. Put yourself in the position of reading with the intention of actually forming, in your context, such a group in the near future. Prayerfully, think in terms of how you personally might apply the principles and ideas outlined here to your own environment, and dream about the possibilities of what God might do through your efforts. See yourself, with the help of an apprentice or two, starting your own group specifically designed for seekers. Imagine identifying an ideal setting, maybe in your church, your workplace, or your neighborhood, and inviting seekers to join you on a regular basis for a discussion about spiritual matters. Envision yourself leading seekers to Christ through a seeker small group.

If you will agree to take on this challenge, you will put yourself in a better position to more fully digest the ideas in this book. You will find yourself growing with excitement about the possibilities. And you will achieve greater retention of the material because you will be more highly motivated to figure out how you can apply it to your situation.

Are you up for the challenge? Are you in? I hope so. Because if you're on board, you're in for the ride of your life. So grab a partner and get ready to roll, because you're about to embark on the exciting adventure of launching your very own seeker small group.

## Your Response

Once you have accepted this challenge, hundreds of questions and obstacles or even fears may enter your thoughts. What hurdles jumped to mind? What are your initial hesitancies? What roadblocks can you foresee? The first step in overcoming these obstacles is to simply identify specifically what they are. Other potential leaders have gone through this exercise over the years, and perhaps you can identify with some of their initial concerns.

- I wouldn't know where to start.
- I'm not an evangelist.
- I'm not a leader.
- How much of my time will it take to lead a seeker group?
- Where do I find seekers for my group?
- I don't have any non-Christian friends to invite to a group.
- How do I avoid viewing seekers as my projects?
- How do I keep from having an agenda with my non-Christian friends?
- Why would seekers make the time to come to a group?

- How do I get seekers to show up for the group meetings?
- Is it really possible to get people who are far from God to come to a spiritual discussion?
- If seekers do show up, what do I do with them?
- I'm not good at leading a group discussion.
- I'm not knowledgeable enough about the Bible to do this.
- I wouldn't know how to prepare for a group discussion.
- How would I deal with tough questions the seekers would ask?
- I'm lacking any apologetic skills.
- How do I adequately care for the seekers in the group?
- What happens to the seekers in the group after they become Christians?
- Where will I find support for questions I have about leading this group?

The bad news is that this list of concerns may look long and overwhelming; the good news is that hundreds of leaders have discovered the solutions to overcome these obstacles. And you will too. In fact, the primary goal of this book is to address these barriers, and other related issues, one by one and to disclose the breakthroughs many have already found. My prayer is that as you read on, you will become fully equipped and supported to move forward with your dream to see seekers come to faith in Christ. And the best news is that you are *not* alone — as you take steps to launch a seeker small group, God is right there with you. "For God did not give a spirit of timidity, but a spirit of power, of love and of self-discipline" (2 Timothy 1:7).

# CLAYTON LEE'S STORY

*Property Manager*
*Folsom, California*

*M*y seeker small group experiences have been fantastic. In all my life I've never seen God work so powerfully or so swiftly in the lives of seekers. I discovered that more than anything else, group leaders need to be open, accepting, trustworthy, and real—because leading these groups effectively has more to do with one's heart for seekers than one's ability.

Four years ago, I led my first seeker group at my church with absolutely no training or experience. But thankfully, that lack of knowledge and skill didn't seem to matter. God demonstrated the special place he has in his heart for seekers by doing some amazing things anyway. Nearly everyone in that group made a decision for Christ—twenty-two people in all! Good thing I didn't wait until I was completely ready to start—because that day never would have come. Instead I had to step out and take a risk.

Penny came to the first meeting dragging her husband, Dave. He sat in the chair with his arms crossed and a smug look on his face. Given the chance, he would have gone for my jugular. I could see it in his eyes—he was out to get me. From the outset, I tried to explain that our group was an open forum where everyone could explore Christianity at his or her own pace. I told them I'd challenge their thinking, but I'd never push them beyond what they were ready to do. After I gave those disclaimers, Dave seemed to relax. At the next meeting Dave tried very hard not to participate, but he did listen.

By the fourth session I could see his heart start to soften. After the meeting I suggested we get together sometime. "Great," he replied. "Let's go out and have a cold beer." His response threw me for a loop. But the next day, over a beer, he told me all about his favorite pastime—watching ball games and getting plastered with "the boys." He added that he didn't enjoy any other activities.

A few weeks later, as I began our group discussion, Dave interrupted me. "I want to tell you all something," he said. This was practically the first time Dave spoke up during a meeting, so we were all eager to hear what he was going to say.

*"You know, after listening to these group discussions, I've come to the conclusion that it's not so much what you know. It's more about where your heart is."* Silence. *At that moment I wanted to jump out of my chair and dance around the room! I contained myself, however, and calmly replied, "Dave, you have uncovered a mystery that very few people understand."*

*Not long after that he accepted Christ into his life. He's a committed Christian now, with no desire to go back to the life he had before.*

*Another guy hauled to our small group by his wife was Marty. He had a reputation for being a party animal. At our meetings he would brag about his drinking episodes, drug addictions, and womanizing* in front of his wife. *In private conversations with me, he shared repulsive stories about his life.*

*Marty was very argumentative — he disagreed with just about everything anyone said. And I had a difficult time figuring out how to address Marty's questions without riling him. Finally, I took him aside and promised to fully address his issues privately if he would give me two or three weeks to research them. He then backed off from instigating so many arguments. He started to listen more, and I began to notice a glimmer of transformation happening within him.*

*At the end of one meeting I decided to take a very big risk with Marty. Almost every week I closed our discussions with a twenty-second prayer. This time I asked Marty if he would say the prayer. To everyone's surprise, he prayed — out loud! I was totally flabbergasted that someone so far away from God would pray publicly.*

*About a week later he announced that he had decided to make some drastic lifestyle changes and pursue a relationship with God. Eventually he became convinced that Jesus Christ was the only way to obtain complete forgiveness and true fulfillment and turned his life over to him. Today he's growing strong in Christ.*

*Dave and Marty are just two examples of the amazing transformation that took place in the lives of those in my seeker group. But there are so many more amazing stories. God answered prayers and changed people for eternity through that group — and I got to be a part of it!*

# DAVE VOSS'S STORY

### Retired High School Teacher
### Folsom, California

*I*'m a very private person and I've always had a difficult time opening up about my deeper feelings — especially those of a spiritual
nature. I knew that in Clayton's small group I would be expected to
talk, so I was very reluctant to go. But my wife, Penny, convinced
me to give it a try.

Even though I showed up, I remember sitting in the meetings
with my arms folded in a defensive position. I had all kinds of questions that I doubted Clayton would allow us to discuss. But instead
he welcomed my skepticism — and I couldn't believe that. I felt my
heart soften. In fact, I even started to read the Bible.

The friendships Penny and I have developed in that group are
so much deeper than anything I've ever experienced before. And
Clayton and I just seemed to click right away. It's not a typical thing
for me to open up like I did — I'm more standoffish. But the more I
got to know Clayton, the more I admired his Christian example. I
tend to analyze all sides — weighing this and that — before making
a decision. But it wasn't too difficult to draw a conclusion about
Christ after spending time with Clayton.

It's impossible to describe how grateful I am that Clayton invited
me to search for answers in his group in spite of all my doubts. During our discussions I had a growing sense that something was missing in my life and marriage. Deep down I knew I was ultimately
looking to fill that void with something spiritual. That's when I
became more receptive to Clayton's suggestions that I seriously consider Jesus. Eventually I invited Jesus to forgive me and take away
my emptiness.

Since receiving Christ, I've become involved in ministry-related
activities. Penny and I attend a Thursday night Bible study with four
other Christian couples, and I joined a men's accountability group.
Also, since I play guitar, I enjoy worshiping God through music. Two
Sundays ago I performed during the services with the worship team. I
did a lot of praying and practicing beforehand, and it went well. I know
I had extra help from God. That was an amazing experience for me.

*I've been volunteering for other service activities at church, like directing traffic on Sunday mornings. I've helped with Communion services too. I'm fifty-nine years old now — and I've served God and others more in the past year than in the other fifty-eight years of my life combined. And finding ways to honor and love God is exactly how I want to spend all my remaining time.*

# MARTY SPEER'S STORY

### Architectural Assistant
### Folsom, California

*G*rowing up, I had never known anything about religion or church. I was far away from God and never even had a clue about who Jesus was. In high school I was a drinker and a hard-core partier. At twenty-one I started smoking weed regularly, as well as doing all kinds of other drugs. I was doing so much partying on a daily basis that I started drinking and doing drugs as soon as I woke up. In my first marriage I had multiple affairs. The guilt from that is something that I still live with today. I was a really bad guy. And I never imagined God would ever want anything to do with me — except maybe to get rid of me.

But one day my wife took me to a seeker small group. A guy named Clayton led it — and it was a great small group experience. To be honest, I have to admit that I was the biggest skeptic in the group. I asked a lot of very hard questions — and even some stupid ones. But they were things I really wanted to know. I liked to think that I kept the discussions interesting! For the first time ever, things in my life started to look up.

Over time Clayton and that small group challenged me to invite Jesus Christ into my life — and into my heart and soul. What a profound turning point it was for me when I asked Jesus to forgive and transform me — because he did just that. I was a broken man. I still am to a degree, and that's why every day I renew my invitation to the Lord to come into my heart, take over my will, and give me guidance. Now, thanks to the influence of that group, that's what I want more than anything.

# Chapter 2

# Build Strong Bridges

*Pray for us, too, that God may open a door for our message, so that we may proclaim the mystery of Christ, for which I am in chains. Pray that I may proclaim it clearly, as I should. Be wise in the way you act toward outsiders; make the most of every opportunity. Let your conversation be always full of grace, seasoned with salt, so that you may know how to answer everyone.*

COLOSSIANS 4:3–6

*If Jesus Christ be God and died for me, then no sacrifice is too great for me to make for him.*

C. T. STUDD

I first met Jay Pass in middle school. As we began to hang out together, we would occasionally look each other straight in the eye and see both a friend and a competitor. We were in a lot of the same classes, where we would battle for the better grades. As it turned out, we both played trumpet in the band, and time after time we would shoot each other a grin before vying for the higher chair by playing a piece for the band director. "Jay, you're outta here," I'd say as I headed for the music room. And I'd beat him — only to be outdone by him the next time!

Most of all, we enjoyed competing in sports — baseball, wrestling, football — to list just a few. We thoroughly enjoyed this friendly kind of warfare; he'd slap me on the back as we entered the gym for a wrestling match and say, "Hey, man, you're such a good friend, I'll almost feel bad when I pin you in ten seconds flat!" During our baseball games, if I picked up a bat and hit a home run, you'd better believe Jay would try his best to do the same. And if he snagged a fly ball with an impressive dive, I'd run all the harder to make an even more aggressive catch. Whatever the activity, we turned up the competitive heat.

But there was only one thing we didn't have in common — faith. I was a Christian; Jay, an atheist. By the time we were in high school, Jay was quite vocal about this major difference between us. And he didn't have any hesitation about mentioning this fact to all who would listen. "God is just a figment of your imagination for your own convenience, to pacify you," he'd state. "There is no God. It's just something your parents talked about to scare you — and foolishly you bought into it." It almost got to the point where he acted like some kind of "atheistic evangelist."

Even in this area our competitive natures emerged. As Jay eagerly explained his lack of belief in God, I openly told others about the God I trusted and followed. We were each equally confident about our own stance and demonstrated a strong conviction regarding what we believed. Yet it was hard for me to fathom how someone with whom I had so much in common could feel so differently — exactly the opposite — about God.

One day a group of us were on a road trip to a sporting event, and Jay decided to make things interesting. He had already gained a reputation for being an animated guy who enjoyed stirring up a crowd, so it didn't surprise any of us when he began to liven up our long bus ride through the flat farmland of northern Indiana.

He stood up in the front of the bus and yelled out a challenge. "Listen, you guys. To make this ride more interesting, I think we should split up and have a big debate. So whoever believes in God, sit on this side, and whoever doesn't believe God exists, sit on the other side." Curiosity — and an appreciation for Jay's courage and creativity — split us up just as he suggested. As we shifted from one side to the other, Jay continued. "I'll represent all the atheists, and Garry here will represent those of you who believe in God. Let's settle this once and for all!"

I went along with the idea and stood up next to Jay. Surprisingly, there were an equal number of kids on both sides of the aisle, and for the rest of the trip that entire busload of students engaged in an exciting, intense discussion about the existence of God. I no longer remember all the specific arguments, but I do know that convictions ran deep and emotions were charged.

The last week of our senior year, Jay and I, plus about twenty other classmates, scrambled for our desks in our advanced math class and anxiously prepared to take the final exam. The teacher had not yet arrived, and Jay determined that if any of us were going to make it through this big test, what we really needed was some divine intervention. So he stood up in front of the class and led us in a kind of mock prayer. "O God, up there in the sky, I know you're not really there, but if you are, we sure could use your help with this final exam. Help us, help us, help us!" he implored. The whole class roared with laughter. We all knew Jay was an atheist, and saw the irony of his plea.

As Jay took his seat next to mine, I leaned over and whispered, "That was a mighty fine prayer for someone who doesn't even believe God exists." Jay turned, looked me right in the eye, and said, "That was the first time in my life I ever said a prayer."

That summer Jay and I played a lot of tennis in the evenings at the local park. We had some pretty fierce games — including some very competitive doubles matches. But, typical of us, we were almost always on opposite teams. Often our matches lasted late into the night.

By the time we finished, we'd frequently be the only two left on the courts. So we would shut off the lights, walk over to the parking lot, sit on the hoods of our cars, and just talk. We conversed about whatever was on our minds — you name it, we covered it.

Eventually Jay would bring the conversation around to spiritual things. "Now, you know I don't believe in God," he'd begin, "but if he *did* exist, why do you think . . ." Then he would dive into some intellectual spiritual issue. He seemed genuinely interested in exploring the implications of God's existence. I'd try my best to address some of his disputes surrounding the existence of God, but I knew that his disbeliefs were deeply ingrained in his thinking. It would take, well, a *miracle* to change his mind.

At the time, I figured Jay's questions were random thoughts he had about Christianity. But looking back, I realize that his objections dealt mainly with the whole issue of God's existence and his miracles. In fact, Jay's concerns centered around the outlandish claims that make Christianity unique: God coming to the earth and living as a human being, even a baby; the resurrection of Jesus from the dead; and the entire concept of God's forgiveness secured by the death and resurrection of Christ. It was all too much — too supernatural and miraculous — for Jay to believe.

The last time I saw Jay that year was at the end of the summer, just before we left for colleges in two different cities. After an exceptionally fierce tennis match, we shook hands, tossed our rackets into our cars, and had yet another of those animated spiritual discussions. But this one was different. Jay seemed more intense than ever before, and his comments and questions seemed more focused — as if he were urgently looking for some answers. For the first time, he even appeared open to the idea that God might exist. Our conversation lasted until just past midnight, when we finally said goodbye and parted ways. Jay drove off in his car and I climbed into mine and headed in the opposite direction.

As I came to a stop sign inside the park grounds, though, I suddenly couldn't drive any farther. An overwhelming sense of compassion for my friend welled up inside me and I was unmistakably drawn to pray for him. I threw the car into park, and in front of that stop sign bowed my head on the steering wheel and said, "Oh, God, please help Jay know that you're here. He seems so close and yet so far. His eyes are blinded to the truth about you. Open his eyes and help him to truly see you as you are."

It's hard to explain and impossible to prove, but in that moment of prayer I sensed that God overwhelmingly cared for Jay. And that night I felt like I encountered the heart of God toward all seekers.

## If We Build It, Will They Come?

Have you ever had a moment like that? Do you allow your heart to grow tender toward those who are not yet convinced? As you open your eyes to see seekers as Jesus does, you are being prepared to authentically reach out to them with his message of good news.

But where do you begin? And what path offers the greatest potential for launching and leading a successful seeker small group? Let's assume you are open to the challenge of starting a small group for seekers. You like the idea of leading non-Christians in discussions, so you've made all the necessary preparations. You have the date, place, and time of the first meeting firmly established. You have a nice meeting room arranged with comfortable chairs, and refreshments are waiting for all your guests. You've even identified a couple of Christians to partner with in this endeavor — one to serve as the host for the evening, and the other to act as your apprentice (or coleader). You have all attended training sessions for leading seeker groups and prayed together about reaching out to seekers through this group. You're about as ready as you can get, but as the three of you sit in a circle, waiting to launch the group, the question begs to be asked: "If we build it, will they come? Will the group simply fall into place?"

The answer is a resounding *no.* In fact, it's more accurate to say, "If we build it, they will *not* come."

Getting seekers to attend a seeker group is not a slam dunk; just because you decide to launch a seeker group does not mean that non-Christians will come running up and ask to be included. In fact, usually just the opposite will be true. Seekers will most likely pay you no attention, look the other way, and avoid your group at all costs — unless an essential structure is firmly in place. Without it your seeker group will never get off the ground.

What's missing? The bridge is missing. A bridge of trust between you and the seekers you want to reach needs to be securely in place before you can successfully invite them to be part of your group. When it comes down to it, two kinds of seekers are potential group members — those you know reasonably well and those you hardly know at all. Which type of seeker do you think is more likely to accept your invitation? Most definitely, the ones who know and trust you will be the ones drawn to your group. Once you have made a relationship connection and a foundation of trust is firmly established, you will then have earned the right to invite seekers to visit your group. And that's what this chapter is all about: building bridges with seekers. What follows may be the single most important secret behind the successful launch of a seeker small group.

My friendship with Jay became one of those life-changing experiences that set the stage for me to discover and develop some important principles behind building bridges of trust with seekers. Over the years, I have condensed those ideas into four simple "handles" for effectively building relationships with unchurched people.

Ultimately, your grasp of these handles will determine whether or not seekers will attend your group. So hold on tight and watch the trust level of seekers soar.

## Hang Out Together

The first handle to grasp is the development of authentic, caring friendships with seekers, and this is best accomplished by spending time with them on a consistent basis. It's a simple handle conceptually, but it is all too often missed practically. In fact, of the four handles, this is commonly the greatest obstacle for Christians.

It seems the longer we have been Christ followers, the fewer and fewer non-Christian connections we maintain. This is sometimes referred to as the holy huddle syndrome. We are busy people and our limited time forces us to be selective about whom we will share this most valuable commodity with. Given the choice, we Christians usually hang out with fellow believers, simply because we have more in common with them. We attend church with them, join small group Bible studies with them, and socialize with them. When we take a new job, we pray that our coworkers will be Christians. When we move into a new neighborhood, we hope there will be other Christian families on our block with whom we can interact and develop friendships. But as the years go by, we look back and discover that we have systematically eliminated most of our associations with people far from God.

But this is not the example Jesus modeled for us. In fact, when it came to developing friendships with seekers, he was accused of spending *too much* time with the "sinners." Wouldn't it be his desire for us that the longer we have been walking with him, the more tender our hearts should become toward those outside the kingdom of God? Wouldn't it honor him if we were to take time to gather more — not fewer — seekers around us?

This first handle reminds and challenges all of us to break out of our holy huddles and hang out with non-Christians, rubbing shoulders with them on a regular basis. One of the best ways to start is to identify areas of *common ground* that we have with non-Christians and focus on engaging in those activities together. In other words, if you enjoy playing golf and know that some of your coworkers like playing a round now and then, make it a point to include them instead of golfing only with your Christian associates. Go out to eat, go to the movies, attend sporting or social events just as you normally would, but invite your seeking friends to go with you. You don't have to rearrange your schedule or add another item to your to-do list. Just continue to do the things you usually do, but simply be more inclusive about whom you do them with.

It's important to note that the purpose behind hanging out with seekers is to develop authentic, caring friendships with them. In 1 Corinthians 9:19, 22–23 Paul wrote, "Though I am free and belong to no man, I make myself a slave to everyone, to win as many as possible. . . . To the weak I became weak, to win the weak. I have become all things to all men so that by all possible means I might save some. I do all this for the sake of the gospel, that I may share in its blessings."

To follow Paul's example, you will want to remember to do those commonsense things that foster a solid, growing, and sincere relationship. Things so simple as remembering people's names (along with their correct spelling and pronunciation) go a long way in showing that you care about the details that matter to them. Good friends express genuine appreciation in seeing one another by greeting each other with smiles and direct eye contact. People who care ask sincere questions and are good listeners. Philippians 2:3–4 emphasizes this point well: "Do nothing out of selfish ambition or vain conceit, but in humility consider others better than yourselves. Each of you should look not only to your own interests, but also to the interests of others." In other words, remember to be a good friend.

A good resource for sharpening skills in this area is Dale Carnegie's *How to Win Friends and Influence People.* Assuming that the motives behind using this tool are purely to build genuine, authentic, caring friendships, this book is an outstanding guide. Our goal, as we associate with seekers, is to build bridges of trust and respect. This means we must be careful not to harbor a condescending or judgmental spirit, as such attitudes will quickly dismantle the bridges of trust we are trying to build. After all, our calling is not merely to "put in our time" with non-Christians but to give them our hearts as well. Paul set the standard when he wrote in 1 Thessalonians 2:7–8, "We proved to be gentle among you, as a nursing mother tenderly cares for her own children. Having thus a fond affection for you, we were well-pleased to impart to you not only the gospel of God but also our own lives, because you had become very dear to us" (NASB). Proactively look for ways you can authentically demonstrate your love and concern for the spiritual seekers in *your* life.

If you need to make improvements in this area, devise a strategy to facilitate changes. This may mean altering your whole way of thinking so you're making it a priority to spend more time with non-Christians and hanging out with them whenever you can. Or it may mean writing out a list of names of non-Christians in your life and circle of influence, then starting to pray for them on a regular basis. Pray that God would give you the eyes to see them as they really are — people who matter to God. And ask God to give you the vision to see that as you spend quality time with non-Christians, you're building bridges of trust. With that vision sealed in your mind, may you be filled with the inspiration and motivation you need to make a difference.

## Drop Clues Right Away

Two acquaintances worked at the same office complex for an entire year before they discovered they were both Christians. Why did it take so long? Neither had ever offered any clues about their spiritual interests and involvement. They had never even mentioned that they attended church, had kids in the youth program, or were involved in a Bible study. Such hints about our spiritual lives are simple ways to identify ourselves with Christ, and the longer we put off sharing them, the harder it becomes to do so. Just as hanging out with seekers builds bridges of trust, dropping clues about your interest in spiritual matters builds platforms from which you can eventually launch deeper discussions about the Christian message.

The second handle for building relationships that make a spiritual impact is to let the seekers you're developing friendships with see aspects of your spiritual side. This is best done gradually, but be mindful to let them in on what makes you tick, spiritually speaking, early in the development of your relationship. Also make sure the intensity and extent of your clues are appropriate. Don't overwhelm someone in your attempt to enlighten him or her about your spiritual interests.

Now, it's critical to note that the underlying motivation for dropping clues about our spiritual lives should be to simply give others, in a sincere and open way, a glimpse into what matters most to us. This should really go without saying, but it's too important to assume it's understood: dropping clues is *not* about using manipulation tactics. It's *not* about tricking someone into spiritual conversations. It is, rather, all about being vulnerable, open, and honest about who we are and what we're about. It's genuinely and sensitively letting people see inside our hearts and souls. And if it sparks interest or curiosity that someday leads to something deeper, that's wonderful.

All too often the tendency among Christians is to sink back in fear and purposely hide one's spiritual side from people. That fear of rejection then winds up quenching in others any inquisitiveness that otherwise might be present. It is far more effective to be an authentic person about *all* of who you are. Don't attempt either to hide or overly display your spiritual nature; just respond naturally with what's in your heart.

With this motive firmly in mind, here are two examples of spiritual clues you might drop:

1. Offer to pray for the needs of seekers, and then do so later privately. Say something like, "Would you mind if I prayed for you and the situation you just mentioned? If it's all right with you, I'd like to keep that in my prayers. And by the way, if there's ever anything else you'd like me to pray for you about, just let me know." What you're doing here is dropping a clue, a little hint, that you're a spiritual person or that you believe in God or that you believe in prayer.

2. Be open about your church activities and involvement. If somebody asks what you did over the weekend, your description could go something like this: "Well, I saw a movie with my wife and another couple, and then we had dinner at a great new restaurant. Sunday morning we went to our church and in the afternoon I played golf. Do you play?"

Your seeking friend will most likely register a mental note about the hints you drop in your offer to pray or your brief description of your weekend activities. Depending on where he or she is spiritually, a variety of reactions could occur. On one extreme, you might get labeled as a religious fanatic—and even find yourself avoided in the future. On the other extreme, your hint might prompt a direct question or comment from someone who's exploring spiritual alternatives. Or you may notice a somewhat mixed response. For example, if you are someone that person is enjoying getting to know but your clue sent signals that triggered a preconceived negativity toward "religious" people, your friend may not know exactly how to respond. Don't be too concerned about this. If you are building a solid bridge of trust, your friendship will withstand the temporary perplexity. And your openness may be the very thing that sets your new friend's spiritual journey in motion. Despite the potential risk of scaring someone off with an honest yet sensitive disclosure about your spiritual side, it is better to be true to who you are than to hide your identity in Christ.

Although a few non-Christians may initially reject a friendship with you due to their discovery of your spiritual nature, they may turn out to be the very ones who double back at some point in the future. If they come upon hard times or for some reason acquire an interest in spiritual things, it may very well dawn on them that you were the one person in their pathway who demonstrated spiritual sensitivity. They may remember your reference to prayer or church and wonder if you would be willing to talk them through a current difficulty or spiritual question. That has happened to me time and time again. But it's really only a possibility when you and I are willing to drop hints here and there about our spiritual identity.

Now, of course, we all have different personalities and styles that will dictate the way we go about this. I've seen some Christians appear to take out a baseball bat and hit people over the heads with their "clues." They place religious bumper stickers on their cars, carry around big Bibles, wear buttons stating religious clichés, or use heavy religious jargon. Those are all ways to make a statement about one's religious inclination. But I prefer more subtle approaches. And you must decide for yourself the best way to go about dropping clues—just be sure to employ some common sense and sensitivity and to place seekers' needs before your own.

Dropping clues about your spiritual interests is a simple way to identify yourself as a Christ follower. It builds bridges of openness with your seeker friends. Coupled with the first handle of spending time with seekers and building bridges of trust, this second handle offers a powerful spiritual dimension to your growing friendship. As you model and practice being open and vulnerable about who you are, you will establish the avenue for seekers to someday do the same with you.

One final caution bears keeping in mind. The longer you wait to let somebody see who you are in Christ, the harder it will be. If you've ever had the awkward experience of opening up about your spiritual life for the first time with someone you've known for years, you know exactly what I mean. In a sense, you've been hiding something for far too long. Who could blame your friend for thinking, *You mean to tell me that I've known you all these years and you've never mentioned anything about this before? How can it be that important?* Of course, even though it can be awkward, it's really never too late to be forthright and drop clues about your true identity. But insofar as it is possible, let people know about your spiritual side early in your relationship.

At this juncture I'm compelled to offer a flat-out guarantee. If you will take a firm grip on these first two handles — if you will regularly hang out with seekers and drop clues about your identity in Christ along the way — it will be only a matter of time before you will have tremendous opportunities to talk with friends about spiritual things at a much deeper level! And isn't that what Christ asks us to do — engage people with the gospel? Once you make hanging out and dropping clues central to your lifestyle, keep your eyes open, because opportunities are coming your way. Which is exactly what the next handle is all about.

## Look for Open Windows

The third handle for building bridges with seekers is this: Look for open windows of opportunity to engage your seeking friend in conversations about Christ. It may sound obvious, but are we really on the lookout? Do we truly seek occasions to interject a spiritually significant comment or ask questions that could spark further conversation? Deeper levels of dialogue can and will happen, but first we have to identify and pursue those spiritual-conversation-starting opportunities that come our way.

These possibilities often come upon us like a fork in the road. We can choose to ignore the option of engaging in a spiritual conversation and instead move on to other topics. Or we can choose to test the openness of our seeking friends by asking a probing question or making a spiritually significant comment or two. Seizing the moment like that could trigger a positive response that could in turn take us down the path of discussing spiritual topics at a much deeper level. The choice to check out a seeker's receptivity to spiritual conversations is really ours to make.

This doesn't mean, however, that we must always select the road that leads to a spiritual conversation. Sometimes we must wisely decide *not* to take that option, because the timing is off or the person is not ready. But it has been my observation that most of us let those golden opportunities slip by, simply because we are not even aware that they are before us. Our eyes are closed. If we are to build significant spiritual bridges with seekers, we must always be on the lookout for the opportunities to turn the conversation toward spiritual things.

Lee Strobel, author of *The Case for Christ* and *The Case for Faith,* pointed me to a great approach to stay on our toes and remain aware of the opportunities that come our way. It's a simple technique for putting our minds to work for us. Have you ever heard of the reticular activating center, located deep in the human brain? Lee explained that this portion of the brain is responsible for triggering our minds to remember specific occurrences. It somehow alerts us to whatever stimuli that we (either consciously or subconsciously) have programmed it to notice.

Has this ever happened to you? You get a new car — let's say, a Ford Mustang — and suddenly you find yourself always noticing other Ford Mustangs out on the road. Your reticular activating center is at work, simply flipping those switches in your brain to pick up on and respond to any Ford Mustang you encounter. In a similar way, you can sort of "preprogram" or condition your mind to be on the lookout for opportunities to engage your seeking friends in conversations about spiritual things.

Most of us do not realize how many times a day we let those opportunities pass us by, simply because we're not looking for them. Through prayer, though, God can help us adjust our focus, shift our priorities, and keep ourselves aware and on the lookout. With some determination we can activate our minds to flag those windows of opportunity and bring them to the forefront of our thinking.

And once you're in lookout mode, you'll be amazed at how frequently those windows will open up right before your eyes. They may open unexpectedly and then may open only a small crack, but if you're patient and test the waters at appropriate times by asking probing spiritual questions or making comments or observations, the window could open quite wide. Before you know it, you'll be engaged in a thrilling conversation about Christ, at a much deeper level than you thought possible.

Of course, there will be times when you will find a small opening and make an attempt to connect in a spiritual conversation, only to have the window abruptly slam shut. When that's the case, it's important to recognize a closed situation and back way off. Don't try to force something to happen unnaturally. Realize that you can only go as far into a spiritual discussion as the other person will allow. In some cases an apology may even be in order. If someone says that he or she isn't interested in discussing spiritual matters, simply say something like, "Oh, I'm sorry, I didn't mean to offend you. I was just wondering about your spiritual perspective on things, but I didn't mean to come across as being pushy or too personal."

Sometimes, when we take the risk to test our seeking friends' receptivity, the window flies wide open! Capitalize on that with a sensitivity to the Spirit's leading. Ask a probing question about the person's religious background, beliefs about God and his Son, or recent religious experiences. Keep in mind that at this point your role is really more about asking questions and discovering where a seeker is coming from than about giving out snappy answers. Prayerfully and carefully ask your seeker friend more probing spiritual questions or gently drop more clues about your interest in spiritual matters. As you continue to discuss these kinds of things, you'll realize that you can engage your friend in spiritual topics at deeper and deeper levels, eventually finding yourself explaining why you find fulfillment in God, why Christ means so much to you, and other eternal and significant matters.

Most likely, the only way a conversation about spiritual things will happen is if *you* get things started. And you *can* choose to be a person who engages others in conversations about Christ. That's a decision you can make. As you go about your life, you can pray, "Lord, if there's an open window of opportunity, give me the courage to explore it. And if there's any willingness on the part of my seeking friends, give me the wisdom to know how to follow through and see what you will do. I'll trust you, Lord, for the results. If they slam the window in my face, that's okay; I'll back off. If they're open, I want to be ready and prepared." You can do that.

So hang out with non-Christians, rub shoulders with them on a regular basis, and do life with them. And as you spend time together, appropriately drop clues about your own faith in some form or another to let them see who you are in Christ. Then take the many significant opportunities that will come your way to dialogue with seekers at a deeper level about what it means to know Christ.

## Get the Message Down

As you develop friendships with seekers and share spiritual conversations with them, you will eventually have a chance to explain the gospel message. It is imperative that you know that message so well that you can share it in a clear and compelling way. So start preparing now!

And that's the fourth handle: Get the message down. Understand the gospel message so well that you can explain it to others in simple terms. Know it backward and forward. Know how to explain it in thirty seconds or thirty minutes. You need to be able to present it using various illustrations to help people understand exactly what it means to accept Christ. On the flip side, of course, there's some danger in memorizing gospel illustrations so well that you find yourself going on autopilot. Be careful to tailor your approach so you can personalize your explanation to the other person's specific needs and issues.

In Colossians 4:2–6 Paul wrote, "Devote yourselves to prayer, keeping alert in it with an attitude of thanksgiving; praying at the same time for us as well, that God may open up to us a door for the word, so that we may speak forth the mystery of Christ.... In order that I may make it clear in the way I ought to speak. Be wise in the way you act toward outsiders; make the most of every opportunity.

Let your conversation be always full of grace, seasoned with salt, so that you may know how to answer everyone."

This ought to be our prayer as well. We need to be very wise in our approach to building bridges with seekers. We need to be fully leveraging the opportunities that come our way. And we need to be fully prepared to clearly articulate the gospel message and address our seeking friends' specific questions and concerns about it.

In presenting this challenge, 1 Peter 3:15 reads: "Always be prepared to give an answer to everyone who asks you to give the reason for the hope that you have. But do this with gentleness and respect." For most of us, the best way to be prepared is to obtain some formal training in evangelism. We must look for ways to get equipped, so we become confident in our ability to clearly articulate the gospel and to assist seekers to positively respond to Jesus Christ. The *Becoming a Contagious Christian* course, for instance, is an outstanding evangelism training tool. It provides guidance, for example, regarding how to use several gospel illustrations effectively. (Take a look at the example on the next page from this helpful resource.)

Another resource, called *The Three Habits of Highly Contagious Christians,* is a training tool I developed to inspire and equip Christians to get intentional about effectively reaching out to seekers. The three short sessions are primarily designed to get small groups of believers discussing practical ways to *apply* the principles outlined in this chapter.

As you work to master these four handles for building bridges with seekers, ask yourself which of them you're already confident using and which of them need the most improvement. Then do your best to make all of them a way of life, because these handles really are the prerequisite to inviting people to visit your seeker small group.

Practice them on a consistent basis. If you drop clues as you hang out with seekers, and look for open windows to engage others with a clear presentation of the gospel message, you can earn the right to invite them to a discussion about spiritual things. And that's why seekers will come to your group. They will come because of *you,* not because of anything else (besides the work of the Holy Spirit, of course!). They will accept the invitation because they know and trust the one extending it. You may even be surprised, but they *will* come.

# DO VS. DONE

| NARRATIVE | OUTLINE |
|---|---|
| The difference between religion and Christianity is: | |
| Religion is spelled "D-O." It consists of trying to do enough good things to somehow please God, earn his forgiveness, and gain entrance into heaven. This self-effort plan can take on many forms, from trying to be a good, moral person to becoming an active participant in an organized religion— Christian or otherwise. | **RELIGION**<br>• Is spelled "D-O"<br>• Trying to do enough good things to please God |
| The problem is, we can never know when we have done enough. Even worse, the Bible makes it clear that we can *never* do enough in Romans 3:23: "For all have sinned and fall short of the glory of God." Simply put, the "D-O" plan cannot bring us peace with God, or even peace with ourselves. | **THE PROBLEM**<br>• We can never know when we have done enough<br>• The Bible says that we can *never* do enough (Romans 3:23) |
| Christianity, however, is spelled "D-O-N-E." In other words, that which we could never *do* for ourselves, Christ has already *done* for us. He lived the perfect life we could never live, and he died on the cross to pay for each of our wrongdoings. And now he freely offers us his gift of forgiveness and leadership for our lives. | **CHRISTIANITY**<br>• Is spelled "D-O-N-E"<br>• Christ did what we could never do<br>  — Lived the perfect life we could not<br>  — Died on the cross to pay for our wrongdoings |
| But it's not enough just to know this; we have to humbly receive what he has done for us. And we do that by asking for his forgiveness and leadership in our lives. | **OUR RESPONSE**<br>• It's not enough just to know this<br>• We have to receive what he has done for us by asking for his forgiveness and leadership in our lives |
| (At this point, ask a follow-up question like "Does this make sense to you?" or "What do you think about what I just said?") | **THEIR RESPONSE**<br>• Does this make sense to you?<br>• What do you think about what I just said? |

Excerpt from *Becoming a Contagious Christian Participant's Guide* by Mark Mittelberg, Lee Strobel, and Bill Hybels. Copyright © 1995 by the Willow Creek Association. Used by permission of Zondervan.

Remember my high school friend Jay? After that last tennis match it was two years before I heard from him again. One day, out of the blue, I heard his voice on the telephone:

"Hey, guess what!"

"Jay, is that you?"

"Yes. Guess what!"

"*What?*"

Jay related his story. "When I got here to college, I became friends with some students who happened to be Christians. Right away they invited me to join them for some small group discussions about the Bible and Christianity. So I decided to take them up on it, and of course I brought all of my tough questions with me — you know, the same ones you never seemed to be able to answer!" (His competitive spirit was still intact.)

"After intensely wrestling with those spiritual issues," he continued, "I took a big step and decided there really might be a God out there after all. I started trying to figure out what he might be like and why he might act the way he does. I got to the point where I became convinced God not only existed but that he actually cared about me. Eventually I discovered it was possible to get to know God on a personal level, so I decided to ask Jesus Christ to be the forgiver and leader of my life. It took me two years to get to this point, but it was well worth the journey."

I was amazed — and thrilled! To think that I may have played a small role in seeing Jay come to Christ and have his whole life changed for all eternity was mind-boggling! A short time later I stumbled upon a passage of Scripture that reminded me of my interactions with Jay. Psalm 126:5–6 reads, "Those who sow in tears will reap with songs of joy. He who goes out weeping, carrying seed to sow, will return with songs of joy, carrying sheaves with him." This promise came true for me and has become for me a great source of encouragement with my ongoing efforts in evangelism.

And although I received that "Guess what!" phone call from Jay many years ago, to this day it still motivates me to keep reaching out to seekers. I'm reminded to hang out with non-Christians and drop those clues about my spirituality right away; to keep on praying and looking for open windows of opportunity to explain the gospel; and to invite seeking friends to church services, seeker small groups, and other outreach events.

And as if I needed additional motivation, I got a knock on my office door a while back from a pastor visiting Willow Creek during one of our conferences. He introduced himself and said, "I wanted to stop by and thank you for something. You see, your friend Jay led *me* to Christ. And it changed my life forever. I've been so impacted by the love of Christ that I left the marketplace and now I want to do everything I can to help others find Christ too. So thank you." That conversation settled it for me. Nothing compares with living a highly contagious Christian life.

# DAVE PACK'S STORY

*Sales Account Manager*
*Des Plaines, Illinois*

*M*y spiritual journey really started with my desire to meet new people and develop friendships.

Through my school years, you might say I'd been a "holiday visitor," attending church on Easter and Christmas but giving it very little thought the rest of the year. In my late twenties, though, I got more intentional, visiting churches and eventually finding Willow Creek. I'd attended weekend services for a couple months when one morning I heard an announcement inviting spiritual seekers to stop by the welcome center after the service.

There I met Paul Mylander, who asked me how long I had attended Willow, what my church background was—things like that. He and his wife, Nancy, were starting a seeker small group to explore what the Bible had to say about living life, and he wondered if I'd like to join them. That sounded promising, because to tell you the truth, I'd recently broken up with my girlfriend and I thought to myself, If this guy has some women in his group, count me in!

I attended the group right away. It quickly became a great opportunity to build friendships. We met on Wednesday nights, and on the weekends the group sat together for the services—always in the same spot, so even if you were running late, you'd know where to find familiar faces.

When we arrived for our 6:00 meetings, Paul and Nancy would be so glad to see us, greeting us with handshakes and hugs and eagerly asking how things were going. Their interest was very sincere. Nancy was warm and friendly and Paul was never rushed. When 7:30 rolled around, he'd never say, "Well, we'd better all go home now." If you needed to talk, he had the time. He'd stay right there with you if you needed him to.

We discussed various topics from the Bible, but unless someone had a question about something, we didn't spend a lot of time on it. Paul would say, "What questions do you have about this issue?" He seldom answered those questions with his own opinions, though. Instead he'd say, "Let's hear what others think and read what the

Bible says about that." We'd look to the Scripture and most of the time find the answer right then. If we couldn't, Paul would say, "I'll look into that and get back to you." And he always did. I began to see that the Bible was a book I could trust. I was amazed that it addressed the issues we had.

As for me, I really didn't have many burning questions. Instead I did a lot of listening. And I watched Paul—carefully. I wondered who his friends were and what he did with his time. I admired the patience he demonstrated. I watched how he reacted to people, and wondered what accounted for the joy he seemed to get out of leading this group.

To be honest, part of me was thinking, "If he drops the ball, I'm outta here." But he never did. Instead he gave me an understanding of what it means to have a relationship with Christ. Time and again he demonstrated his heart for his God and for people. And when he told us the story about his decision to accept Jesus, he became a living example of God's grace and the power of God to turn a life around. He'd say, "Here's what God did for me and here's what God can do for you."

The need to decide one way or another about God was always in front of us. Sometimes Paul would ask, "On a scale of one to ten, if five is where you cross the line of faith, where are you?" It was a very safe thing—there was never any pressure to give a "right" answer. In fact, I remember one group member who'd say he was "about a negative one"! I'd usually say I was around a three or four.

A few months later I was having dinner with Nancy and Paul one night before the group was to meet. Paul got up to see if anyone else had arrived yet and Nancy stayed with me. We talked a little while and then she asked me a question I'll never forget. She said, "So where are you these days with your decision to trust Christ?" That was the first time I realized it was really up to me. I had a choice to make.

I've come to be a big believer in asking that kind of question. It's especially effective in getting a person to think about the answer—and the need to step up to it. For me, that happened on July 22. I finally decided there wasn't anything standing in my way of receiving Jesus Christ right then and there. I'd been going to the group long enough that all my objections had been satisfied. So on that rainy

*July afternoon, I prayed to accept Christ into my life. I called Paul right away and he congratulated me over the phone; then he asked me to share as much about my decision as I wanted at our next group meeting.*

*That was almost seven years ago. Now Paul has retired to North Carolina and Nancy has gone to be with the Lord. But their example continues to inspire me. They modeled a Christian lifestyle that gave me the inspiration to develop one myself. And today, thanks to Paul's challenge, I'm leading a small group for new Christians.*

# RUTH STARRETT'S STORY

*Retired Teacher*
*Wayne, Illinois*

*F*rom time to time my neighbor Pat stops by my home for a visit. She's always so kind and sincere and I enjoy our conversations. One day she invited me to try out her women's neighborhood Bible study group. She knew I was not a religious person and had not been to church in years, but she thought I would enjoy it anyway. I told her I was somewhat interested but couldn't attend, because I was working for my son, who is a doctor. But shortly thereafter I had a mild stroke and took that as a sign that it was time for me to retire— I was, after all, eighty-four. It wasn't long before Pat was calling me to see how I was doing, and once again inviting me to join her small group. This time I said yes.

I have always liked to read, but I had never read the Bible for either pleasure or study. I thought it was about time I made an effort to actually read the Bible. So out of intellectual curiosity, I decided to attend a small group Bible study for the first time ever. I hoped that this group experience would be interesting and informative. I also went because I trusted my friend Pat—I just knew she wouldn't steer me wrong.

Since I no longer drove, Pat was kind enough to pick me up and take me with her to the small group meetings. Each week's discussion was interesting and informative. Even though I felt welcome to participate in the discussion, at first I preferred to do more listening and observing. But everyone made me feel comfortable no matter how much or little I contributed.

The thing that surprised me most was the depth of the women's openness. They talked and even complained about issues I had always considered simply a part of life and certainly not things to share in a group setting. But this kind of interaction gave me a chance to get to know them at a much deeper level than I had expected. It was refreshing to hear people be so genuine. I was particularly touched by the love and prayer expressed for Joanne, a young woman struggling with cancer.

*During one of the most memorable meetings, a woman named Margaret, who was just a few years younger than me, shared her story. I had recently seen radical changes in her life and was interested in what she had to say. She told about being completely transformed by Jesus Christ. She explained that the Bible describes her experience as being "born again." That's what I wanted. I needed what she had.*

*I have come to understand who God is and what the purpose of life is really all about. I personally accepted Jesus Christ as my Savior and Lord just a couple years ago — at the ripe old age of ninety-two! Of course, my only regret is that I didn't know about God's great gift to us many, many years earlier.*

*In addition to Margaret, I have been amazed to see drastic changes in the lives of many other women through the years — including the changes that have occurred in me! I have learned so much. I used to want total control, but I have learned to put my life in God's hands and trust him. Now I see through a different set of eyes because I see the handiwork of God in so many ways that I never even noticed before.*

Part 2

# ATTRACTING SEEKERS
# TO SMALL GROUPS

With the principles from the last two chapters firmly in mind, you're now ready to zero in on how to form and launch your seeker small group. Chapter 3, Extend Irresistible Invitations, focuses on identifying the fears your seeking friends may have about attending—and addresses those fears so seekers can feel safe enough to give your group a try. In this chapter you will learn how to make an invitation to your seeker group clear and compelling. Chapter 4, Conduct the All-Important First Meeting, lays out a detailed plan for how to conduct your first meeting and includes a sample session with explanations of each of the recommended components.

## Chapter 3

# Extend Irresistible Invitations

✦

*The Spirit told Philip, "Go to that chariot and stay near it."*

*Then Philip ran up to the chariot and heard the man reading Isaiah the prophet. "Do you understand what you are reading?" Philip asked.*

*"How can I," he said, "unless someone explains it to me?" So he invited Philip to come up and sit with him.*

Acts 8:29–31

*Now go; I will help you speak and will teach you what to say.*

Exodus 4:12

hat on earth am I doing here?" Ken muttered under his breath. Fist poised to knock on the front door, he nearly gave up without trying. In fact, he had done exactly that, *twice*, just a few days earlier. As he walked through his neighborhood to invite men to try out a new seeker small group he was forming, he focused on those he knew best — the ones most likely to say yes. No way was the guy on the other side of this door going to accept his invitation.

But Ken couldn't shake the feeling that he was *supposed* to ask this neighbor. He sensed the tug of God about this one. So on this third trip up these particular front steps, he took a deep breath and knocked.

Ken Wilson and his friend Bruce Kramer, who had agreed to host the upcoming seeker group meetings at his home, spent two hot July weeks inviting neighborhood friends to visit their new small group. Between them they asked about forty men, challenging even the skeptical ones to check out at least one meeting. "We gave them a handout that included the date and time, and showed them a copy of a book we were going to use as a study guide," Ken explains. "When someone hesitated, we urged him to show up just once, and if after that it wasn't his thing, that was fine. We didn't want anybody to feel pressured into joining something they weren't ready for."

Later that summer fifteen men showed up for the first meeting. And to Ken's surprise and excitement, they included the very neighbor he had been so reluctant to approach! "He came as kind of a curious spectator," Ken says. And as it turned out, the timing of his visit would be critical.

"That first meeting was low-key, more relationally than spiritually focused," Ken remembers. "Part of what I did was assure everyone they were not going to be asked to pray or read the Bible or even say anything if they didn't want to. Nobody had to ever worry about being put on the spot." The whole group, though, did participate in the icebreaker exercises, in which each man answered a few get-to-know-you questions, including, "In an emergency, how many friends would you feel free to call in the middle of the night?"

"Most of the guys named one or two people, but the neighbor I almost didn't invite admitted he had absolutely no one he could call," Ken recalls. "But less than a week later, at midnight, this man received some devastating news concerning his son, and the first thing he did was to make phone calls to Bruce and me. That very night the three of us gathered at his home. We prayed and even shed a few tears together, and he was so thankful he had people he could trust to help him through what turned out to be a very difficult situation. Later that year, after several other group members had taken the step to invite the Lord into their lives, he too made that life-changing commitment. The man whose house I almost skipped may well have been impacted more by that small group than anyone else there."

Back up and freeze-frame in your mind that picture of Ken's clenched fist poised to knock on his neighbor's front door. That image, right there, captures the most difficult step in launching a seeker small group — extending the invitation. There Ken stood, filled with doubts, ready to drop his arm and turn to walk away for the third time. But the prospect of an accepted invitation and the onset of a journey of a lifetime drew him to knock and ask.

Without a doubt, the toughest part of launching a seeker small group is extending the invitation. It is in those moments that you set yourself up to potentially encounter your greatest discouragement and disappointment. The very act of offering an invitation to someone puts you in the vulnerable position of facing rejection. But as Ken's experience demonstrates, it's precisely within a seeker small group setting that real life-change can occur. So it's well worth every calculated risk we take to carefully extend invitations to seekers. The invitation *must* be made; it's where the rubber meets the road — no one will ever come to your group without it. It's as simple as that.

## Seekers' Fears Matter

In this chapter we will examine some ways to extend irresistible invitations to seekers. But before we consider this further, we must return to our initial premise and ultimate motivation for starting seeker small groups. We must remind ourselves that *seekers matter.* They matter to God and they ought to truly matter to us. And if they really *do* matter to us, we must first wisely and prudently take into account the feelings and fears seekers have about receiving an invitation to attend a seeker small group.

As you imagine inviting seeking friends to your small group, what reservations do you think they might have about accepting your invitation? What concerns and reactions can you envision? What obstacles might they encounter as they consider attending your group? After leading scores of seeker groups and interviewing hundreds of seekers over the years, I've accumulated the following list of some of the most common categories of these fears and reservations.

### Fear of the Unknown

Most seekers have never been to a small group discussion, let alone one focused on spiritual matters. They don't know what goes on in a typical meeting and have no idea what to expect, and that's a big concern for them. So as they consider attending, all kinds of questions fill their minds. How many other group members will be there? What are the others like? How long will the meeting last? What topics will be discussed? Is singing and praying involved? How much knowledge is required? What needs to be understood or believed already? Are people lectured at or preached to? These kinds of questions inundate seekers and cause them to proceed slowly and cautiously.

### Fear of Exposing Ignorance

Most seekers have not read much of the Bible and may not be very familiar with the teachings of Christianity or other religions. No one wants to put himself in the awkward position of looking or feeling stupid in a group setting — another good reason to decline an invitation.

### Fear of Being Put on the Spot

The last thing seekers want to do is put themselves in the uncomfortable position of being asked to pray out loud or to turn to an unfamiliar portion of Scripture and read words they cannot pronounce. Will they be called on to answer questions they feel are too difficult or too personal? Will they be pressured into telling everyone their deepest, darkest secrets and forced to open up in ways that would be uncomfortable? These kinds of scenarios and questions run through their minds as they consider attending a group meeting, and often their conclusion is to avoid it like the plague.

### Fear of a Long-Term Commitment

Seekers have the idea that if they attend just one meeting, they might then be locked into attending a whole series of meetings for many months to come. The fear of feeling trapped in an unsatisfactory group situation, with no way out, is enough to keep them away.

### Fear of Not Fitting In and of Being Judged

Seekers have concerns about not having much in common with any of the other participants. They doubt they will connect well with the others and may also feel that opening up about their lifestyles or beliefs will mean being looked down upon. Perceiving disapproval and judgment from you and the other members of the group is not something seekers want to deal with.

### Fear of Change

Seekers are afraid that if they get in too deep with a small group, they will be asked to make drastic changes in their lifestyles, give up all their current friends, and "get converted." They are not especially open to making radical changes in their lives, especially if they feel that things are going along just fine the way they are. Some also have the perception that Christians are fanatical and odd — traits they do not wish to emulate.

### Fear of Joining a Cult

A very real (and legitimate) concern seekers have is that by visiting a spiritual group, they will be getting involved with a religious cult or some odd gathering with strange and scary practices. This thought will no doubt send them running for the hills.

### Fear of Wasting Time and Money

Everyone is busy and seekers worry that the group will simply be a waste of time. There's the additional concern that the group is going to somehow use pressure tactics to collect money for some "worthy" cause.

### Fear of Confidentiality Leaks

Seekers are concerned not only that things they share in the group will not be kept confidential but also that their attendance in the group meeting will be made known.

### Fear of Rejection

As seekers consider attending your group, something of a catch-22 can go on inside their minds: If they decline your invitation to participate in your seeker group, they will disappoint you. But if they accept the invitation, there's still the possibility of jeopardizing their relationship with you by not responding the "right" way during group discussions. Either way they are faced with the possibility of being rejected by you, which leaves them in a difficult dilemma.

These and other fears hinder your seeking friends from accepting your invitations to visit your seeker small group. So it is essential to carefully identify and address them *before* you extend any invitations. One of the best ways to prepare yourself for this is to reflect, with your apprentice leaders (as well as other seeker small group leaders), on any and all barriers your seeking friends might encounter as they consider attending your group. Spend some extended time thinking about this, because it's crucial to understand the mind-set of your seeking friends. Put yourself in their shoes and ask, "How would I feel about going to this group meeting? What barriers would I encounter?"

And don't stop there. Get on the *solution* side. Take the next step and consider ways to alleviate and dispel those fears not only in the group discussions, but also in the invitation process. Figure out how to extend the invitation in such a way that you relieve seekers of the fears you've identified. Your invitations will be compelling if they communicate an understanding and compassion about what would make the group safe for your seeking friends.

Before most seekers will accept your invitation to attend your group (and continue to come back), they must be convinced that you as the leader can be trusted. Gain their trust and respect by first taking the time to fully understand your friends and where they are coming from. Your trustworthiness in their eyes will grow by leaps and bounds as they see you going out of your way to ensure safe opportunities for them to investigate spiritual matters.

## Invitation Guidelines

Now you are ready to extend invitations to your seeking friends. The best way to start is simply to develop a list of all the seekers you and your apprentices could invite to your group. (Besides offering support and encouragement, an apprentice effectively doubles your network of potential group members. You'll find a more detailed discussion of the role of an apprentice leader in chapter 8.) Spend time together praying through your list, asking God to go before you to prepare the hearts of the seekers you are considering inviting.

Here are ten suggestions for making irresistible invitations.

## 1. Earn the Right to Invite

Without a doubt, the most important determining factor behind extending an irresistible invitation is the degree of depth in your relationships with the seekers you invite. Most of us will agree to devote at least a limited amount of our time to a trusted friend's cause or request, especially if we are convinced it is only a one-shot deal and includes no pressure for an ongoing commitment. So put those seekers you and your apprentice know best at the top of your list, as they are the ones most likely to accept your invitations. Add to that those seekers with whom you have already had a few spiritual conversations. If you're not sure who you have earned the right to ask to your group, you may want to go back and review chapter 2 about building bridges of trust with seekers. The greater the level of trust you have with your seeking friends, the greater the chance that your request for a onetime visit to your group will be honored.

Last spring my good friend Neil invited me to join him and his two buddies for a round of golf. It had been a very long time since I had played, and I really had no interest in picking it up again. Besides, I was too busy writing this book! But Neil persisted and said, "Come on, man, just join us for nine holes. You never know, maybe you'll hit a good score and like it more than you think." I joined them that day and he was right — once I got out there on the course, I really did have a good time.

Why did I end up golfing that day? Two reasons: First, because someone *invited* me. I would never have initiated hitting a round of golf — I needed someone to *ask* me to go. Second, I went because I enjoy Neil's friendship. When he gave me the invite that day, my thought process went something like this: *I know for sure I'll shoot a miserable score, and I'm not really into golf anymore, but at least I'll enjoy the company. And even though I've never met the other two guys who will be there, I trust Neil enough that I'm sure I'll have fun hanging out with the three of them.* The whole thing hinged on my friendship with Neil. My decision was directly influenced by how much I trusted him.

An effective invitation to a seeker small group works in a similar way. A friendship is established. Trust is built. An invitation is extended. Fears are diminished as the invitation is explained. No threats are ever made and no pressure is exerted about making any commitments beyond the first gathering. And because a fairly significant relationship exists, the invitation is accepted.

As you can see, it is best to focus your efforts primarily on those you've gotten to know well enough to build bridges of trust. Now, of course, this does not mean you should never invite seekers you don't know. There's always the chance that they just might respond positively to a considerate and appealing gesture. But be careful. Don't risk alienating someone and preempting the process of building future bridges of trust. Repairing the damage is sometimes difficult once someone's trust has been violated.

When you do approach seekers with whom you lack much of a connection, be extra sensitive and acknowledge that fact as you invite them to visit your group. Say something like, "I know we don't really know each other that well, but I thought I'd let you know about something I'm doing anyway, just in case you're interested. I'm planning to get together a small group of us from the neighborhood for an hour discussion about the Bible and spiritual things, and it would be great to have you join us. It's open to anyone and everyone, no matter what perspective people are coming from. Would you have any interest in checking it out once?"

## 2. Never Say No for the Seeker

Because extending an invitation to attend a seeker small group can be so challenging, there is a tendency to predetermine who will and will not accept. But in so doing, we could exclude seekers who may very well be eager to attend. So do your best to avoid saying no for someone else by not offering an invitation at all. Also steer clear of phrasing the invitation negatively, such as "You probably wouldn't want to come to my meeting, would you?" In reality it's almost impossible to predict who will accept or decline our invitations, so it's best not to rule out anyone — even those we don't know especially well. You'll be surprised. The very ones you think would never, ever come may end up being the first ones through the door.

## 3. Ask Face to Face

It's best to make the first invitation *in person*. This communicates a level of sincerity and importance not really conveyed through any other means. Stop by their homes, take them out for lunch, or set up appointments, but make every effort to invite your seeking friends in person.

### 4. Be Warm and Friendly

Extend an invitation with kindness and gentleness. An upbeat, enthusiastic approach is important, but always be willing to back off if the person you're inviting expresses a lack of interest.

### 5. Be Very Specific

Communicate exactly what it is you are inviting someone to attend. Describe your gathering as a small group discussion format involving eight to ten people. Explain that the focus of your discussion will be on spiritual issues — using the Bible as a primary resource — but since your group is open to anyone, all perspectives are welcome. Further explain that the emphasis will be on getting to know the others in the group and understanding one another's spiritual perspectives. Give specific details about the date, starting time, ending time, and place of your meeting. It's important not to pull a bait and switch — in other words, don't promise one thing in the invitation and deliver something completely different at the meeting. Be open and honest about what the group will be like.

### 6. Dispel Seekers' Fears

Remember all the fears and obstacles we identified that seekers could have regarding attending a seeker small group? Those concerns need to be addressed and dispelled at some point during your invitation. Usually it's a matter of clearly explaining that your seeker group is designed to be a safe place. Then give your seeking friends assurances that your group will *not* be all that they dread, and especially refer to any specific concerns relevant to them. (Identifying and understanding a seeker's concerns is obviously much easier when you really know the person you're inviting.)

Suppose your friend Dennis is fearful that a small group experience may reinforce his perception that he doesn't understand much about the Bible. On top of that, he is quite shy and doesn't like speaking in front of groups. Though he may not express it, you know he will want to avoid your group for fear that it might set him up for some embarrassing moments. So as you ask Dennis to consider visiting your group, it is absolutely crucial to emphasize that he will never be pressured into talking. Assure him that he can be just an observer, watch how the group works, and only participate if and when he feels ready. Furthermore, reassure him that this group is *designed* for people who are not "Bible know-it-alls"; it's meant for those just starting to investigate spiritual issues. Explain that no one will ever be put on the spot; people will feel completely free to decline if they are not ready to share their observations and opinions. Make it clear that participants are encouraged to investigate at their own pace — in a safe context where the Bible's claims are discussed and discovered one step at a time.

Suppose Amy has shared with you her frustration about past encounters with overly judgmental religious people. In addition, she is concerned about a family member involved with a strange religious cult. As you extend an invitation to her, stress that she'll be able to express any opinions or beliefs, no matter how different or unconventional they may seem, without the fear of being put down or condemned. Emphasize that the whole purpose of your gathering as a group is to give people a forum in which they can be completely open and honest about their true thoughts and feelings, no matter where they are coming from. Also clearly communicate that your group is not affiliated with any cult or "controlling" organization and that group members not only are encouraged to investigate at their own pace but are of course free to come and go as they please.

In the scenarios above, the invitations include assurances that your group will be a safe one to visit. You will need to go out of your way to convince your seeking friends that their particular concerns will be taken into account as you lead the group. You will then need to follow up by doing everything in your power to deliver on that promise.

### 7. *Always Give a Disclaimer*

Since almost every seeker will wonder about the extent of his or her obligation if they visit your group, I strongly recommend that every single time you invite a seeker to your group, let him or her know there is no requirement to return. Here's a great way to express this disclaimer: "Just come one time and check it out. That's all you have to do. Try it once and if it's not for you, you have no obligation to ever come back. But if you do enjoy the time, of course you are welcome to visit again. So why don't you check it out just this once?" This approach assures your friends that they can come for a single, no-obligation visit and that you'll never use any guilt tactics to get them to come again.

### 8. Ask for a Yes or No Response

Even though you'll never want to twist someone's arm to visit your group, I do think it's important to ask for a yes or no response. Avoid using an open-ended invitation like, "Hey, I'm starting up a discussion group and it would be nice if you could come. Our first meeting is next Tuesday night and I sure hope you can be there." That approach sets you up for an ambiguous response: "Okay, thanks for letting me know."

It's much better to request a response one way or the other. "I'm planning a little get-together with four or five other couples in my home in a couple of weeks. We're going to discuss spiritual issues for about an hour over coffee and dessert. There's no obligation to attend any future meetings, and it's made up of people just like you — people just starting out on their spiritual journey. We'd love to have you join us and I think you'd enjoy it. What do you think? Would you and your wife have any interest in joining us? Would you be able to attend?" Try to ask for a decision one way or the other without being too pushy. If your seeking friends need time to decide, offer some reassurances that you understand. Then contact them again to see what they intend to do.

When someone declines, simply state that you totally respect that decision and that it's not a problem. Add something like, "I sure hope I didn't offend you by asking; I just wanted you to know that you are very welcome to attend the group. So if you ever change your mind, please know that you are more than welcome." Assure your friend that declining your invitation in no way alters your friendship.

### 9. Be Patient — Never Give Up

One reason why extending an invitation to a seeker is such a challenging exercise is that the uncertainty factor is so high. It's risky business to invite someone to a seeker gathering; there's always the chance that he or she will decline. That is often difficult to take, especially if it happens over and over again. But rejection is something you need to be willing to face—it comes with the territory. People will say, "No way, I'm not really interested" or "Thanks, but no thanks" or "Sorry, but religion is a personal thing with me." The no comes in many different forms, but it most certainly will come.

At other times seekers may indicate that they are interested in coming but then not show up. They may be immobilized by their fears. But don't be discouraged; recognize and remember that there is a spiritual battle going on. "Our struggle is not against flesh and blood, but against the rulers, against the authorities, against the powers of this dark world and against the spiritual forces of evil in the heavenly realms" (Ephesians 6:12). "The god of this age has blinded the minds of unbelievers, so that they cannot see the light of the gospel of the glory of Christ, who is the image of God" (2 Corinthians 4:4). Seekers have this amazing tendency to act a lot like seekers, which means they may struggle with making progress in their spiritual journey. Their interest and progress may appear inconsistent. It may seem as if they take three steps forward and two steps back.

But know that in many cases it's really just a part of the seeking process. Seekers may initially decline your invitation because they are just not ready—and then surprise you later by asking about coming to your group. More times than I can count, I've had seekers turn down my invitations, only to reinvite themselves a few months later. Sometimes our seeking friends need to go through one or more of life's valleys before they are ready to talk about spiritual things. But when they are ready, they'll remember the invitation you offered them and in many cases contact you about your group. So take the risk and make the ask. The potential positive outcome is well worth it.

From time to time during weekend services here at Willow Creek, we invite seekers to fill out a card to indicate their interest in checking out a seeker small group. Right away our small group leaders contact everyone who expressed an interest, hoping to get them connected into one of their groups. Over the years we have found that on average, for every ten cards we get, only five individuals are still open to attending a group. Isn't that interesting? When it comes down to actually accepting the invitation, five seekers will balk at taking the next step. They probably think to themselves, *Why in the world did I fill out that card? I wish I never had. Now what am I getting myself into?* Their fears and reservations crop up, and they change their minds and back down.

And now, to give you another reality check, think about this: of the remaining five seekers who *do* accept the invitation, on average only three will actually show up at the meeting. (Keep in mind that these seekers were generated from impersonal sign-up cards, *not* existing relationships with the leaders.) Something will come up or their fears will take over. Even though they promised to be there, not all will make it. This is a common pattern for many seekers, so don't be surprised if you get similar results.

Additionally, of the three who do come to the first meeting, only one or two will return for the second gathering, not so much because they didn't like the experience but because a schedule conflict came up or another fear about being in the group came to mind. It's very challenging sometimes for seekers to stay focused on taking another step in their spiritual journeys. But this is a natural tendency and it's important that you know up front what to expect.

On the other hand, there will be those who will say they *don't* want to come to the group, but then something happens; they change their minds a few weeks later and decide to show up after all. Ernie and Ginny tell the story of one seeker who attended two group meetings, then didn't return. But Ernie and Ginny never completely gave up. Without being pushy or forward, they continued to call their friend and extend an invitation to come to the group. From time to time they even sent little notes of encouragement. For six months they let him know he was welcome to come back for another visit.

Ernie and Ginny also never gave up praying for him. And after six months without a positive response, the man came back to the group. He attended for three weeks in a row and then gave his life to Christ, and his whole life was changed! As a seeker small group leader, know that seekers are sometimes inconsistent and you really can't predict what they'll do. But as you continue to pray and to be patient and diligent, you'll never cease to be amazed by how God will use you and your group in the lives of your seeker friends.

### 10. Follow Up with Every Seeker You Invite

Do your best to confirm your seeking friends' responses to your invitations, contacting them to see if they have any questions or concerns you can speak to. Those who have accepted your invitation will need a reminder a few days before the meeting. You might even arrange to travel together to the meeting. A phone call, email, or postcard can be an appropriate, nonintrusive way to touch base. Again, you'll need to use good judgment and not come across as too aggressive, but even those who decline your invitation might appreciate your checking in with them from time to time. Test the waters to determine whether a person is indicating, "No, I'm not interested, so don't ever bother me about it again." If so, respect their position. But if they're saying, "Not now, but feel free to ask me again from time to time," it's probably appropriate to do so.

Much of what you should do depends on the kind of friendship you've established with the person. If your connection is a solid one, you might be able to use a little humor to keep the door open. "You know, one of these days you're going to visit the group — you know that, don't you?" Sometimes seekers just need a little challenge to persuade them. Keep praying about which people to continue to invite.

To further illustrate the care and awareness required to make an effective invitation to seekers, consider the following two scenarios. Suppose you took your five-year-old nephew Will out to lunch the other day. You called him earlier in the week and promised that you'd take him to his favorite restaurant. You told him to make sure it was okay with his mom and dad first, and of course you had a conversation with them about it too. When you arrived, Will was so excited to see you that he ran outside before you even got out of the car! You walked him back into the house, checked in with his mom, found his coat and shoes, and finally headed back to the car. After helping him into the backseat and fastening his seat belt, you were off. You found the restaurant Will described as "the one with all the games and stuff." When his favorite order — including fries and a chocolate shake — was brought to the table, he politely asked you to cut the hamburger in half, just like Mom does. It was fun to hear all about his neighborhood friends, his favorite toys, and his half days at kindergarten. While you were paying the server, he ran off to greet a school friend playing a video game on the other side of the room. When you found him, you had to repeat, "Time to go, Will" several times before he got the idea you were serious. As you settled back in the car to head home, Will thanked you with a very tight hug around your neck. You told him he was welcome with a high five and made him giggle nonstop when you kept pulling your hand away so he'd miss. When you arrived at his house, Will's mom was waiting at the door with a big smile, and he raced to greet her, never noticing your waves goodbye. Lunch with Will is always an experience.

Now imagine that the following day you invited your brother Jim to grab some lunch. You left him a voice mail about where to meet and said that unless you heard otherwise, you'd be there. You were running late, so you were glad he had already gotten a table. Over lunch the two of you talked business, finance, and sports before tackling the heart-wrenching topic of putting Dad in a nursing home. When the bill came, you managed to convince Jim it was his turn to pick it up. He gave in when you informed him that it would cover these free consultation sessions you've been giving him! He was still laughing as you cut out to make your next meeting on time.

As you continue to figure out the best ways to invite your seeking friends to attend your small group, think about this: inviting a *seeker* to a small group is a lot like taking your nephew out to lunch — and inviting a *believer* to a group is similar to meeting your brother for a meal. Believers know the routine. They don't need a lot of extra care or concern. They won't freak out if you're running late or leave them to handle the details on their own. But with seekers it's a whole other story. They don't know the ropes. They need you to meet them right where they are and not assume they're very confident about this spiritual journey thing. Take nothing for granted. Treat them with extra special care because they're not experienced enough in the seeking process to know how to make things go smoothly. After all, they're not yet convinced!

# KEN WILSON'S STORY

*Bridge Engineer*
*Zelienople, Pennsylvania*

*E*vangelism is not in my gift mix and I have had very little training in apologetics. But after completing a training course at a
Willow Creek conference, I knew I wanted to give leading a seeker
small group a shot. I was excited about the possibility of somehow
making an evangelistic impact, and I figured that this was something
I could actually pull off.

So after a lot of planning and praying with Bruce, my apprentice
leader, we began going door to door throughout our neighborhood,
inviting men to join us for a group discussion around spiritual matters. This was not an easy process—eighteen guys turned us down.
Eighteen times we heard the words "No, thanks" or "Sorry, not
interested." We had eighteen solid reasons for calling it quits and giving up. But the discouragement didn't last, because the ones who
responded positively more than made up for the disappointment of
the rejections.

As we reflected on this later, we realized that those we didn't
have a strong relationship with usually did not accept our invitations.
And the ones we invited after we had already built a bond of friendship most often accepted. The key ingredient to our successful invitations was an existing relationship with good rapport.

We wound up meeting twenty-four times between mid-September
and late May, with an average attendance of about ten guys. (I kept
detailed attendance records, which later served as a great way to reflect
on and celebrate all that God had done.) The book we studied covered
issues applicable to the group's participants—how men could be better
husbands or dads, for instance, or how they could best grow their
friendships. It felt very natural when that in turn led the group to investigate what the Bible had to say about those topics.

As friendships deepened and more men joined in the discussions,
my comfort level in facilitating the group developed as well. Even
dealing with a stutter in my speech didn't prevent me from boldly
leading some spiritually significant discussions. I constantly looked
for ways to make sure that the message of Christianity was offered

in a friendly, nonthreatening way. I have had friends who have been hit over the head with the gospel, so I worked hard to make sure that didn't happen in this group.

My style was not only approachable, it was effective. One group member, who described himself as a "true jock," came to the meetings believing that Christianity was "for women, old folks, and weaklings — but not for real men." That wall was slow in coming down. However, over several months of seeing respected friends share their lives and struggles in the group, his attitude changed. But by the time the group broke for the summer, he still hadn't crossed the line of faith — a fact that initially left me discouraged. Then a few weeks later my apprentice and I were over at this guy's house sharing a relaxing evening, and he gave his life to the Lord. How cool is that?

Another significant event occurred in the life of a group member's former drinking buddy, who started attending the small group meetings halfway into the year. Divorced, estranged from his children, and leading a very lonely life, he craved the camaraderie and friendship he found at these meetings. Then one night he allowed thirty years of bottled-up struggles and hurts to emerge, sharing them in a torrent of tears and confession. He then invited Christ into his life and returned home a new man. A few months later he had a major stroke, and as many of the guys rallied around him, I wondered where he would be without this group. Now on the road to recovery, he is leading a seeker small group of his own!

The stories vary but they share a common beginning: an invitation. A knock on a door even when you "know" it's a dead end. A phone call to say, "Just come once and see what you think." Extending those invitations launched my first seeker small group, and leading that group of guys became one of the greatest privileges of my life. As a result, I'm hoping and planning to lead a seeker small group every year for the rest of my life.

# LAURA ATCHLEY'S STORY

*Office Manager*
*Atlanta, Georgia*

*F*or the past seven-and-a-half years I have been on a long journey, seeking a relationship with Christ — although I didn't know
what I was really looking for. During this time a coworker continually invited me to join her and her Christian friends for church services, outings, or get-togethers. I honestly never fully understood her
beliefs but I admired her commitment. So I concluded that we would
simply have our differences and that was that.

But last year I received a phone call that changed the total trajectory of my life. It was a friend calling to tell me about a group he
was starting — a seeker small group. For years he and my coworker
had taken time to answer all my "Why this?" and "Why that?"
questions about Christianity, so it wasn't too surprising to get his
invitation. But even though I trusted him, I was a little scared
because I didn't want to get pulled into some kind of weird situation
and I'm not a "jump on the bandwagon" type of girl. Beyond that
I was afraid of looking foolish because I didn't know much about
Christianity.

I enjoyed the group meetings a lot and I tried to attend as often
as I could. Eventually, though, my dedication to my job left me no
choice but to drop out. After several months I reconnected with the
group, thanks to the ongoing invitations from the leaders — and this
time I was determined to make every meeting. I had a renewed passion to know God. I had a burning desire to find the truth. I looked
forward to finally making studying and reading the Bible a priority.
I trusted the people in my group and felt very comfortable being open
with my struggles and weaknesses. For example, I didn't understand
the Trinity and I didn't even know that Genesis was the first book in
the Old Testament. My small group members were also vulnerable
about their personal struggles. They embraced me and encouraged
me in my search to find Christ. And they ultimately helped me
through one of the darkest periods of my life. I lost my grandmother
in December and lost my thirty-eight-year-old brother in March. I
had never felt such overwhelming emptiness and sadness. It was in

*facing these losses with my group members at my side that I placed my faith in the love of Christ. Without his forgiveness, love, and strength I would not be standing today.*

*Since my decision to receive Christ, I no longer feel alone in this world. I'm learning to change my priorities and really look at what is important in life. I am in awe of the love that Christ has for any and every one — and they need only accept his gift.*

# Chapter 4

# Conduct the All-Important First Meeting

*✦*

*"Begin at the beginning," the king said, gravely, "and go on till you come to the end; then stop."*

LEWIS CARROLL,
*ALICE IN WONDERLAND*

*Get your preparation done. I can't emphasize that too much ... we are out to persuade [people] with a body of truth, to persuade their minds as well as to touch their hearts and reach to the center of their being which is their will.*

BILLY GRAHAM

Our biggest fear was that no one would show up," recalls Ginny Johnson. She and husband, Ernie, of Knoxville, Tennessee, describe the first meeting of their seeker small group — a group that ended up lasting seven years and impacting hundreds of seekers.

The couple had just completed training sessions for seeker small group leaders and were eager to start. "During services one weekend," she continues, "our senior pastor challenged seekers to take a step to further investigate Christianity in small groups designed especially for them. Many responded with interest. We were given some of those names to call, and we also invited other friends who had voiced some interest. But we didn't know how many — if any — would follow through and actually show up."

When six people did, Ginny and Ernie were ready for them. "We followed what we'd been taught about making people feel comfortable," Ernie says. "We didn't pressure everyone to participate or force anyone to say a prayer, just to make sure we didn't turn anyone off. Instead we started out with a nonthreatening icebreaker question, and we even had a couple of backups ready — just in case the first one flopped!"

Once the icebreaker interaction helped make everyone feel comfortable, the Johnsons explained what their group would be about. "Very gently we asked people to describe what 'truth source,' if any, they based their spiritual beliefs on," explains Ernie. "Then we said that for the purposes of our discussions, the Bible was the main place we'd be getting our information to address whatever spiritual questions or issues came up."

Ginny and Ernie ended that first meeting by inviting people to respond to this question: "If Jesus were to walk into this room right now, what would you most want to ask him?" For participants who returned (and Ginny remembers that not everyone did), those questions became the basis for future discussions. "Each meeting we would bring up a topic someone from the group was concerned with, and we'd invite people to share their perspectives on it," Ernie says. "Then we'd tell them, 'Next week we'll talk some more about this and see what the Bible has to say,' and Ginny and I would research it and come back prepared to lead a discussion around what we'd learned."

This approach worked well, and although members of the group seemed to have little in common, they began to form close bonds. "We were young and old, single and married, professionals and minimum-wage earners," Ernie says. "And we loved it that way! It was easy to invite anyone to join us — a brother or mom or friend or neighbor. Everyone fit in."

As the group continued to meet week after week, hearts grew open and receptive to the truths of the Bible. Lives began to change. As people accepted Christ into their lives, Ernie and Ginny helped them transition into groups for new Christians or into other ministry areas. The Johnsons, in turn, continued to welcome additional seekers into their group. "At one point during our second year, we had twenty-one people, which was just too many," remembers Ernie. "However, one of our apprentices was ready to lead, so we split the group in two and from that point on limited our numbers to no more than ten or twelve."

As it turned out, "that point on" lasted every week for five more years, during which scores of spiritual seekers crossed the line of faith. But Ernie and Ginny remember that first step into a seeker small group ministry as if it were yesterday. What advice do they offer people just beginning that process? *Pray a lot and lead with patience and tender loving care.*

In addition, Ernie recommends visiting a successful seeker group to get a sense of the dynamics involved as people explore issues of faith. He and Ginny also advise new leaders to do everything possible to build and strengthen their relationships with group members. "In addition to our weekly meetings at the church, we'd sometimes host get-togethers at our house and invite special speakers, or just have simple social events," says Ginny. She adds that sometimes family and friends of group members would visit for the first time at those events. "They weren't necessarily seeking spiritual things; they were just really curious," she says, laughing. "But after a few such nonthreatening events, many actually joined our group for future discussions."

The Johnsons make it clear, though, that while their practical advice might be useful, it must be accompanied by reliance on God. "You can get worried about all kinds of things — what if no one shows up, what if we don't know how to address their questions, what if the people don't get along, what if a hundred other things," says Ginny. "But you just have to stop worrying and say, 'What do I know that's true? That I can do *nothing* without Christ.' That was true with us. We just turned it over to the Holy Spirit and said, 'You know what? It's *your* group. We're going to make ourselves available, but you're going to have to help us with this.'"

And the Johnsons would tell you there's nothing like the excitement of watching him do exactly that.

## Only One First Impression

You've established high levels of trust with your seeking friends, you've extended invitations, and people have agreed to try out the group at least once. Everything is set. Now, what in the world will you do in the first meeting? Whatever you decide, let one thing be clear: if you invited people to come and check out your group without any obligation to ever come back, you'd better make sure their very first experience is a good one! That first meeting will make or break any possibilities for future gatherings, so it's absolutely *crucial* that your first meeting go well. You only get one shot at making a first impression.

The guidelines in this chapter are designed to give you and your participants the best first meeting experience possible. These suggestions have been developed and refined over many years, and they have proved to be very helpful in launching seeker groups. At Willow Creek we ask every leader of a seeker small group (whether it meets in the marketplace, the neighborhood, or the church) to follow this format as closely as possible — just because we have seen it work so effectively. For your reference, a summary of the following guidelines for leading the first meeting of a seeker small group is included in appendix A. Of course, don't hesitate to make any adjustments as needed to better serve your particular group.

## The Setting

First of all, select the right setting for your group's meetings. Make sure the location is easy to find and convenient, and make sure it's a nonthreatening place. In other words, if your seeking friends come mainly from your neighborhood, don't meet at your church — instead let one of them host the group in his or her home. If most of your seeking friends are from your church, they would probably be more comfortable meeting there at first. Choose a location familiar to your guests.

Sometime before the meeting, set aside some time to pray with your apprentices. Pray about your discussion time. Pray for those planning on coming, that nothing would get in the way of their showing up. Pray that the Holy Spirit would work in their hearts as they take steps in their spiritual journey.

Eliminate as many distractions as possible. Turn off phones, answering machines, televisions, and sound systems. Make sure pets are kept quiet and away. You may want to organize child care so parents are not interrupted and distracted. Even the "little things," such as a comfortable room temperature and fresh flowers, can go a long way toward shaping the overall success of your group.

Arrange comfortable chairs in a circle to facilitate good eye contact, and do your best to help everyone feel relaxed. Your attitude and demeanor will determine the tone for the meeting, so be friendly, positive, and natural. To help keep things fun and loose, it's a good idea to have some light snacks and drinks available. Of course, keep in mind that you need to honor your friends by sticking to the agreed upon start and end times. I recommend that you limit your total discussion time to no longer than an hour and fifteen minutes, but plan to interact informally afterward with those who wish to linger.

## Welcome

Be at your designated discussion place early enough so you and your apprentices can warmly greet people as they arrive. When it's time to start, ask everyone to find a seat. Thank everyone for coming and acknowledge that it's kind of a scary thing to attend a small group like this without really knowing what to expect. Assure your guests you're glad they came and that you think they will enjoy themselves. Predict that they will have a good time getting to know each other and discussing important topics.

## Introductions

Give everyone a chance to share names, places of residence, occupations, and favorite hobbies. You should start things off to demonstrate the depth of response you're looking for and set the pace. This initial time of interaction should be very informal, fun, and easygoing; there are no "wrong" answers and no one should feel put on the spot.

As people take their turns, keep an ear open for any potential connections that might exist among group members. Frequently group members will discover they have things in common. If two people find they both live in the same suburb, for example, don't squelch the connection and stifle the conversation by asking them to wait their turn before making comments! Instead encourage group members to interact with each other and discover more connections. You could say something like, "I wonder if you two live near each other. What neighborhoods do you live in?" Then see what discoveries result. From the onset encourage communication among group members and send clear signals that group interaction does not always have to go through you. Such interaction does wonders to help the group gel and build bridges of trust and openness.

As the facilitator, look for ways to provide a safe environment for members to get to know each other. In a group of six to eight people, it should take about ten minutes to welcome people to the group and give everyone a chance to share something about themselves.

## Icebreakers

Next tell the group you have an idea for keeping the interaction flowing. There's a tool for getting discussions jump-started called *The Complete Book of Questions: 1001 Conversation Starters for Any Occasion.* The first one hundred of those questions are light-hearted and easy to answer, so they are the best ones to begin with. Have someone pick a number between one and one hundred, read that question, and answer it. (You can make a joke that the bravest one in the group should go first.) Then ask the next person to pick another number — or if someone prefers, let him or her select one that has already been used. Follow that pattern for about ten minutes until everyone has answered a question.

Here are some examples of the kinds of icebreakers found in the section of *The Complete Book of Questions* called "Light and Easy."

Do you squeeze the toothpaste tube or roll it? What's the advantage of your method?

What's one of your nicknames? What do you prefer to be called?

What's something your parents used to say to you as a child that you promised yourself you'd never say — but now you catch yourself saying all the time?

What books on your shelf are begging to be read?

What's something that people do in traffic that really bothers you?

How many siblings do you have? What's your birth order?

How do you get rid of pesky phone calls from telemarketers?

Who performs more random acts of kindness than anyone else you know? Give the details.

Using only one word per person, what was your first
impression of each person present with you now?
What's the first thing that comes to mind when you hear
the word "fun"?

This time spent responding to these safe, nonthreatening yet
enlightening questions should bring about lots of laughter and fun
and create a comfortable atmosphere in your group meeting. Then
move on to the next section of the icebreaker book called "Personal
Profile" (questions 101–200). Follow the same procedure and spend
another ten minutes or so tackling this set of get-to-know-you questions. Here is a sampling of questions from that section.

Are you a hugger or a non-hugger? Why?
In what situations are you most likely to procrastinate?
Are you serious-minded or a jokester? Why?
Are you more likely to avoid conflict or engage in it head-
on? Why?
What do you consider your best quality?
Are you a leader or a follower? How do you know?
Are you more of a rule breaker or a rule keeper? Why?
Would you describe yourself as an extrovert or an introvert?
Give an example.
Would you describe yourself as more of a feeler or a thinker?
Why?
Are you usually late, early, or on time? Why?[1]

Those two sets of icebreaker questions should take about twenty
minutes altogether to complete, which will leave about thirty to
forty-five minutes before the meeting should be brought to a close.

## Transition Icebreaker

Next comes a pivotal transition in your small group discussion,
when you should move your group from a time of lighthearted
interaction to one of greater significance. This can be accomplished
with what I call a "transition icebreaker." Like other icebreakers, a
transition icebreaker is nonthreatening — but it sets up the group to
take on a discussion around deeper issues. It's a tool to assist you in
turning the corner with your group and getting more focused on the

topic you want to discuss. The transition icebreaker that I strongly recommend you use for your first seeker small group meeting is this: If you could ask God one question you knew he would answer right away, what would it be?

This is a question that seekers typically love to answer, but nonetheless you should always allow people the option to pass if they want to. And let people answer in random order rather than moving around the circle. This will alleviate the pressure that builds as each person's turn grows closer and closer. But, as I've seen over and over again, this one question can break your discussion wide open, especially if you've set the stage by initiating the discussion with the less-threatening icebreakers. And best of all, the answers your seeking friends provide can give you great insight into where they currently are in their spiritual journey. You'll be able to immediately identify their issues and hang-ups about God and spiritual things.

As with the introductions, you should answer the question first to model a response and set the pace. Come prepared to share an authentic and meaningful question you have for God. For example, if I were to answer this question in a seeker group setting right now, I would share that recently our family had to make the incredibly difficult decision to place my father in a nursing home. He has had Parkinson's disease now for twenty years, and the strain on my mother as she has cared for him has become too much for her to handle. So my question for God would be, "Why are my parents having to suffer through such a difficult battle with this dreadful disease?"

Remember that you're setting the tone for the kind of response you're looking for from the rest of the group. If you notice an extended period of silence when it's time for the others to share, don't panic; people are probably thinking and need a little more time. A good facilitator doesn't fear silence. It's a good idea to ask the group for permission to write down their responses for future reference — so you can remember who asked which question. As people share their answers, be sure to affirm their responses and thank them for sharing. Let them know how interesting and important their answers are. Offer encouragement by informing them that the points they raised are most likely similar to questions other group members (including yourself) have either had in the past or still have now.

In these moments you will approach one of *the* most critical junctures you will face. As people open themselves up to the questions and issues they have about God, you will be tempted to respond by addressing their issues. Don't do it! Bite your tongue if you have to, but *don't* attempt to answer their questions or you'll short-circuit the seeking process.

Giving two-cent answers to million-dollar questions cheapens those great questions and can shut the seeking process down. (Of course, this is *not* to say that solid, compelling answers could not be given in a short amount of time. It is quite possible to provide succinct, significant answers, but in the context of a seeker group discussion I'm suggesting you hold off from that practice.) Be patient. In time you'll have opportunities to adequately address group members' issues, but this first meeting is not the time to do that.

Instead, once you've affirmed their responses, try asking *why* their particular questions came to mind. Draw out the reasons *behind* their responses; look for the emotion *behind* their intellectual questions. But whatever you do, don't suggest possible solutions during this first meeting. Your role as the facilitator is to help your seeking friends articulate for themselves their issues and questions concerning God. For some, this is something they have never done! Chances are, they may have never stopped long enough to even think about it. Your goal is to create enough interest so they'll want to return and seek out the answers for themselves in future meetings. Your job is to provide opportunities for them to figure out ways to discover the truth for themselves, and in upcoming chapters we'll look more closely at how to do that.

By acknowledging their good questions and thanking them for their open participation, you are building bridges of trust. As you probe a bit deeper into what's going on behind their questions and they experience a safe place to be open and honest, you are reinforcing those bridges. Let group members know that you respect them for their willingness to respond and you appreciate why they chose the question they did. Accept them right where they are, without judgment, and eventually you'll see them grow hungry for the biblical answers to their questions.

When it comes to discussions of faith, seekers are often forced to hear answers to questions they are not asking, and they get the feeling that Christians are not really open to hearing about where they're coming from. Indeed, we Christians usually view evangelism as an experience in which non-Christians must become our audience and listen to us do all the talking and preaching. *But a seeker small group setting reverses that tendency — and just the opposite happens.* A seeker small group is centered on letting nonbelievers voice their issues and questions while Christians become the audience. *We* are the ones who do most of the listening and probing. We ask questions, then draw seekers out with follow-up questions. Few non-Christians have ever had that kind of interaction with Christians, but in their seeker group they will discover a place where they receive very high levels of honor and respect.

## Scripture

The transition icebreaker exercise should take about twenty minutes to complete. After everyone who wants to has had a chance to share, let the group know it's almost time to bring things to a close. Indicating that you are aware of the time shows you are in control and providing good leadership, which helps put seekers at ease. Inform the group that before you wrap things up, you'd like to get their knee-jerk reactions to some verses you'll read aloud from the Bible. After they hear the passage, ask them to share what it means to them or what stood out or how it impacts them. Again, there are no "wrong" (or out-of-bounds) responses here. You're just looking for the group members' reactions to what you read.

Select a verse or two you think might be relevant to your specific group members, and don't select a passage that is too controversial or difficult to understand. (Psalm 25:4–5, John 7:37–38, John 11:25–26, 1 Timothy 1:15, and 1 John 4:9–10 have worked well for several of our seeker groups in the past.) Read the passage a couple of times, then ask people to respond. In some cases you may need to ask group members if they would be willing to temporarily suspend their belief that the Bible is not from God, just for the sake of discussion. Given that caveat, they may more readily enter into the discourse. Let people respond for five minutes or so, but not much longer. Let them know that this is a taste of what it's like to engage in a short discussion about something the Bible says.

# Conclusion

At this point your group has probably been together for fifty-five to sixty minutes, and it's time to draw things to a close. You may be tempted to let the discussion continue past your end time, but don't do it. A lesson I learned from my dad, an outstanding amateur magician who performed tricks with doves, rabbits, and silks that simply amazed his onlookers, was to always leave the audience wanting more. I think that rule of thumb also applies to seekers in small groups. You never want to give them more than they can handle.

As you close, remind your friends that there's no obligation for them to gather again, but if they *are* interested in doing so, you're open to that possibility. Suggest that you would be willing to take the "questions for God" they just shared and organize them so the group could discuss a different one each time you meet. Offer to provide verses from the Bible that relate to their questions, with the goal of stimulating good discussion around each topic so each person could draw his or her own conclusions. But assure them that if they would prefer not to meet again, that's quite all right. If these guidelines for leading the first meeting are closely followed, seekers usually have such an enjoyable time that they not only want to meet again but desire to meet more frequently than the leaders do!

Make it clear that you will let the *group* make that decision. If they want to meet again, have them decide how frequently (weekly, every other week, three times a month, etc.), then ask them to commit to a relatively small number of meetings (four or five is reasonable). Assure them that at the end of that run they can reevaluate. This is a very important exercise for the group, because it transfers ownership from you to them. It's somewhat risky, of course, because they could decline to ever meet again. But if they decide to continue, you have given them greater ownership, and their commitment to the group will be much stronger. High ownership is crucial to the successful launch of your group, so sit back and listen as the members discuss what they want to do.

If they decide to continue meeting, ask them to agree on a couple of simple ground rules. The first is that this should be an open group, which means that anybody is welcome to invite others to come and visit. Seekers are the best inviters of other seekers, so you will never want to shut down that flow of fresh people coming into your group. Encourage them to bring their friends!

Let them know that you have one or two apprentice leaders you'd like to invite into the group at some point. Hint that if the group grows, you may have to split the group in two and have an apprentice assist with leading the discussions. Assure them that if that happens, you'll handle it well, but you just wanted to give them a heads-up about what could occur as the group grows. Remind them that growth is a good thing because it means more people may benefit from the discussions. (See chapter 8 about issues relating to adding seekers to your group, and the role of apprentices). Informing your friends of this possibility up front makes expectations clear and gives you the freedom to plan for growth so more seekers can participate.

You can express the second ground rule as a favor you want to request. Ask them to inform you when they are unable to make an upcoming meeting, so you can let everyone else know where they are. Since your group has already begun to bond, everyone will wonder what happened to someone if they don't show. Assure them that there's no pressure intended and you understand that things do come up, but explain that it's helpful to hear from them in any case. Then be sure to give out your contact information. Creating this accountability factor will serve your group well. It's not about manipulation; it's about holding them accountable to something they said they wanted to do. This will give your seeking friends one more reason to come back and keep their commitment — you'll be wondering about them if they don't show! Most of all, you'll want to make the seekers in your group feel valued as you demonstrate you really care about them.

Finally, thank everyone for coming. In some cases you may want to say a short prayer to close, but in other cases it may be wise to pray only with your apprentices afterward. Dismiss them with an expression of appreciation for the chance to spend time together getting to know each other better and hearing one another's stories. Allow people to stick around, maybe offer some refreshments, and just hang out. When group members linger after the meeting, it is usually because they really enjoyed their time with the group. Savor those moments.

# JOSIE GUTH'S STORY

### Stay-at-Home Mom
### Wheeling, Illinois

*A* few years ago my husband, Jim, and I, along with our three children, moved into a new subdivision that included a lot of young families. When we first arrived, everyone was very eager to meet and socialize. And I was looking for ways to honor Christ in my neighborhood. I was happy to watch a child if a mom was in a bind, I was always willing to drop a meal off if someone had a baby or was experiencing a hardship, and occasionally I even invited some non-Christians to various outreach services at church. Everything I did was what I would call "safe." That all changed one Sunday—"safe" was no longer good enough.

God spoke to me! I was in church listening to a compelling message about getting out of our comfort zones, and God began challenging me to start a seeker group in my neighborhood. "No way!" I thought. "I would never want to push my beliefs on anyone, and besides, what would everyone think?" I ignored the idea for about four months, until God gave me a reminder of what he wanted me to do. But this time I said maybe. I rationalized that if I could find one other Christian who would start the group with me, I would do it. Otherwise forget it! I got my nerve up and called the only other Christian I knew in my neighborhood and told her my idea. She said no. Phew, was I glad. I was off the hook.

But God had other plans for me. Little did I know that he was already at work preparing the heart of a seeker. One afternoon she came over to my house and asked if I had ever considered starting a Bible study in our neighborhood. I smiled politely and said, "Well, we would have to find someone to lead it, first." It was no use—I knew that leader had to be me.

Now came the hard part—actually asking seekers to come. My initial thought was to send a flier so no one would have to say no to my face. But then I realized that I had built too many solid friendships in the neighborhood to just take the easy way out. So I decided to personally invite each woman.

I will never forget the butterflies in the pit of my stomach when I picked up the phone to call Lisa. I really didn't know her that well, but every time I would pray about the Bible study, God kept placing her name in my mind. Reluctantly, I made that call and asked her to come to the study just once. I assured her she didn't ever have to come back again. Fully expecting to hear a "No thanks, freak," I heard Lisa say, "Yes!" (Later I learned how her sisters, who had become "really into Jesus," had been inviting her to attend a Bible study with them and she didn't want to go. But because the location of my group was so close and convenient, she decided to come. She's been a huge inspiration to me because she is full of questions and so eager to learn.) After that interaction with Lisa, I had the courage to ask anyone and everyone.

At the first meeting five seekers showed up. Wow! I decided to start out light and informal. I prepared two icebreakers that I thought would spark good conversations. But they turned out to be anything but light. Within the first twenty minutes one woman was in the bathroom crying because someone had offended her. Just when I thought I had successfully smoothed that over, I decided to ask the next question. "If God walked in the room right now, and you could ask him any question, what would it be?" The first woman said she would ask God what heaven would be like for the Muslims, Hindus, and Jews, since there is no such thing as hell. I took a deep breath and started sweating bullets. Another woman jumped in and stated that she didn't think a group like this was going to work out, because everyone was too different. I assured her that it really could work but that we all had to have a nonjudgmental attitude. She started crying. Then the woman who offended the other woman started crying too—because she felt so bad. I felt like crying. But thankfully, I held it together, and God gave me words of comfort that were not my own. To my surprise, they all came back the next week.

That was seven weeks ago and they are all still hanging in there with me. We completed our first study guide. At the end of the last session I checked in with everyone and asked if they wanted to continue. They unanimously said yes and asked if they could invite two other seekers. Amazing.

Leading this group has been the most rewarding thing I have done in a very long time. It has given my life more purpose and has caused me to get all fired up about Christ and his power to change lives. He has pushed me out of my comfort zone and is pulling me out of the spiritual rut I have been in for the last several years. I can't wait to see how he will move next in the lives of each one of the women in my group—including me.

# JOE AND CATHY D'ALESSANDRO'S STORY

### Chef and Teacher
### Bartlett, Illinois

*A*bout two years ago my wife, Cathy, who had begun to pursue spiritual answers, suggested that we try out a seeker small group she'd heard about. I was reluctant. We both had grown up in religious families, but Cathy was restless. She was impressed by the peace and contentment she observed in the lives of her sister and certain other friends, but she never quite understood why they were so fulfilled. Deep down I also knew something was missing inside me, but I refused to admit it.

And so I surprised her (and myself!) by agreeing to go. We looked forward to the upcoming meeting with some mixed emotions. Cathy was fearful that it would be too preachy and that her lack of Bible knowledge would be made apparent. I was sure we would be pressured into some kind of crazy conversion experience. But in spite of our hesitations, we were determined to attend.

The first meeting was informal and relaxed. I was surprised to feel totally accepted and not judged! But the thing that really surprised me was how much I was willing to talk! It seemed the more I felt understood, the more I opened up. To be in that kind of an environment was very important to me; I had confided in Cathy ahead of time that if the group became a forum for the leader to give a judgmental lecture, that would be my first and last small group experience ever. I had enough bad experiences with religious fanatics who were more concerned about pushing their own opinions on everybody else — that was something I didn't need.

However, we ended up returning week after week for eleven months. We were free to express our doubts and disbeliefs, and at the same time we were learning what the Bible says about God's plan for our lives. I had never cracked opened a Bible in my life, but the lessons I learned provided wisdom and insights unlike anything I'd ever seen before. We became thirsty for more.

Our group interactions centered around spiritual topics and issues we'd never thought about — much less discussed with others.

*And I was amazed at how all of us opened up so much to each other. Sometimes we got a little heated and emotional, but we always respected each other no matter what differences of opinion existed.*

*The greatest realization I had was this: the distance from God I felt was real, and there was nothing I could do to bridge that gap caused by my sin. I began to understand that, essentially, any attempt I make to gain God's favor is an insult to what Jesus did on the cross. But that was the hard part for me—that his forgiveness was free. How could I not try to make a trade or earn my way? I eventually discovered that I didn't have to wheel and deal anything—God wants me just as I am.*

*During our involvement in this group, our faith grew to the point that we both gave our lives completely to Christ—Cathy first, then me about a month later. What triggered my decision to follow Christ was a conversation I had with the leader of my group. On that particular night I was overwhelmed with a series of hardships I was facing. Everything seemed to be crashing down on me all at once. In desperation I called my leader and asked him if there was any way possible he could meet with me to talk right away. I was relieved that he was available, because I really needed to get everything out in the open and I knew of no one better to do that with than him—I just knew I could count on him to listen and understand.*

*For over two hours I poured out all my frustrations and concerns. Just having someone there to hear me out like he did softened my heart. Tears came to my eyes as I realized that all these years I had been trying so hard to manage my life without God—but it was not working. My leader offered to pray with me to receive Christ and turn my life over to him, but I needed to do so alone with God. So I drove to a nearby park and under the night sky I made the greatest decision of my life.*

*Recently my wife and I were both baptized, along with several others in our group. Cathy and I cannot contain the overflowing joy and peace we have found in Christ, and we will be forever grateful for the difference this group has made in our lives. The impact has been powerful and beautiful. We are true believers now and we can see our spiritual lives developing every day. We cannot imagine our lives without Christ and we are doing our best to make him the center of our family. I feel his presence and trust him with everything. I have found my place in this life—and the one to come!*

# MARK MITTELBERG'S STORY

*Evangelism Specialist*
*Trabuco Canyon, California*

*I*n the car on the way to his home, Garry and I received some last minute coaching from an anxious host. But I didn't blame him — after all, his living room was filled with his closest seeking friends who were waiting for us to arrive. "Now remember, we're British, which means we're known for our 'British reserve.' We're not like you Americans who talk so openly about your personal beliefs. Especially the two friends I've warned you about. They are going to be really offended if you put them on the spot and try to force them to talk about their religious opinions. They'll never want to come back to my house again! So play it cool and don't push them, okay?"

I was fascinated to see what would happen later that night, as Garry tried to calm the fears of our English friend. We were on a teaching tour of the UK, and prior to our coming to Southampton, Garry had been asked if he'd be willing to come to this leader's home to facilitate a seeker small group with some of this man's coworkers and neighbors. Now this leader seemed to be getting cold feet! I knew that was natural, given the high value he placed on his relationships and the huge spiritual stakes that were involved. But I also knew that Garry wasn't going to be easily talked into squandering a great opportunity to engage some seekers in some open spiritual dialogue!

Well, the night turned out, to use a British term, "brilliantly." After sharing hors d'oeuvres and informal conversation for an hour or so, Garry asked our group of about fifteen together to sit in a circle of chairs. Then he got us all interacting around some light icebreaker questions — and the group really opened up! In no time we were all talking, laughing, telling stories, and just enjoying being with each other.

Then the crucial moment came. Garry, in a very relaxed and natural manner, transitioned from the safe realm of mundane icebreakers to the more serious subject of spiritual realities. He said something like, "Thanks for your great responses to those questions. That was a lot of fun! Now I'd like to ask you something I'm really *curious about. Imagine this: If you could talk to God and ask him any question, and you knew he'd give you an answer right away, what would you ask him?"*

*During the brief ensuing pause, I have to admit I avoided eye contact with our host, who I'm certain was starting to sweat! But as I held my breath for what turned out to be only an instant, a woman spoke up and said, "I'd ask him why he allows innocent people to suffer."*

*"That's a really good question, Laura," Garry responded. "Can I ask what makes that question the most important one to you?"*

*"Well, when I was just seven my grandmother died suddenly," Laura volunteered. "And she was such a wonderful person. I just couldn't understand why God would allow that to happen."*

*"That must have been really hard for you, Laura, especially at such an early age," Garry gently replied. "I'll bet some of the rest of us have similar questions to Laura's ... John, what question would you ask God if you had the chance?"*

*John responded with a thoughtful question. Then someone else did as well. And another. And so the evening went. For the next ninety minutes there was not even an uncomfortable pause! People felt freed up to talk about their spiritual questions and ideas because such a safe and accepting environment had been created. And when it came around to those two friends we'd been so clearly warned about — we could hardly get them to stop talking about their questions and issues!*

*I left that night convinced more than ever of the evangelistic power and potential of seeker small groups — and, I must admit, I thoroughly enjoyed listening to Garry's good-natured ribbing of our host as he drove us back to our hotel!*

# Part 3

# LEADING
# SEEKER
# SMALL
# GROUP
# DISCUSSIONS

Now, before we turn our attention toward how to lead subsequent meetings, it's time to hit the pause button and explore two critical skills that support the effective facilitation of seeker group discussions. Chapter 5, Ask Great Questions, takes an in-depth look at the process of asking thought-provoking discussion questions. Chapter 6, Listen Well, analyzes the dynamics of a good discussion and the need for leaders to develop outstanding listening skills. Become a skilled practitioner in these two areas — asking great questions and listening exceptionally well — and you'll be well on your way toward mastering the art of facilitating great seeker small group discussions. Then in chapter 7, Facilitate Captivating Interactions, we'll push play and examine how to prepare group discussions and outline a detailed game plan for leading seeker small group interactions beyond the first meeting.

The material in the following three chapters is based on the author's years of thought and experience along with concepts from the following resources: *Lead Out; Stephen Covey, The Seven Habits of Highly Effective People;* Em Griffin, *Getting Together;* Russ Korth, *Lively Discussions;* Karen Lee-Thorp, *How to Ask Great Questions;* and Norm Wakefield, *Between the Words.*

# Chapter 5

# Ask Great Questions

*

*When I came to you, brothers, I did not come with eloquence or superior wisdom as I proclaimed to you the testimony about God. For I resolved to know nothing while I was with you except Jesus Christ and him crucified. I came to you in weakness and fear, and with much trembling. My message and my preaching were not with wise and persuasive words, but with a demonstration of the Spirit's power, so that your faith might not rest on men's wisdom, but on God's power.*

1 CORINTHIANS 2:1–5

*Judge a man by his questions rather than by his answers.*

VOLTAIRE

*The important thing is not to stop questioning.*

ALBERT EINSTEIN

*Can I ask you a question?*

SOCRATES

Quick question: Who turns and says, "Just one more thing ..." followed by a hard-hitting, probing question? He's a popular television character — a blundering, disheveled, but endearing kind of fellow who is almost always wearing a beat-up trench coat and putting a cigar in his mouth. Do you know who it is yet?

If not, don't give up. This man seems to constantly get phone calls at someone else's house or office. He's well known for expressions like "Excuse me," "Just a formality," and "Sorry to bother you." He frequently explains that he is "just tying up loose ends" as he's caught snooping around inside someone's house without invitation or warning.

By now you've probably guessed that I'm referring to Lieutenant Columbo, TV's version of a Los Angeles homicide detective, marvelously portrayed by Peter Falk. Created by William Link and Richard Levinson, *Columbo* was one of the seventies' most popular television shows. A total of forty-three episodes were shot between 1971 and 1978, but every once in a while a new episode is created and released, even now.

Have you ever wondered what people like so much about this show? I think one of the secrets to its appeal is Columbo's fascinating ability to get the criminal to confess. He solves his cases through persistent and careful attention to all the clues, but his apparently disorganized and bumbling manner disguises his razor-sharp analysis — and causes everyone to underestimate his competence. This inevitably leads to the killer's undoing.

Every Columbo episode follows a similar pattern, commonly referred to as the Columbo Formula. It starts by showing the murderer meticulously executing his plan. Later, while crime investigators scurry about, in walks Lt. Columbo. Knowing full well who is responsible, viewers observe the ensuing battle of wits between the crafty villain and the brilliant detective. We are captivated as Columbo begins to suspect the true killer and then systematically and steadily wears that person down to the point of confession.

You may have noticed that Columbo rarely *tells* anyone anything. All he ever does is ask questions — in a style all his own. From a self-deprecating position, he pauses dramatically for a moment, rubs his bottom left eyelid with his right index finger, and finally raises a penetrating question. Then he carefully listens to the response, scratches his head, and offers the killer another opportunity to shed more light on the crime. Presented by Columbo almost as an afterthought, his "just one more thing" questions catch their victims off guard. His prudent and profound queries force the killers to admit the truth of their own wrongdoings.[1]

Columbo reminds me of another somewhat-odd yet brilliant character — this one from the fifth century B.C.

Barefoot and shabby in the streets of Athens, Socrates was fond of initiating dialogues about the meaning of life. Probably the greatest philosopher of his time, he posed question after question, deeply challenging the thinking of his fellow Greeks. He drew fascinated crowds by countering responses to his questions with ones even more intriguing. People were riveted as Socrates forced them to think and search for truth in ways they had never experienced. He refused to simply hand out wise insight; rather, he preferred to spur others on to pursue and find the answers for themselves. And the people of his day loved it. This style of interaction and dialogue has come to be known as the Socratic Method.

This method, in which questions are used to awaken curiosity, serves as a logical, step-by-step guide that enables students to discover insights, develop thoughts, and draw conclusions for themselves. Most of the questions are prepared in advance, but follow-up questions, based on responses, can also occur extemporaneously. The facilitator essentially challenges people to use their own logic as they reflect on the questions to make deductions about the ideas (either erroneous or more accurate) that shape their belief systems.[2]

In a way, a leader of a seeker small group needs to become some combination of Lt. Columbo and Socrates. Of course, without the backdrops of love, mutual respect, and authenticity, any technique is rendered useless. But that understood, a great leader facilitates discussions in such a way that seekers discover biblical truths for themselves and decide exactly what they do and do not believe about spiritual matters.

Most seekers have never fully considered what they believe or why they believe it. But once those starting points are established, the leader can formulate a series of questions that require group members to move logically from one point of understanding to another in their thinking about God and their relationship with him. The leader uses these sets of questions to carefully invite seekers to systematically analyze their belief systems and compare them with a biblical perspective — and eventually draw their own conclusions.

## The Power of Questions

Jesus was the world's greatest teacher. He amazed crowds with the stories he told and the depth of his wisdom. But what really made his teaching style so unique and powerful was his mastery of the art of asking great questions. Throughout the Gospels we discover how Jesus' questions caused people to stop and think.

> "Why do you break the command of God for the sake of your tradition?" (Matthew 15:3).
>
> "Who do people say I am? ... But what about you? ... Who do you say I am?" (Mark 8:27, 29).
>
> "Which of these three do you think was a neighbor to the man who fell into the hands of robbers?" (Luke 10:36).
>
> "What good will it be for a man if he gains the whole world, yet forfeits his soul?" (Matthew 16:26).
>
> "Why are you thinking these things?" (Mark 2:8).
>
> "If you love those who love you, what credit is that to you?" (Luke 6:32).
>
> "What do you think?" (Matthew 17:25; 18:12; 21:28; 22:42).
>
> "Which of the two did what his father wanted?" (Mathew 21:31).
>
> "What is written in the Law? ... How do you read it?" (Luke 10:26).

In her book *How to Ask Great Questions,* Karen Lee-Thorp makes the excellent observation that "Jesus' questions were simple, clear, never condescending, always provocative. They made people think for themselves and examine their hearts. Jesus' questions were always fresh and attuned to the unique needs of the people he was talking to. Instead of following a rote method, he seemed to have thought about how his questions would affect his audience."[3]

Questions are great conversation starters. And they force people to think, look within themselves, examine their hearts, and search for answers. Just as questions were a great teaching tool for Jesus, questions are also an excellent tool in the hands of his followers. By simply raising a few good questions with your seeking friends, you can spark in-depth spiritual conversations. "What is your religious background?" "How have your beliefs changed over the years?"

"Where would you say you are now in your spiritual journey?" "What are your hang-ups about Christianity?" These sorts of questions can become the nudge a seeker needs to open up and disclose spiritual roadblocks, take steps to explore the objective truths of the Bible, and eventually overcome those barriers to faith. In her article "Let Me Ask You Something," Becky Brodin writes, "[Just think] what could happen if we would slow down the verbal exchange by asking good questions, listen intently to hear what the other person is thinking and feeling, and, in the spirit of conversation, talk, truly talk, about the Gospel."[4]

Jesus' example of using questions to spark spiritual conversations succeeds not only with individuals but also with groups. And you too will want to ask question after question to facilitate exciting discussions and interactions in your seeker small group setting. This is not the time for you to teach or preach and give a monologue. In fact, your role as the leader consists primarily of asking a series of provocative questions to expose group members to the teachings of Jesus and the Bible, challenge their thinking, and explore the feelings behind their statements. This process provides them with the opportunity to articulate, wrestle with, and discover biblical truths for themselves.

When people verbally respond to good, thought-provoking questions, they are in effect processing their thoughts out loud — which greatly enhances learning, comprehension, and retention. The experience of hearing one's own thoughts aloud is often enough to clear up points of confusion, expose faulty thinking, or confirm sound understanding. Great questions not only create an opportunity for learning but also aid people in *remembering* what it is they are learning, because they are the ones doing the work and struggling to figure things out.

The last thing you'd ever want to do in a seeker small group setting is put yourself in the role of an expert or scholar with all the answers, because that would rob seekers of the chance to make their own discoveries. Your role as the leader is to stimulate their thinking and facilitate their learning process — not to short-circuit it. Keep in mind the adage of Dale Carnegie: "Others are not nearly as interested in what we have to say as they are in what they want to say to us."[5] Moreover, the seekers in your group will remember what *they* say far better than what they hear *you* say. And they will retain what they figure out for themselves more often than what they get force-fed from you.[6] You'll know that the seekers in your group are really starting to understand things when they articulate their findings in their own words. And by asking questions, you give them the opportunity to do just that. Your questions will spark this discovery process and encourage them to say out loud the spiritual truths they are beginning to grasp.

As you cultivate the skill of asking carefully thought-out questions and then patiently allowing seekers the freedom to wrestle with the answers, you put yourself in the position to witness first-hand some amazing "aha moments." When a seeker says, "I've never quite understood things this way before" or "I'm finally getting it!" or "Wow, this is all starting to make sense to me," you can almost see the lightbulb click on and the puzzle pieces fit together. If you work hard at asking great questions, those moments will happen over and over again in your group meetings.

## Formulating Great Questions: The Criteria

Because questions are the springboards for discussion and the vehicles through which a leader assists group members to discover spiritual truths, it is important to cultivate the ability to formulate a series of provocative questions. Even though study guides for seeker groups are available (see chapter 7), a leader's ability to tailor questions to the particular needs and interests of his or her group is invaluable. Here are a few simple guidelines for doing just that.[7]

### Prepare in Advance

Your discussion questions should be carefully prepared *prior to* your meeting. The challenge is to come up with the kinds of questions that draw people out and encourage them to think and reason out loud in order to discover spiritual truths for themselves. As you prepare good questions, keep these things in mind:

- Never *inform* when you can *inquire*. Don't attempt to explain something that group members could discover for themselves if you were to ask the right questions.

- Form questions that build on one another.
- Develop questions that gradually move the discussion toward the biblical truth you hope group members will discover. Let group members draw conclusions for themselves.
- Ask questions that foster good listening by the members of the group.

## Be Clear and Concise

Make sure your questions are clear and easy to understand. They should require little to no explanation or setup. Ask only *one* well thought-out question at a time. The quickest way to cause confusion is to ask two or three poorly worded questions at once. Long, complicated questions will cause your group members to stare blankly at each other, not knowing what to say or do. Of course, asking questions that are *beneath* the intelligence of group members can result in the same silent, blank gaze—because people feel foolish answering questions that are too simple.

## Draw Out Opinions and Feelings

Always use questions that can prompt a variety of "correct" responses. In other words, the best questions to ask are those to which you either do not know the answer or do not require a single, pat answer. Try to form questions in such a way that they enlighten seekers to objective truths of the Bible and elicit their opinions and feelings about those spiritual discoveries. As the facilitator, the last thing you want to do is put yourself on a pedestal, asking your seeking friends "test" questions for which only you know the "right" answers. That approach will put people on the defensive and quickly kill any chance for a good discussion.[8] Instead, put yourself on the same playing field as everyone else and ask about issues and opinions you sincerely want to hear about from the group.

For example, suppose you were to address the topic of how many paths lead to God.[9] Rather than ask your group members the question: "Is Jesus Christ the only way to God?" develop a series of questions that challenge your group, in a nonthreatening and sensitive way, to candidly consider the biblical position and draw their conclusions. Notice that the questions listed below invite opinions without forcing a "right" or "wrong" answer — and yet they require a close examination of the biblical perspective.

> What is your immediate reaction to the verses we just read from the Bible that claim that Jesus Christ is the only way to God? How do you suppose most people react to this claim?
>
> What are some objections that come to mind concerning the claim that Jesus is the only way?
>
> Describe a path of salvation that is *not* exclusive, and that would make more sense to those troubled by the "one way" proposal.
>
> How does concluding that there is more than one way to God make a mockery out of Christ's death?
>
> If Jesus Christ really is the only way to God, what impact would wholeheartedly believing this have on our lives and relationships?

In his book *Lively Discussions,* Russ Korth gives this advice to leaders: "Be sure not to use questions to focus attention on your own answers. Once people discover you are leading them only to your conclusions, they will feel pressured and resent it. Others will try to figure out what you have in mind rather than share their own thoughts and ideas. When this happens, any applications people make will be based on your idea — not their own. True growth will not take place."[10]

When the time comes to challenge group members' thinking on a particular issue, respectfully ask how they're able to put what the Bible has to say together with what they are saying — how they are able to reconcile the differences between those two points of view. Most seekers have never had to give a reason for why they believe the way they do. They've never thought it all the way through — they just believe what they believe and that's that. Now, for the first time, you're asking them questions about their opinions and helping them to think through their answers.

### Keep Things Open-Ended

Do you know the difference between open-ended questions and closed-ended questions? I just asked a closed-ended question —

one that requires a simple yes or no response. Most closed-ended questions do not stimulate much discussion and are often too insulting for anyone to bother to answer. Examples of questions that do not promote good discussion include: "Do you think the Bible teaches that all people are sinners?" "Can you relate to this verse?" "Is this verse significant to you?" "Do you understand that our sin separates us from God?" Instead always use questions that elicit a variety of appropriate responses, like "What do you think these verses imply about the condition of the human race?" or "In what ways do you think our sin impacts our relationship with God?" Open-ended questions bring out better interaction in a group setting because they require further explanation or comments from your seeking friends.

*Clarify the Responses*

Your discussions will also be enhanced by follow-up questions that draw out more clarification when needed. Ask things like "What do you mean by your comment?" or "Could you give us an example to further clarify your point?" or "Why do you feel that way?" Also, keep your ears open for opportunities to ask others in the group follow-up questions to the responses they heard: "Do the rest of you agree or disagree? Why or why not?" Sometimes people hold back until they're sure their opinion is really wanted. When you ask for more, you communicate that you care about what your seeking friends think and feel. (In chapters 6 and 7 you will find more information about ways to follow up on your group members' responses.)

## Formulating Great Questions: The Choices

Listed below are several kinds of questions you can use in your seeker small group discussions.[11] Your prepared discussion questions should include at least one or two of each type. Appendixes B and C of this book include sample lessons taken from the Tough Questions Series, a curriculum specifically designed for seeker small groups. These two sample sessions illustrate each type of question described below. (In chapter 7 you will find a more detailed explanation of the Tough Questions Series and how it can be used as a guide for your small group interactions.)

## Ask Icebreaker Questions

Always start your group discussions with one or two light-hearted, nonthreatening questions that everyone can feel comfortable answering. This type of question provides a fun and easy way to get members of the group to open up and talk about themselves, drawing out all kinds of interesting information about group members' likes and dislikes, experiences from the past, opinions about issues, and other facts. This allows everyone to get to know one another better and feel more connected, and seekers enjoy this time because it's a safe and easy way for them to participate in the discussion. Most important, icebreakers help break down barriers and build bridges of openness and trust between you and the seekers in your group.

Icebreakers are an absolute necessity, especially in the formative stage of your seeker small group. Notice that in the guidelines for the first meeting, provided in the last chapter, most of the time is allotted for icebreakers. Feelings of trust and connection within a newly formed group take time to develop and grow, and it is critical to establish this foundation early in your seeker small group. Without it no spiritual conversations of significance can occur. Be careful, however, to closely monitor the time each person spends answering these questions, as it's easy to let the time slip away. Icebreakers should be used every time the group meets, but the total time spent on the icebreaker questions will decrease with each meeting because the need for them will diminish somewhat. Also keep in mind that the longer your group has been meeting, the more in-depth and personal the icebreakers can be.

As the leader of the group, you might want to answer the opening icebreaker question first, setting the pace for response time and modeling the depth of vulnerability you want to see. Karen Lee-Thorp gives a good example of this for the question, What is one thing you're good at? "If your answer is, 'cooking,' you will probably get a series of single-phrase, not-very-vulnerable answers from the rest of the group. That's fine if people aren't ready to open up very much. If your answer is, 'I was the Student Activities chairperson at college, so I can throw a heck of a party for three hundred people,' group members may smile and loosen up a bit in their answers. If you say, 'I am good at listening compassionately to people in pain because I've had a lot of pain in my life and I know how it feels,' you'll set an entirely different tone. This is a serious, self-reflective, and bittersweet answer that will work only if your group is really ready to get down to business."[12]

As referenced in the last chapter, *The Complete Book of Questions: 1001 Conversation Starters for Any Occasion* is a resource filled with hundreds of icebreaker questions usable in seeker small groups. The icebreakers are broken down into ten categories for easy reference, including:

Light and Easy
Personal Profile
Preferences
Blast from the Past
Just Imagine
Viewpoints
Hard-Hitting
From the Heart
Spiritually Speaking
Extreme Spiritual Matters

There are many creative ways to use this book in your seeker group meetings. You could predetermine one or two questions you'd like everyone in the group to answer, or have each member of your group randomly select one from the book and answer it. You could even identify a category of icebreakers you would like your group to use, and they could answer questions from that section. However you do it, keep the icebreaker interaction time fun and creative.

Several years ago the group I led looked forward so much to our traditional opening icebreaker question that when I skipped it one week, they insisted that no further discussion would take place without it. So we brainstormed our own icebreaker, and after that the group designated a member named Dan to always come prepared with the opening question. From that point on, he was affectionately called "Icebreaker Dan." He did a great job coming up with the icebreakers that year, and it was fun to watch him take ownership of his responsibility. (Anytime you can create ways for the seekers in your group to become more involved, you establish stronger bonds of trust and ownership.)

## Ask Transition Icebreakers

The final icebreaker question should become a link from light-hearted interaction to the main topic of discussion. I call this specific icebreaker a transition icebreaker because it assists the group to go a step deeper into the discussion. For example, suppose you were planning to ask your seeker group to discuss the Luke 15 parables of the lost sheep, the lost coin, and the lost son (see appendix B, Sample Lesson 2). You could start out with a couple of light, get-to-know-you icebreaker questions, but as a way to prepare your group for the Luke 15 discussion, you could ask the group to answer the following transition icebreaker: "Describe a situation in which you misplaced or lost something very valuable. What did you do? How did that loss make you feel?"

Or suppose you were going to discuss the question "What happens to people who've never heard of Jesus?" A possible transition icebreaker question could be "Do you believe in the phrase 'ignorance is bliss'? Why or why not?" Or, if you were going to interact around the issue of the severity of humanity's sin problem (see appendix C, Sample Lesson 3), a possible transition icebreaker might be "Do you think Christianity dwells too much on the negative, because of its apparent emphasis on sin, hell, and judgment? Explain your answer."

These kinds of questions allow the group to shift gears and get into a better mind-set to process the topic at hand. They give your discussion a jump start, in nonthreatening terms and in a general way, regarding your intended topic.

## Ask Observation Questions

"Who is the main character in this story?"
"Where was Jesus when he told this parable?"
"When did the main event occur?"
"What events transpired in the parable?"

Observation questions, such as those listed above, help seeker group members identify what they see and notice, inviting seekers to give their attention to the way things really are. They are the who, what, where, and when questions that draw out facts, or a particular truth, in a passage of Scripture. In some cases these questions enable seekers to become aware of spiritual truths they have not previously recognized. Observation questions address the basic content of a topic or passage and determine the direction of the upcoming discussion.

Try to develop good, thought-provoking questions that encourage seekers to make key observations, without boring or insulting them. Lee-Thorp illustrates it this way:

> Imagine that you are teaching someone to play tennis. You can say, "Keep your eye on the ball." The person thinks, "Thank you for the insightful advice. I never thought of watching the ball." He believes he *is* watching the ball. You can ask, "Are you watching the ball?" He might respond internally, "Of course, you idiot," or "No, I'm distracted by your dumb questions." But if you say, "How high is the ball when it passes over the net?" you have given him something to focus on. He now has something to be aware of, a reason to engage his brain and notice something that was there all the time. A good Observation Question draws the group's attention to facts (like the height of the ball) that are significant and worthy of focused awareness.... It's not feasible to ask all potential Observation Questions during a group meeting. Hence, you'll need to do your own careful observation ahead of time and then select a few key questions that you think will draw out the most important things the group needs to observe.... In as little as five minutes, you can discuss the key details and move on to what people really want to talk about: what it all means.[13]

After the group has read the parables in Luke 15, these observation questions could create some good interaction (see appendix B, Sample Lesson 2):

> "Describe the reaction common to all three stories when the missing valuable was finally found."
> "According to Jesus, what do these three stories teach concerning how much God values lost people?"

Here are a couple of examples of observation questions from the discussion about the problem of sin (see appendix C, Sample Lesson 3):

> "According to your understanding of the Bible, what separates people from God: a propensity to sin, a lack of knowledge about God, or both? Explain your answer."

"Do you believe that people are for the most part basically good, basically bad, or somewhere in between? Explain."

(For additional observation questions, see question 3 in appendix B, Sample Lesson 2, and questions 4 and 10 in appendix C, Sample Lesson 3.)

## Ask Interpretation Questions

The usual next step in a group discussion is to draw out the meaning behind the observations that have been made. Interpretation questions attempt to clarify a deeper understanding of the topic or Scripture. They encourage the group to go beyond the initial observations and make some sense of the facts discovered.

Some examples of interpretation questions include:

"What does this mean?"
"How is this significant?"
"What do you think is the main point behind what you see?"
"What conclusions can you draw ..."
"Why do you suppose ..."

Interpretation questions can help point out comparisons, contrasts, and connections between two or more observations. They get seekers thinking more intentionally about the main point or significance of a set of observations. Good interpretation questions also encourage seekers to focus on the cause and effect of the events they observe. Keep in mind that in a seeker small group setting many interpretation questions really need to draw out the *opinions* of your group members, rather than "right" or "wrong" answers. Expect group members to have differing points of view about the meaning behind their observations — this is normal and promotes great discussions. Asking members to further explain their interpretation of things can open the door to some lively interaction, as it challenges them to rethink their conclusions about biblical truths in a way that honors them in the process.

Here is an example of an interpretation question for the Luke 15 discussion (appendix B, Sample Lesson 2):

"Think back to your description of how you felt when you lost something very valuable. How does your reaction in that situation compare with how God must feel toward those who are not yet part of his family?"

For the discussion about the problem of sin (appendix C, Sample Lesson 3), note these three interpretation questions:

"The Bible teaches that the penalty of sin is spiritual death. What do you suppose it means to be spiritually dead?"

"The Bible teaches that our sin causes us to become God's enemies (Romans 5:10) and that we are then alienated from him (Colossians 1:21). How might people who appear to be indifferent or neutral toward God really be his enemies?"

"Some say God rates people using a scale. He places all the good things you've done on one side of that scale and the bad stuff on the other. Whichever side outweighs the other determines whether you are a good person or a bad person. Do you agree with this analogy? Why or why not?"

(For additional examples of interpretation questions, see questions 4, 5, and 7 in appendix B, Sample Lesson 2, and questions 7 and 9 in appendix C, Sample Lesson 3.)

## Ask Reflection Questions

Questions that elicit various group members' emotions are what I call reflection questions. These questions get at the heart of the matter concerning how people really feel about the topic at hand. A good group discussion focuses on both the intellectual and the emotional side of an issue. Sometimes you can ask questions that invite seekers to put themselves in the shoes of another person and share how they would feel. Other times simply asking how your group members feel about a certain discovery will open up a great time of interaction.

Some members of your group may feel a bit uncomfortable sharing their feelings, while others may be unable to adequately articulate what they feel. Always give your group members the freedom to decline sharing if they would rather not. Reminding the group of several possible emotional responses from which to choose, however, may encourage them to identify and describe their feelings. Appendix E, Emotions Word List, illustrates one way to identify and categorize some of our emotions.

Remember, there is no such thing as a wrong response to a reflection question. And sometimes the most important discovery a seeker will make during your small group meeting will be how he or she really *feels* about a certain spiritual issue. Occasionally, the source of an apparent intellectual objection is not intellectual at all, but really a smokescreen for an unresolved, unwilling heart attitude. So your ability to effectively encourage seekers to make a connection with their feelings could very well aid them to overcome roadblocks and propel them to make biblical discoveries further along in their spiritual journey.

Here is an example of a reflection question from the lesson on the Luke 15 parables (appendix B, Sample Lesson 2):

> "How do you feel about the idea that God hosts a heavenly celebration when a single person like you comes to him and is found?"

And here is an example from the lesson about the severity of our sin problem (appendix C, Sample Lesson 3):

> "How do you respond to the biblical claim that the sin in your life is so offensive to God that it has spiritually separated you from him?"

(For additional examples of reflection questions, see questions 2, 10, and 11 in appendix B, Sample Lesson 2, and question 12 in appendix C, Sample Lesson 3.)

### Ask Application Questions

Questions that invite seekers to articulate how they will respond to newly discovered spiritual truths are application questions. These questions are crucial in helping people think through how they will apply what they have learned to their lives. These questions in fact may be the most important part of the whole discussion, as seekers contemplate possible courses of action they may or may not want to take. Application questions challenge people to take some next steps and act on what they are beginning to understand and believe. James 1:22 stresses the importance of this step: "Do not merely listen to the word, and so deceive yourselves. Do what it says." However, be careful not to ask these questions in a way that puts your seeking friends on the spot in some intimidating way. Here are a few good examples of application questions:

"What spiritual discoveries have you made?"
"How have these discoveries impacted you?"
"What, if anything, will you change in your life as a result of today's discussion?"

If interpretation questions stress the "So what?" behind an issue, application questions emphasize the "Now what?"[14] Giving seekers an opportunity to identify a truth to believe, a command to obey, an example to follow, a pattern to avoid, or a promise to trust is an amazing process to watch. This is when things get exciting for the leader of a seeker small group. This is when you will start to see your group members grow closer to one another and make movements toward lasting life-change.

For the lesson on the Luke 15 parables (appendix B, Sample Lesson 2), here is an application question example:

"What would God need to do for you to feel loved by him?" (A good follow-up question would be "What is your understanding of what he has done already?")

Here are two application questions from the lesson on the problem of sin (appendix C, Sample Lesson 3):

"Do you have a tendency to minimize or maximize your sin by comparing yourself with others? Explain."
"How have you or will you deal with the sin problem that the Bible claims all of us have?"

(For additional examples of application questions, see question 13 in appendix B, Sample Lesson 2, and question 15 in appendix C, Sample Lesson 3.)

The quality of your group's interactions rests heavily on the questions you prepare. Think in terms of leading your group and assisting them to make spiritual discoveries, simply by asking a series of key questions. Carefully think through every question you will raise and just watch how your group responds. Chapter 7 will take an in-depth look into how to plan and prepare lessons to address the topics and questions that interest the seekers in your group. But before we turn to that process, an issue of critical importance needs to be covered. As important as it is to ask great questions, nothing compares with the significance of developing the skill discussed in chapter 6 — effectively *listening* to seekers' responses.

# JOAN SMITH'S STORY

*Office Manager*
*Hoffman Estates, Illinois*

*E*ven though I grew up attending church with my family, I never found my place there. I remember questioning what life was all about. Why am I here? What is the meaning of life? And if there is a God, where is he? I felt so alone. I became depressed as those questions weighed heavy on my heart. I was searching. Searching for answers and some kind of inner peace.

A few of my friends were Buddhists and they invited me to attend a meeting with them. I thought perhaps this could change my life and give me the inner peace I so desperately longed for. During that time I got married and my husband and I had a daughter.

I practiced Buddhism for eighteen years but that missing inner peace never came. And I was tired. Tired of trying so hard with no results. Tired from the pressure of having to make it on my own. Buddhism left me empty. I still felt unfulfilled and all alone. So I stopped practicing Buddhism altogether.

At that point, I decided I could simply be spiritual my own way, without the help of organized religion. I didn't trust religious institutions anyway. However, being so alone, I ached for some sort of connection with others. I really didn't think I could connect with Christians, because you had to believe in God for that and I was far from believing in God. I also felt that Christians were self-righteous and judgmental types — like it was some private club and there was some political agenda. That attitude really turned me off.

But my eleven-year-old daughter had many friends who were Christians, and I felt bad that my prejudices might affect her. So when the mother of one of my daughter's friends asked me to attend an Easter service last year, I decided to be open, accept her invitation, and attend with my daughter. I thought to myself, "I can handle an hour of Christianity, but nobody had better come up and start talking to me!"

To my surprise, I was overcome by emotion! The music filled me and the video about Jesus struck me like fireworks inside my heart. The message was about being on a "spiritual journey" and how important it was to make progress and take steps forward. Now, that I could handle. I left that service in awe.

I remember confiding in a friend of mine at work that I went to a Willow Creek service and that I liked it, but I pleaded with her not to tell anybody! She smiled and said, "I won't tell a soul." I attended services every week after that. Then after the services I used to sit up by the bookstore just to watch people, waiting for one false move. But all I saw were normal people doing normal things. Within a couple of months, my skepticism diminished and I knew this church was a safe place.

Shortly after, I was ready to take a next step. I learned that there were seeker small groups for people just like me who were searching. So I signed up. The group I visited quickly became a safe place for me and the other members to ask our questions and discuss the possible answers. It was great! The leaders really embraced me and respected me and where I was coming from. I felt like they trusted God because they did not try to manipulate my journey or try to use pressure to push me along. I made progress one step at a time, at my own speed. But they stood by my side all along the way, and if I needed them, I knew they were there.

One night I felt God spoke to my heart, saying, "Open your life to me! Open your beautiful heart to me and I will give you the peace and fulfillment you are looking for." My life opened up! I said to my seeker leader that the Jesus I was hearing about was the Jesus I wanted to know. I started reading the Bible and telling everybody about the experience I had. I wanted to learn as much as I could, because I knew it was just a matter of time before I would open my life up to Christ and follow him. But I had to be sure.

Then life took a turn. It was Tuesday, September 11, 2001. I was at work. I am the office manager for a small school. One of the moms rushed in crying, saying that terrorists had hit the World Trade Center. We didn't have access to a TV, so I turned on the radio. The teachers had to be with the children, so it was my job to keep them informed throughout the day. When the Pentagon was hit, I just stood by my desk and said to myself, "What am I waiting for?" Life is so precious and yet so fragile. I thought I knew how to live. I thought I had the answers. But I realized I had evil in me too. I needed God's forgiveness and acceptance. "Lord," I prayed, "I receive you, Jesus, into my life! Thank you for dying on my behalf and paying the price for my sin. Now show me your way and I will follow!"

Life has never been the same. I have that inner peace now. And I know that I am not alone, for God is with me. And now as I get baptized this week, I say to Jesus, "Thank you for forgiving and accepting me. I want to receive you into my life as my one and only Savior. Thank you for filling me with that missing inner peace. You've made it all possible. Thank you."

# MEL ALGER'S STORY

*Custodian*
*Palatine, Illinois*

*A*round here I am what they call a "seeker." I believe there is a God, but I don't have a strong understanding of who he is or how to get connected with him. But I'm searching.

Religion for my family was something that happened only on Sundays. I grew up in a large family, the fourth of seven children in a pretty chaotic environment. I've often heard the middle kid referred to as the lost child, a designation that describes me perfectly. I truly was lost for many of those early years, yet I didn't want to be found or noticed. Over time the chaos took its toll and my family began to unravel.

I was married and divorced, then tried marriage again. Shortly after my daughter's birth I became aware of a big void in my life — still feeling like the lost child and not knowing where to look for answers. I was abusing alcohol on a regular basis, a habit I picked up early in life. For several years I felt stuck in my own depression, and frequent arguments with my wife and other family members created a distance between us.

One morning, about six months ago, I received a phone call from my older brother telling me that our father was dead. My dad, who had struggled with alcohol his entire life, had sold the family business and moved, along with my mom, to Florida only three weeks earlier. And now he had taken his own life. The only way I can express what I felt is this: "total numbness." The already big void in my life grew larger.

Finally, I arrived at the conclusion that I had been constantly turning in the wrong direction. I had made poor choices based on my wants and needs, seeking only to satisfy my own selfish desires. Once again I hit bottom. My life and my marriage were at the breaking point.

I was lost inside myself. I felt estranged from my wife, family, friends, and most certainly God. In the midst of my pain, my wife and I happened upon a newspaper ad for a new series of services starting at Willow Creek Community Church. Called "Surviving the Storms of Life," the series promised to address loss, betrayal, failure, and disappointment. We were certainly in the midst of a storm. They say pain is a great motivator, and things were so bad that I was willing to try anything — even church. I found my way to the last row way up in the balcony — I didn't want to be converted or anything; I just wanted to hear what they had to say.

What I heard that Saturday night moved both my wife and me to tears. It opened up a flood of emotion unlike anything I'd ever felt before. We came back the next weekend and I remember secretly thinking, "I hope that happens again." And it did — each week for the rest of the series. I began to think that God might actually be answering my meager prayers.

I had a Bible at home with a lot of dust on it, but I didn't know exactly how to read it. It's kind of overwhelming, so I thought that joining a seeker small group might be a good place for me to start. But how do you do that? I mean, how do you go there and say, "I know absolutely nothing; I'm a real basic beginner at this and I need a lot of help"? I was worried the group would be too diverse — too far ahead or even too far behind me. After much discussion, lots of hesitation, and some fear of the unknown, my wife and I decided to take the plunge and actually attend one meeting. We would start with that and see where it led. So we did. We filled out a card, requesting information about seeker small groups, and put it in the collection basket, hoping that somehow God would lead us and that he might have a plan for us.

To make a long story short, it's been a wonderful experience. Someone from the church called and suggested that we try Ted's small group, which met in the atrium at 5:30 P.M. on Saturdays. We arrived early and spotted a big sign on one table that read, "Ted's Small Group." I thought, "This is it, this is the place, here goes nothing." We sat down with some people who were roughly our age, amidst a whole conglomeration of people with different thoughts and ideas and philosophies and backgrounds. I felt welcomed, not pressured, and accepted for who I was and not judged for being spiritually inept.

At first I had a lot of questions and I worried that they were so basic that I might be in the wrong place. Over the next couple of months, though, I eventually got them all asked. Now I find myself midweek looking forward to the weekend meeting and thinking,

What questions am I going to bring to the discussion group? *It's all out there in the open now and that feels great. I was surprised (and pleased) to discover that even my wife is at the same place spiritually that I am.*

*It's been an exciting journey for me, as each day brings something new and at every meeting I learn a little more. I've come a long way spiritually. I'm not totally there yet but I want to keep on going. I'm open to the idea of accepting Jesus into my life, but I don't know quite how to do that or how to formalize that and actually cross that line and make the connection. I'm almost to that point, but I realize that it's a process.*

*What I lack in knowledge, I make up for in willingness. I'm reading the Bible now and finding answers there to questions I've asked my whole life. Our group is growing closer, thanks to Ted, who is a very patient leader. And I'm finding that I'm not alone. While each person in our group is there for a different reason, we have a common goal. We're all hoping to find some answers.*

*I'm also hoping to find the peace and contentment that I see in Ted and in so many others here at Willow Creek. I think I will, because each day as my journey unfolds, I am closer than I've ever felt to finally filling that big empty void in my life — thanks mainly to my seeker small group.*

# Chapter 6

# Listen Well

*

*Be quick to listen, slow to speak.*

JAMES 1:19

*Listening is so much like loving, it's hard to tell them apart.*

UNKNOWN

*The first duty of love—is to listen.*

PAUL TILLICH

*'Tis better to be silent and be thought a fool, than to speak and remove all doubt.*

ABRAHAM LINCOLN

Our group had been meeting every Wednesday night for just over four months, discussing the questions for God we had raised at our first meeting. We talked about God's existence, his attributes, and his love and concern for us. We had intense, interesting dialogues about the problem of evil, hell, and the Devil, the authority of the Bible, and the role of Jesus in the world today. And through our discussions we became a close group of friends.

Pat, Kasy, Marty, Leslie, and Cindy always arrived early to eat together before things got started, and it wasn't long before most of the rest of us started to do the same. After the meetings, Keith and I frequently headed out to a nearby pool hall to shoot a game or two and take our group's discussion to the "next level." Sue and Barbara (my apprentices) usually stuck around to hang out with anyone who wanted to talk further. Between meetings we stayed connected through emails, phone calls, or impromptu get-togethers. Sometimes we sat together as a group during church and then met for a meal. We celebrated the birth of Cathy and Joe's second son and grieved the tremendous loss of Laura's brother. We sympathized with Gloria's struggles as she cared for her physically challenged child. Over time these and various other shared life experiences, along with our gatherings outside our regular meeting times, strengthened the bonds between us.

But the thing about the group I enjoyed most was the interaction that took place during our actual meetings. I appreciated how we felt so safe and free to be ourselves and share openly and honestly what we were really thinking about spiritual matters. The group discussions gave me an inside track to the significant spiritual issues my seeking friends were wrestling with, offering me a firsthand view of their struggles with what they could and could not believe about God and the Bible. To me, there is nothing more exciting in the world than an up-close look at the process seekers go through to take steps of spiritual progress.

I remember one night our discussion got so passionate that when I tried to end the meeting at the usual time, no one left. I suggested that we pick up the discussion next time, but apparently no one was willing to put things off until later. *Everyone* stayed for overtime. An hour or so went by, but then I had to go. When I told them to "carry on" and then left, the fact that they didn't need me to continue the discussion was a secret victory. They had become seekers earnestly in search of the truth, and I knew now it was only a matter of time.

A few weeks after that legendary marathon session, something amazing happened that I will never forget. Everything I had done so far set me up for this; all the prayers I had offered, all the bridges I had built, all the questions I'd asked, all the listening I had done had brought me to this very moment.

It came about during a discussion on how a person actually becomes a Christian. Our interaction that evening was exceptionally fast-paced and energetic. No one seemed to agree on anything; everyone expressed something completely different. But I just kept pressing them to contrast what the Bible was saying with what they thought. I asked questions designed to challenge their thinking. Questions like:

> "When you first heard about Christianity, what did you think was its message? To the best of your understanding, how would you summarize that message now?"
>
> "Do you think becoming a Christian is an ongoing process, something that happens at a specific point in time, or a combination of the two? Why?"
>
> "If salvation is a free gift, isn't it automatically applied to everyone — even atheists? Why or why not?"
>
> "What is the difference between an intellectual assent to a set of beliefs and an actual acceptance of those same beliefs?"

I urged them to draw comparisons between the Bible's claims and what they were ready and willing to believe. My silent prayers were a steady flow heavenward as I followed up with questions like "How does your response make you feel?" and "What reasons can you give for drawing your conclusions?" or "Do the rest of you agree with that? Why or why not?" The times of silence between some responses indicated their struggle to decide one way or another; I watched my friends carefully as they weighed the issues at hand. I drew some of the quieter ones out so everyone could benefit from their thinking.

Then it happened, without any warning. One of the seekers stopped herself midsentence and paused. The whole group grew silent, turned and looked at her. Slowly she looked up at me and asked, "But what do *you* think, Garry?"

You could have heard a pin drop. Someone else spoke up. "That's right, what do *you* think it means to be a true Christian?" Then another agreed and said, "You rarely tell us your thoughts. Tell us now. What do *you* have to say about this?" One by one, each person in the group insisted I share my thoughts and beliefs. This amazed me!

Can you imagine such a scene? When was the last time you had nine or ten seekers sit up, lean forward, look you straight in the eye, and demand that you share the gospel with them? When was the last time you had seekers hang on your every word as you explained what it means to receive Christ as the forgiver and leader of one's life?

I took a deep breath to savor the moment and soak it all in. My friends had pretty much talked themselves out, and my turn to give my point of view had finally arrived. For four months I bit my tongue to keep from short-circuiting their learning process. I waited and listened to them share their skepticisms, disbeliefs, and new discoveries about God and the Bible. For four months I modeled for them how to ask questions, listen, and learn. And now *they* were ready to ask questions, listen, and learn. They had been sufficiently heard and were now ready and open to give listening to me a whirl. So in response to their invitation, I gave the most concise and compelling explanation of the gospel I could muster.

Now, to be clear, I *had* participated in the past discussions from time to time just like everyone else, especially with the icebreakers. And I *had* offered my thoughts and opinions as appropriate, including brief explanations of the gospel message here and there as the opportunity presented itself, but for the most part I asked question after question and listened intently to their responses. I demonstrated respect, acceptance, and patience toward each member of the group by giving him or her my undivided, uninterrupted attention. This attitude was instrumental in bringing each of them to the point of trusting me enough to eventually ask me about my beliefs. Finally they were ready, and even eager, to hear and understand what the Bible teaches about knowing God. Without pressure, manipulation, or arm-twisting, I had earned the right to be heard. And I earned it by being a good listener.

By the time our group had been together for about a year, almost every seeker came to the place of putting his or her faith in Jesus Christ — and I had the wonderful privilege of baptizing many of them. Looking back, I feel I didn't *talk* any of them into the kingdom; I *listened* them in! Of course, I know that ultimately no one comes to Jesus unless the Father draws him or her (John 6:44), and no one can believe in Jesus without hearing about him (Romans 10:14, 17). But my role of doing more listening than talking, more facilitating than teaching, and being more relational than intellectual played a crucial part in the process of bringing them to the point where they were ready and willing to learn spiritual truths from the Bible.

And that's exactly the point of these seeker small groups. As leaders, our hope is to take our already established relationships with seekers and utilize our group time to strengthen those bonds of friendship even more. We want to give our seeking friends an opportunity to identify their toughest objections and obstacles to faith in Christ — and, by thinking out loud, process them within the safety of our group. We want to provide a forum in which our seeking friends can safely address their toughest spiritual questions and investigate the claims of Christ at their own pace, and we want to do so in ways that build stronger bonds of trust with each group member. *And nothing develops the level of trust with seekers better than practicing the art of listening.*

## The Power of Listening

Think of a time when a person turned to face you squarely and displayed a sincere desire to fully hear and understand you. Chances are, that kind of undivided attention made quite an impact on you. More than likely, you felt accepted and encouraged to say whatever was on your mind. You may have even been open to hearing some counsel or advice from that listener, because you felt so understood by him or her. Listening at this level provides a foundation of trust necessary for producing stronger interpersonal relationships, because it expresses unselfish love and concern (see Philippians 2:3, 4 and James 1:19).

It seems to rarely occur, but whenever we are heard at such a deep level, we feel the freedom to safely express and process our ideas, problems, impending decisions, and emotions. Such listening communicates how much the listener really wants to know and understand us. And that's quite a gift.

As seeker small group leaders, we gain overwhelmingly positive benefits through the practice of concentrated listening. As we listen intently, we receive greater insights into the lives of our seeking friends, enabling us to effectively focus the small group discussions more directly on their needs and concerns. But the real question before us now is this: How can we become better listeners? Are we equipped and trained to really hear our seeking friends at this level?

In his book *The Seven Habits of Highly Effective People,* Stephen Covey puts the question this way: "Communication is the most important skill in life. We spend most of our waking hours communicating. But consider this: You've spent years learning how to read and write, years learning how to speak. But what about listening? What training or education have you had that enables you to listen so that you really, deeply understand another human being from that individual's own frame of reference?"[1] I am convinced beyond any shadow of doubt that the very best seeker small group leaders not only know how to ask key, provocative questions but, even more than that, understand how to truly listen to the hearts and souls of seekers.

## Listening Aids

Since listening is a skill that needs to be intentionally cultivated and utilized — and for most of us, not something that happens naturally or without much effort — here are several basic skills that, if developed, will help you become a better listener. Think of these suggestions as a starting point in your mastery of the art of listening.

### Engage the Listener

Eliminate any distractions that prevent you from really listening to your group members. Put yourself in the right frame of mind and let your body communicate that you are fully engaged to truly listen. Be attentive and eager. Give good eye contact to speakers, facing them squarely and looking genuinely interested to hear what they have to say. Give an approving smile or nod as each person shares. Verbal affirmation gives seekers confidence and helps draw them out more. Making comments like "Yes," "That makes sense," "I understand," and "That's helpful" can be a great encouragement to them.

The book *Lead Out* explains that "President Kennedy made you think he had nothing else to do except ask you questions and listen, with extraordinary concentration, to your answer. You knew that for the time being he had blotted out both the past and the future for you."[2] Listen like *that*.

### Listen with Your Eyes

Communication researchers estimate that only between 7 and 10 percent of what a person communicates is expressed in words; 30 to 38 percent is conveyed in sounds of the voice, such as inflection, rate, and volume; and 55 to 60 percent is represented in body language.[3] As you listen, observe the body posture, facial expressions, and gestures of your friends. Pay attention to their voice quality, which may give additional meaning and understanding to the words you hear.

Nonverbal communication is sometimes difficult to interpret, so be careful about drawing conclusions too quickly. In some cases it's appropriate and necessary to ask for clarification about the significance of any nonverbal cues. I remember, in one group discussion, picking up on a seeker's lack of eye contact. She just didn't seem herself. When I asked if everything was all right, this group member told the rest of us about a painful loss she had recently experienced. As a group, we were then able to offer words of encouragement and even support her in a short time of prayer.

## Listen with Your Heart

Try to discern what emotions you're picking up from those in your group. Remember that feelings are not always easy to determine, so be cognizant that your judgments might be inaccurate. Encourage your group members to share their feelings by asking reflection questions (see chapter 5). Often people are not aware enough of their own feelings to know how to express them, so your questions may aid them tremendously in discovering how they really feel.[4] But in any case, try to understand what emotions are being communicated behind the words expressed.

## Never Interrupt

Interrupting communicates that what you have to say is much more important than what the other person is saying. It's a habit worth breaking. When you interrupt, you reveal that you are thinking more about your response than anything else. Did you know that some people save their most important idea until the end of their response? If you interrupt someone before he or she is finished, you may well miss the most significant point![5] On very rare occasions you might need to rein in someone heading into a long tangent (see chapter 7), but for the vast majority of the time, it is extremely important to avoid interrupting the speaker. The only time I interrupt someone is to stop another person from interrupting by saying something like "Hold on just a second, please. Let's hear the rest of what was being said."

*Silence Is Golden*

Don't be afraid of silence. Once you've put a question out there, the best thing to do is patiently wait for group members to respond. Keep in mind that people are most likely thinking about how they might answer. Your ability to wait and let the group members think long enough to formulate good responses demonstrates your care and concern. And be aware that the signals you send during the silence will greatly influence how the rest of your group feels. If you become uncomfortable and nervous about the silence, your group will be ill at ease. If you determine to be confident and relaxed during these periods, your group will react accordingly. Simply wait it out. If, however, the silence grows unbearably long, you may be able to prompt a response by restating the question or asking in what way the question was a little unclear. Sometimes a little humor, like "Don't all jump in at once, now!" can serve to put everyone at ease. Including you!

*Use Follow-up Questions*

While your original questions should be planned ahead of time, follow-up questions cannot be preplanned — they must come to you in the moment. Lee-Thorp describes follow-up questions this way: "Once the discussion ball is in the air, secondary or guiding questions keep it moving. They build on the primary question so the discussion resembles a good tennis match (serve, return, volley, volley, volley) instead of a dull one (serve, point; serve, point; serve, point)."[6]

These questions flow out of the discussion at hand and take on many different forms. For example, if you sense that someone in the group has more to add after they finish responding, you may want to follow up with that person by asking something like "Did you have anything else to add?" Or you can move on to others, asking, "What do the rest of you think?" or "Does anyone have a different response?" Do your best to link what was previously stated to your next question. Even articulating some of the same words or phrases that members used will create a sense of acceptance and continuity within your group.

When someone responds with a short answer, a good follow-up question like "Can you tell us more?" might be the only nudge the person needs to elaborate. When someone responds with a lengthy reply, ask that person or someone else in the group to rephrase or summarize what was said, so everyone is clear. The idea here is to value each group member enough to really understand what he or she is saying. But as you ask clarifying questions, remember to be careful not to put people on the defensive. You don't want them to think you are asking them to defend their position, when all you really want to do is more fully understand their point of view.

## Empathic Evangelism

I am so convinced of the critical importance of good listening to the success of seeker small groups that I will devote the rest of this chapter to exploring a level of listening that goes well beyond the basic skills listed above. As the leader, you will need to practice and model a deeper kind of listening — a gift most of your group members will have never fully experienced before.

In his book *Between the Words,* Dr. Norm Wakefield challenges his readers to become "perceptive listeners." He defines a perceptive listener as someone who simultaneously practices these five kinds of listening:

- hearing the words
- watching the nonverbal
- discovering the meaning of the message
- identifying defined or undefined emotions within the message
- discerning the full message behind the verbal and nonverbal communication[7]

Similarly, Stephen Covey identifies "empathic listening" as the highest level of listening. In his book *The Seven Habits of Highly Effective People,* he describes five progressive levels of listening:

1. ignoring
2. pretending
3. selective listening
4. attentive listening
5. empathic listening[8]

Covey summarizes his fifth level of listening this way: "Seek first to understand, then to be understood." These kinds of listening principles, outlined by Wakefield, Covey, and others, encapsulate what I have been attempting to cultivate in myself and other seeker group leaders for more than twenty-five years. Whether you call it perceptive listening or empathic listening, this high level of listening defines exactly the kind of listening that needs to be put into practice by seeker small group leaders. Although we have significant theological differences, I greatly respect Covey's insights and concepts regarding listening. So what follows now is a summary of Covey's principles of empathic listening applied to the task of engaging seekers in conversations about spiritual matters. It is vitally important that you, as a leader of a seeker small group, cultivate this habit.

## Supply Plenty of Acceptance

According to Covey, the greatest psychological need of human beings is "to be understood, to be affirmed, to be validated, to be appreciated." As your group members share their hearts, they need to feel your grace, acceptance, and encouragement even when you disagree. If they don't, it will seem as if they are left gasping for air, psychologically speaking. But when you listen in such a way as to meet these needs, you are in a sense breathing "psychological air" into your group members, freeing them to focus on solving problems, making discoveries, or taking steps of spiritual growth.[9]

Genuinely lavish your group members with praise and support. I cannot emphasize this point too much. On a very practical level, this means sincerely thanking them for their willingness to share, mirroring their statement back to them (as necessary) for clarification, and genuinely expressing approval for their contribution. It is important to note, however, that one can give affirmation and acceptance without necessarily *agreeing* with what was shared. As Wakefield points out, "Acceptance is not to be equated with agreement. Acceptance says, 'I accept your feelings as valid to you. I do not condemn you for having them.' Acceptance is a significant way to express the love of Christ."[10] This attitude of acceptance and encouragement goes a long way toward creating an open and honest environment where spiritual growth and learning can take place. As seekers share, always remember to sincerely and genuinely respond in these three ways:

- Convey encouragement and gratitude (appreciating): "Thanks for responding." "I appreciate your willingness to share."
- Ask for clarification when needed (mirroring): "Is this what you mean . . ." "So what I hear you saying is . . ." "Let me see if I've got that right . . ."
- Express approval and support (validating): When you *agree* with the comment, say something like, "That's a great point." "Excellent thinking." "You make sense because . . ." When you *disagree* with the comment, preface your statements with something like, "I'm not sure I agree with you, but . . ." "Now that's not my point of view, but . . ." "That's not exactly what the Bible teaches, but . . ."

## Diagnose Before Prescribing

As the leader, your natural tendency might be to evaluate, interpret, and solve issues prematurely, without fully understanding where your group members are coming from. The time to point seekers toward biblical answers *will* come, but be very careful not to bulldoze through without earning that right. Wakefield addresses this problem:

> Ninety percent of the time we give our opinion, advice, or counsel:
>
> - before we know all the facts
> - before we know the real problem or need
> - before the person is finished
> - before the person is *ready* for help
>
> Our well-intentioned help falls on deaf ears. If we don't rein in the impulse to fix the person, to straighten him or her out, to solve the problem, we'll accomplish little or nothing. . . . The issue is a question of timing. We try to short-circuit the process by giving our input *before the person is mentally or emotionally ready*.[11]

Covey suggests following this commonsense rule of thumb: "Diagnose before you prescribe."[12] In other words, forget about trying to answer questions seekers are not asking, avoid solving problems they don't have, refrain from throwing out two-cent answers to million-dollar questions, don't attempt to be understood until you first understand, and speak much less than you listen.

*Avoid Autobiographical Listening*

In his chapter "Principles of Empathic Communication," Stephen Covey suggests that most of us listen autobiographically and thus filter our responses in four ways. Based on our own frame of reference,

1. we evaluate (agree or disagree),
2. we probe (ask questions),
3. we advise (give counsel), or
4. we interpret (figure people out).[13]

But responding in these ways hinders our ability to understand the speaker, because we predetermine our spin on the conversation and prematurely draw conclusions.

In an attempt to explain further these kinds of autobiographical responses and, alternatively, the power of empathic listening, I have adapted a set of interactions from Covey's book for our purposes here.[14] What follows is a series of one-on-one evangelistic dialogues I constructed between a Christian and his seeking friend, to illustrate the empathic listening process — for use with seekers both during group meetings and apart from them. Notice in this first example the Christian's autobiographical responses (identified by parentheses).

SEEKER: I don't really see how Christianity would work for me.
CHRISTIAN: Now, why would you think that? (evaluating, probing)
SEEKER: Well, for one thing, there are too many hypocrites claiming to be Christians. I don't want to associate myself with a religion filled with so many people who pretend to be something they're not. That disgusts me.
CHRISTIAN: I used to feel that way, until I did some further investigation. Let me tell you what I discovered. After struggling with this very issue for a long time, I finally realized that Christians are not ever going to be perfect in this world, but you can't hold that against Christianity. Just because some people cheat in golf doesn't mean it's a bad sport. And just because Christianity

doesn't make people perfect doesn't mean it's not the right way to go. (advising)

SEEKER: How can it be the right way to go if it doesn't work? I mean, if Christians can't live up to their own standards, tell me what about that is working.

CHRISTIAN: But it does work; it's working for me and it's working for millions of other Christians. I may not be perfect, but I'm doing my best to live the Christian life, and that's all that God asks of me. Say, maybe you've seen the bumper sticker "Be patient, God isn't finished with me yet." I think that principle applies to my Christian life. (evaluating, advising)

SEEKER: Yes, but I still don't see how hypocrisy would be acceptable in God's eyes, especially by the very ones who claim to be following him.

CHRISTIAN: You can't just focus on that. They're wrong for living hypocritically and God will judge them accordingly. But I wish you could see that you can trust God to make things right. Why don't you just give Christ a try, like I did? Then you would see for yourself that Christianity does work. (advising, probing)

SEEKER: Try? It sounds too risky for me to do that. It may have worked for you, and I'm happy for you. But I'm just not ready now.

CHRISTIAN: It's too risky *not* to try. I'm not sure you know how high the stakes are. We're talking about eternity here. When you say, "Not now" to God, you're really saying no to him. (interpreting)

SEEKER: I know this is important. I think I just need to process things a little more.

CHRISTIAN: I understand and that's great. Just know that I'm always willing to talk more with you about this. (evaluating)

SEEKER: Yeah, I know. Thanks.

Now, of course, this Christian cares about his seeking friend and means well. He really is trying to make a positive impact, but how much did he actually begin to understand his friend? How well did he really listen? Now examine this same dialogue a little closer by noting throughout what the seeker is thinking and feeling all along (identified by parentheses).

SEEKER: I don't really see how Christianity would work for me. *(But I'm open to exploring the possibility.)*

CHRISTIAN: Now, why would you think that? (SEEKER: *Wow, maybe you really do want to know!*)

SEEKER: Well, for one thing, there are too many hypocrites claiming to be Christians. I don't want to associate myself with a religion filled with so many people who pretend to be something they're not. That disgusts me. *(How does anyone live up to such high standards? I know I couldn't live up to them. And I would feel like the biggest hypocrite of them all.)*

CHRISTIAN: I used to feel that way, until I did some further investigation. Let me tell you what I discovered. (SEEKER: *Great, just what I wanted—a lecture with a quick, easy solution to an issue that's not my main problem. I can see this isn't really about me—it's about you! If you only knew how much I wish I could believe, but can't.)* After struggling with this very issue for a long time, I finally realized that Christians are not ever going to be perfect in this world, but you can't hold that against Christianity. Just because some people cheat in golf doesn't mean it's a bad sport. And just because Christianity doesn't make people perfect doesn't mean it's not the right way to go. (SEEKER: *Yes, but what about me—is it the right way for me to go? You don't know my past and how far away from God I feel. I wish I could spell it out for you. But even then I'm not sure you would understand—or if you'd even want to.)*

SEEKER: How can it be the right way to go if it doesn't work? I mean, if Christians can't live up to their own standards, tell me what about that is working. *(It wouldn't work for me to try to be a Christian—I'd fail miserably.)*

CHRISTIAN: But it does work; it's working for me and it's working for millions of others Christians. I may not be perfect, but I'm doing my best to live the Christian life, and that's all that God asks of me. Say, maybe you've seen the bumper sticker "Be patient, God isn't finished with me yet." I think that principle applies to my Christian life. (SEEKER: *That's fine and dandy for you, but you're not me. God may have accepted you, but not me—how could he, after all I've done?)*

SEEKER: Yes, but I still don't see how hypocrisy would be acceptable in God's eyes, especially by the very ones who claim to be following him. *(I still don't see how God could love and forgive someone like me. I feel like I've disappointed him so many times in the past and could never be good enough in the future.)*

CHRISTIAN: You can't just focus on that. They're wrong for living hypocritically and God will judge them accordingly. (SEEKER: *Just what I thought.*) But I wish you could see that you can trust God to make things right. (SEEKER: *That's what I was afraid of — I'm guilty as charged.*) Why don't you just give Christ a try, like I did? Then you would see for yourself that Christianity does work. (SEEKER: *Try? I would like to try, but you're not letting me tell you about my real obstacle.*)

SEEKER: Try? It sounds too risky for me to do that. It may have worked for you, and I'm happy for you. But I'm just not ready now. *(I know God is just waiting for me to give him a try — so he can watch me fail and then punish me for missing the mark.)*

CHRISTIAN: It's too risky *not* to try. I'm not sure you know how high the stakes are. We're talking about eternity here. When you say, "Not now" to God, you're really saying no to him. (SEEKER: *I do know how critical this stuff is; that's why I brought it up with you. But maybe this wasn't such a good idea after all.*)

SEEKER: I know this is important. *(Give me a little more credit.)* I think I just need to process things a little more.

CHRISTIAN: I understand and that's great. Just know that I'm always willing to talk more with you about this.

SEEKER: Yeah, I know. Thanks. *(But I'm just not able to address my greatest concern with you, so what's the use?)*

*Rephrase Content and Reflect Emotion*

Did you notice how much the Christian missed by not listening with more empathy? It's so important to make an intentional effort to listen for and ask about the meaning and emotions behind what is being said.

According to Covey, there are stages to empathic listening. It begins with mirroring back what the person is saying or feeling, and develops into putting the person's meaning and feelings in your own words. Covey draws this conclusion: "Now what happens when you use fourth stage empathic listening skills is really incredible. As you authentically seek to understand, as you rephrase content and reflect feeling, you give him psychological air. You also help him work through his own thoughts and feelings. As he grows in his confidence of your sincere desire to really listen and understand, the barrier between what's going on inside him and what's actually being communicated to you disappears. It opens a soul to soul flow. He's not thinking and feeling one thing and communicating another. He begins to trust you with his innermost tender feelings and thoughts."[15]

Take a look at this next dialogue in the series — one that illustrates the same conversation with an empathic listening twist. Observe the difference this higher level of listening can make. (The seeker's thoughts are again identified by parentheses.)

SEEKER: I don't really see how Christianity would work for me. *(But I'm open to exploring the possibility.)*

CHRISTIAN: Sounds like you're trying to figure out if Christianity makes sense, but the pieces aren't coming together for you. (SEEKER: *Exactly! It would be nice if it would all fall into place for me.*)

SEEKER: Not yet anyway. The biggest thing that's bothering me is that there are far too many hypocrites claiming to be Christians. I don't want to associate myself with a religion filled with so many people who pretend to be something they're not. That disgusts me. *(And if I became a Christian, I'd become the biggest hypocrite of them all.)*

CHRISTIAN: So if you were to become a Christian, you'd be joining a whole bunch of people who don't live up to what they say they believe, which isn't very appealing. You're repulsed because they fall way short of God's standards even though they claim to be his followers. (SEEKER: *Let's see — is that what I'm feeling?*)

SEEKER: Well, it just doesn't make sense to me. Most Christians I know fail to live up to God's standards. How is that acceptable to him?

CHRISTIAN: What I hear you saying is that you're wondering how God could ever accept people who don't live up to his standards. (SEEKER: *Well, I think so.*)

SEEKER: I would think that those who mess up would and should be out of luck. Especially someone like me.

CHRISTIAN: Are you thinking that God might not be willing or able to forgive everybody and that some people are out of luck no matter what — including you?

SEEKER: Well, yes, I guess so. I feel like if God really knew my past and all the bad stuff I've done, there's just no way he could forgive me. I can't even forgive myself for the things I've done. It's like I'm carrying this heavy weight on my shoulders.

CHRISTIAN: So you feel like you're not good enough and are unworthy to receive God's love and forgiveness. You've disappointed yourself so much, you're questioning how God could ever accept you. (SEEKER: *Yes, somebody understands me!*) But if God could somehow totally forgive you, wouldn't that be a huge weight off your shoulders?

SEEKER: Exactly. But not only that, if I were to become a Christian, I'd just feel like one of those hypocrites I despise so much. There's no way I'd even come close to living up to God's expectations — I've messed up so much in the past and I know I'd just fail miserably in the future.

Notice how in this last dialogue the seeker actually begins to verbalize his thoughts and feelings. Because he feels understood, the conversation has become safe enough for him to be more and more transparent. Empathic listening fosters this authenticity and helps build relational bridges. Covey says, "What a difference real understanding can make! All the well-meaning advice in the world won't amount to a hill of beans if we're not even addressing the real problem. And we'll never get to the problem if we're so caught up in our own autobiography, our own paradigms, that we don't take off our glasses long enough to see the world from another point of view."[16] The dialogue continues:

SEEKER: I guess I feel like I'm just not good enough to ever become a Christian. But I also admit that I feel like something's missing and I think I really need God in my life.

CHRISTIAN: You're really caught in the middle — you feel like you haven't measured up, and yet at the same time you know deep down you want a real relationship with God.

SEEKER: I think that's it. What would you suggest I do?

Can you see how the Christian moved toward the seeker, and as a result the seeker moved toward the Christian? What was in the beginning a great distance between the two has been bridged, and the seeker is actually pursuing the Christian, *asking* for his advice. The opportunity the Christian attempted to manufacture in the first dialogue has now happened naturally because of the Christian's willingness to "seek first to understand." And the seeker is now ready for and open to a life-changing conversation. What began as a simple exchange of information has become a kingdom encounter. Read on.

CHRISTIAN: Well, I can think of a couple things you may want to consider.

SEEKER: Like what?

CHRISTIAN: Here's one thing: Jesus himself said that it's not the healthy ones who need a doctor, it's the sick ones. He came to forgive sinners, not those who think they are already good enough (Mark 2:17). So when you say you're not worthy, you're really on the right track, for not one of us is even close to being worthy. But no matter how unworthy we are, every single one of us is invited to receive God's forgiveness—that includes you and me. That's why Christ came in the first place.

SEEKER: I guess that makes sense; I hadn't thought of it in that way before....

### Know When to Step In and When to Step Away

Frequently, when given the opportunity to process their thoughts about what the Bible says, seekers make spiritual discoveries for themselves. But also be prepared to add your input. Covey puts it this way: "Often when people are really given the chance to open up, they unravel their own problems and the solutions become clear to them in the process. At other times, they really need additional perspective and help. The key is to genuinely seek the welfare of the individual, to listen with empathy, to let the other person get to the problem and the solution at his own pace and time.... And watch what happens to you. The more deeply you understand other people, the more you will appreciate them, and the more reverent you will feel about them."[17] This is a good description of what can take place within the context of a seeker small group—I've seen it happen time and time again. As seekers are gradually exposed to the truth of the Bible, they begin to make new discoveries and the blinders begin to fall off. That's the Holy Spirit at work in their lives. Over time, with experience, you will learn when to jump in with your words of encouragement and when to get out of the way and let it happen.

Wherever I go to teach workshops about leading seeker small groups, people inevitably ask me who makes the best leaders. It's sometimes assumed that evangelists and apologists would naturally be the most effective seeker small group leaders, but I don't necessarily agree. Evangelists and apologists can be outstanding seeker group leaders, but they are sometimes more easily tempted to short-circuit the seeking process by dominating the discussion with their knowledgeable answers. Of course, as leaders, providing group members with reasonable answers and objective truths from the Bible is one of our main objectives. And we must always be sensitive to the Holy Spirit's promptings to communicate the gospel whenever he gives opportunity. But I have discovered over the years that unless we take the time to first really hear and understand our seeking friends, we run the high risk of our efforts not being welcome and our message falling on deaf ears.

While evangelism and apologetic training is very useful, it's not the primary key to effectiveness in these group settings. What seekers need most of all is to be listened to empathically. So you may not be a gifted evangelist and you may not be a knowledgeable apologist, but don't let that stop you from forming a group for seekers. You'll find what really makes a significant impact is demonstrating an authentic, caring, and understanding heart toward seekers by the way you listen. And that's definitely something you can do!

# BILL COOK'S STORY

*Technical Programmer*
*Elk Grove, Illinois*

*A*fter years of attempting to resist my wife's best efforts to get me to accompany her to our local church weekly, a set of events occurred that, looking back, are amazing to me.

I'd been discussing and defending my agnostic position with a long-distance friend who challenged me to read the book The Case for Christ. But while I was an avid reader — mostly self-help books, in hopes of finding greater happiness and fulfillment — I wondered if the book's author, Lee Strobel, was a priest, a psychologist, or maybe even an archaeologist. I was floored to learn that he was a pastor at a big church not all that far from where I lived!

I immediately devoured the book and then asked my wife, Jean, to check out this author and his church (Willow Creek Community Church) with me. She wanted no part of it, but after twenty-six years of marriage, she was willing to go in support of whatever it was I was searching for in life. We attended a weekend service, sitting close to the exit so we could make a quick getaway if things got too weird. And while I was there, I read a notice in the program about seeker small groups available on the weekends in the atrium.

The next Sunday I went back alone, looking for one of these groups. I was early, but it happened that a seeker leader was there, and he sat down to talk with me. Another leader came by and I kept the two of them busy as I peppered them with difficult questions. I was really questioning how a good person who didn't know Christ could spend eternity in hell, when a church staff member stopped by. I remember I really respected what he said. He told me, "You know, I also have problems understanding that completely. But there are so many other things that I know I can trust God about, this one issue is not enough to cause me to reject him. I think I can trust God to be fair with this one too."

I was amazed that instead of condemning me for my questions, these guys welcomed what I had to say. Altogether, I spent several hours talking to one or more of these three men that morning. I drove home blown away by their willingness to spend so much of their time with me.

Over the next few weeks, the guys I had met that Sunday in the atrium occasionally followed up just to keep in touch. Eventually I agreed to visit a seeker small group. They gave my name to Ernie and Ginny Johnson, who called and invited me to come to church with them and a couple other seekers from their group. When I got there, it was great to have people expecting me and then going in the service to sit with me. It was almost like being there with your family.

After the service we made our way to a reserved room, where we enjoyed the coffee and cake the Johnsons brought from home. And that's how I got started—having refreshments and appreciating everyone's company. Then Ginny looked at me and said, "Bill, tell us your story." I was shocked. They weren't there to preach at me or tell me what I should do next. They just wanted to listen as I talked about my journey! I told them about my early years in parochial school and my subsequent distance from my religious upbringing. I explained my nagging feeling that there had to be more to this life and told them about the inexplicable circumstances that had brought me to Willow Creek. I even shared Jean's distress and continued unhappiness that I was pursuing this thing. At one point I became pretty emotional, but I remember feeling very supported and even understood.

Every week Jean would leave for her church at the same time I'd leave to attend Willow Creek's services and meet with my group. But while she would get home in an hour, I'd be gone for two or three. What, she wondered, was I doing in that strange place? Who were these people I was spending so much time with? At one point she even went to one of her church's leaders and asked what she ought to do about what was going on with me. (He told her to let me be, saying, "He could be doing a lot worse.")

The people in my group were from a wide variety of backgrounds: a Jewish woman, Catholics, agnostics, and even atheists. But they were seekers just like me, with many of the same doubts but open to taking small steps in their spiritual journey. It was interesting for me to reflect back to my religious experience growing up. There was a teacher who spoke to us kids about God, but it never occurred to me to discuss spiritual things with my friends. This seeker group was the first time in my life I found myself engaging with others about God. It was so unusual for me! For twenty-six years my wife and I would go to a religious service and walk back to our car talking about anything but what just went on back there in that church. A forum to talk about God just was not available to me — and I was not going to initiate such a conversation at work or at any family gatherings. It was such a relief to finally have a safe place to come and talk about my spiritual questions and concerns.

One night Ginny and Ernie held a party for our group at their home, and Jean came with me. She ended up liking these people just as much as I did, and after that she began to attend services and the group meetings with me. For quite a while she continued to maintain strong ties with her church as well, and to tell the truth, some of the things about Willow Creek continued to perplex us. I remember attending the June baptism service held outside in the lake amidst a festive picnic atmosphere. It was hot, humid, and threatening to rain, and she wanted no part of it. She went with me ("kicking and screaming," she says now), praying all the way for a torrential downpour that would keep us from having to get out of the car. We only watched for five minutes — and from all the way across the lake. It all seemed very strange to us.

What a difference a year can make. By the next June we were in the water — both Jean and I were baptized and making a public statement of our faith and dependence on Jesus Christ! And a year after that I became an apprentice leader of a seeker small group who walked alongside a man as he got baptized! I'm such a believer in the concept that, together with the leader, I'm working to create the same kind of warm, welcoming atmosphere I found so appealing in my initial seeker small group meetings.

# RICK PAYNTER'S STORY

*Senior Pastor*
*Gateway Family Church*
*Melbourne, Australia*

*A*lthough I've been a pastor here in Melbourne for over sixteen years, I've never had an experience quite like the one with my friend Rob. We have about a thousand members in our church — which is a large church for Australia, where ninety percent of the population is unchurched. My church has worked hard at putting together places for seekers to connect — sports associations, theater productions, and more. But providing a place for them to get their questions answered has been missing.

I decided to experiment with my own attempts to reach out to seekers. I started by identifying people I do business with at several local shops, and eventually I found myself striking up a friendship with a certain shopkeeper. I made it a point to show up at the shop as often as I could and even began taking some of my personal business to him. I tried to go over there when I knew I had time to chat for a little while, rather than to just run in and out quickly. Very soon Rob, the shopkeeper, asked me what my angle was. I responded honestly that I was part of a church. I kept showing up and we kept talking — not really about anything deep or spiritual, just sharing news about our families and things.

About a month after I'd started this, Rob shocked me. He said, "Where's your church? I think my wife and I would like to visit." Now, you have to understand a few things about the Australian culture to truly appreciate how unusual this is. Convicts shipped from England were the original settlers here in Australia. There were Anglican ministers who came along on those convict ships, but they were also the magistrates, punishing during the week and then preaching on Sunday. Therein lies the whole view of the average Australian on religion. So to have someone pursue going to church was huge!

Rob and his wife began attending our church, and I got him involved on my basketball team. We played together for the season and we saw each other at church. Then one Sunday he and his wife came over for lunch. We'd simply been building our friendship, but that day a significant thing happened. Out of his mouth suddenly came a question about what he'd heard in church that morning — a deep and significant spiritual question. It was great! We talked about it a bit and then I said, "How about we meet for coffee this week and talk about this some more?" He responded positively, and thus my first ever seeker small group was born.

It was apparent that Rob needed a safe place to process through some of his questions about religion, about marriage and family, and about life in general. We met every week for coffee. We'd sit down, chat, and catch up, and then I'd ask Rob what spiritual things were on his mind. At the end of our time I'd say, "Next week? Same time, same place?" He'd agree and we'd meet again.

The first time we met, we didn't speak of anything spiritual or religious until about the last ten minutes. I brought up that he'd had some questions, and suddenly he began pouring forth his experiences and doubts about God. We spoke of his former experiences in church, and he referred to me as his "nonreligious pastor." I liked that.

By the third week I realized that Rob was hoping I'd give him all of the answers, but I knew that he needed to find them for himself. I would guide and challenge his thinking but not spoon-feed him. I encouraged him to begin reading the Bible on his own, and although this was a struggle for him, it was great to watch him persevere. We would talk about what he'd read, and together we would come up with answers to his questions. About the seventh week the lightbulb came on for him; it was a beautiful moment. We'd been talking about the nature of faith, and at one moment he looked up at me and said, "This is all about a personal relationship with Jesus, isn't it?" I wanted to shout, "Yes!" but instead I just smiled and nodded. He got it. That day I led him in a prayer of faith, and I continue to have the privilege of being in his life and talking about issues of faith and love and the gospel.

My seeker small group was a bit unusual, but it only affirms my belief in an unusual God. I think that one of the most vital things I did was to remain open to whatever God had for me. I didn't try to manufacture anything; I simply was available to what God was doing in Rob's life. I also think it was significant that I didn't hand Rob a Bible study that had all the answers; we simply met and talked *about his questions. The direction of our time together came from him, not from me. Lastly, I think that it was deeply significant that I was transparent with Rob. I didn't try to sugarcoat my own life or pretend like I had everything figured out. I was genuine with him and I think he respected that.*

*Rob and his wife are members of our church now and involved in several ministries. It's been a privilege to watch him grow in his faith and start to make an impact on others. I've had the honor of seeing three other seekers come to faith in Christ through my seeker small group, and I'm grateful for that experience. I love to watch God transform lives and it reinforces my faith along the way.*

# Chapter 7

# Facilitate Captivating Interactions

+

*A friendly discussion is as stimulating as the sparks that fly when iron strikes iron.*

PROVERBS 27:17 TLB

*[People] are never so likely to settle a question rightly as when they discuss it freely.*

THOMAS MACAULAY

*The wit of conversation consists much less in showing a great deal of it than in bringing it out in others.*

BEN FRANKLIN

During the summers of my sophomore and junior years in college, I worked as a part-time youth director at a small-town Presbyterian church in Indiana. As you might imagine, I organized numerous social activities for the kids—canoe trips, miniature golf outings, picnics, and more. What you might *not* expect is that early on, the ministry became seeker small group driven. Here's what happened.

My first day on the job, I picked up the names and phone numbers of about twenty-five high school kids on the church roster. These kids were members but only sporadically participated in the youth activities—which mainly consisted of a weekly large-group meeting geared toward those who already were Christians. Only four or five students showed up on any given week, so I decided to initiate a different approach.

I called each student on the list and introduced myself. Then I invited everyone to a midweek Bible study and encouraged them to invite their friends. I designated a different night of the week for each grade level to meet at a specified picnic table at the local park. Everything was set and my anticipation was high as I carefully prepared the first week's discussion questions.

On Monday night I arrived early to warmly greet the throngs of seniors who would show up — or so I thought! At 6:00 P.M. I sat confidently on top of the picnic table. At 6:05 I patiently waited, without a sign of a single soul anywhere in sight. At 6:10 I remained alone, and I was beginning to think I had the wrong picnic table at the wrong park. At 6:15 I looked around carefully, but there wasn't a high school student anywhere to be found. Finally I prayed a prayer of resignation — my plan was a bad idea and nothing was going to come of it.

Just as I was getting up to leave, four cars appeared and screeched to a stop around my table. Chris jumped out first and asked me where I thought I was going! Sherri popped out of her car, apologizing for making everyone else late; apparently, they had all decided to drive to the park together and had been waiting on her. Kathy and Jim, each carrying a Bible, quickly came over and sat at my table. I couldn't believe my eyes. Maybe this wasn't such a terrible idea after all! That evening the five of us had a lighthearted but open and honest discussion about spiritual matters. As we wrapped things up, I reminded them that we could meet again the next week — and that their friends were more than welcome to join us. They seemed receptive to both ideas.

That first week three freshmen gathered on Tuesday, seven sophomores showed up on Wednesday, and five juniors came out Thursday. Not too shabby, I thought, for my first week of ministry to high school students. But that was only the beginning. Not only did these kids come back week after week, but they gradually brought along their non-Christian friends. Throughout that summer and into the next, each of those groups just exploded in growth.

Robin was one of those eventually invited to the senior's small group. She was shy but seemed to enjoy the interactions, and after her first visit she returned each week without fail. Initially she came out of simple curiosity, but she was drawn back by the discussions that opened her eyes to see things she'd never really understood. Later that summer she decided to receive God's offer of forgiveness and gave her life to Christ.

On one particular Wednesday night it seemed as if the sophomores were coming from everywhere to join the discussion. Bicycles were scattered all around, and we had to push several picnic tables together so everyone would have a place to sit. It amazed me to watch these non-Christian students open up and share their deepest thoughts and concerns about God, the Bible, and spirituality. They were hungry to read Scripture and discuss its implications for their lives. That particular night our interaction lasted just past a beautiful sunset. I closed our time together by inviting everyone to join me in a short prayer that the spiritual lessons they learned that night would last a lifetime. That scene is so vivid in my mind; I'm sure I'll never forget it.

Sherri participated in the senior study. She never missed a Monday night discussion, but she had a hard time believing the Bible and accepting Christ into her life. Each week she pored over the verses and voiced her doubts. Even though she raised many difficult questions and barriers to faith, she seemed to be taking small steps forward in her spiritual journey. By the end of the summer she was the only one in the group who had not made a commitment to Christ. Before we disbanded and went our separate ways, however, we had one last special event planned: a road trip to Milwaukee to hear Billy Graham.

The drive to Milwaukee became an extended time of intense interaction and, as it turned out, was just what Sherri needed. That night's sermon brought everything together for her. Even now I could walk you straight to the row at Milwaukee County Stadium where Sherri stood to her feet and went down onto the field to publicly declare her decision to receive Christ. There wasn't a dry eye among our group members as, one by one, we followed her down the steps. Thousands of people were packed shoulder to shoulder on the grassy area, but I blocked all of them out of my mind as I took a step back and watched in amazement and gratitude while this group of high school students huddled around Sherri in prayer. That picture will last a lifetime and beyond!

The experience of leading four student seeker groups each week for two summers sharpened my discussion-leading skills — I had no choice! And, as you might expect, I learned mostly from my mistakes. Yet it seemed that each blunder I made reinforced a new principle or idea for me. And most of what I discovered so many years ago about facilitating small groups continues to serve me well even today.

Perhaps the greatest lessons I learned were about creating discussions that keep seekers coming back for more — a skill you'll also want to cultivate as you lead your own group. And that's exactly what we will focus on in this chapter. As you remember, chapter 4 provided a detailed plan for leading the first seeker small group meeting. Picking up where that chapter left off, we will explore effective ways to create lesson plans and use existing discussion guides that take your group *beyond* the first meeting. Chapters 5 and 6 covered the importance of asking good questions and listening closely to your group members' responses. And now we will turn our attention toward understanding how to put those elements together to craft your discussions. Finally, we will examine some important methods and techniques to keep in mind as you facilitate your group's interactions.

## Beyond the First Meeting

Imagine this scenario: Your seeker friends are totally enthused because your first group meeting was a great experience. The hour-long interaction was invigorating and engaging. But the truly remarkable outcome is that, even though most participants don't know each other very well, they agreed to meet once a week over the next month! You took a risk, gave up control, and let the seekers themselves determine the fate of the group. And they responded with a resounding, "Yes, let's meet again!"

As they leave, you're struck by their anticipation for the next meeting: "Looking forward to it." "This was a blast." "I wouldn't miss this for the world." As the last person exits, you and your apprentice congratulate yourselves with a couple of high fives.

"Wow, wasn't that something?" you ask.

"It was better than I could have ever imagined!" your apprentice agrees.

But suddenly the two of you are gripped by the same realization and exclaim, almost in unison, "What in the world are we going to do *now?*"

What happens next? After you've got the group members all fired up about meeting again, how do you keep the momentum going strong? What's going to keep them coming back? *The discussion.* Learn how to cultivate captivating discussions, and seekers will never want to miss a meeting.

## The Power of Discussion

Chances are, the reason why seekers are willing to risk a first visit to your group is that you have established a fairly significant foundation of trust with them. As a result, they are willing to suspend most of their fears and reservations just long enough to participate in your discussion. Now, as your group forms, you will either build on that foundation of trust or dismantle it. And the outcome will largely be determined by the degree to which you cultivate highly interactive, stimulating discussions — ones that almost always ensure seekers' return visits.

For example, imagine a seeker named Tom who visits your group for the first time. As he takes a seat in the circle, many thoughts go through his mind:

> *Will I fit in?*
> *Will I have the option to just sit back and observe things before jumping in?*
> *Will the interaction be interesting and fun?*
> *Will I get a chance to express my opinions — especially my differences and disagreements?*
> *Will I be respected?*
> *Will I learn something?*

How you conduct your discussion sessions will answer Tom's secret questions, and a well-led discussion can answer each one in the affirmative.

A discussion not only provides an opportunity to elevate the trust level of your seeking friends, it's also a powerful tool for introducing new ideas. In his excellent book *Getting Together,* Em Griffin explains it this way: "The average lecture/message/sermon is about as interesting as watching grass grow. The group member can listen much faster than the speaker can talk. So he slouches down in his chair, shifts into neutral and passively lets the speaker's words wash over him. But discussion calls for response. It takes energy to figure out what you want to say in a constantly changing discussion. The heart begins to beat; the juices begin to flow. I'll be closed to new ideas as long as I can hang back and not express my thoughts. But if you can jog me into debating the merits of my opinion, I may start churning inside. Once my rigid views are thawed, I might be willing to consider a different or even 'wrong' position."[1]

## The Crucial Role of the Bible

Underlying the power of discussion, an important assumption that has been implicit so far throughout this book must be realized: Your seeker small group discussions eventually need to focus on the truths of the Bible. The significant impact the Bible can make in the lives of your group members is unmistakable. As you already know, "all Scripture is inspired by God and is profitable for teaching, for reproof, for correction, for training in righteousness" (2 Timothy 3:16), and "the word of God is living and active and sharper than any two-edged sword, piercing as far as the division of soul and spirit, of both joints and marrow, and able to judge the thoughts and intentions of the heart" (Hebrews 4:12). Without positioning and utilizing God's word as an objective standard of truth within your group, no lasting life-change in your participants can occur.

The last thing you would want to do is reduce your group to some kind of non-directive, self-help gathering without providing a solid foundation of biblical truth. That would miss the point entirely—and offer little help in the long run. Rather, an effective seeker group is designed to be a place where intellectual questions are addressed with concrete answers based on the absolute truths of the Bible. Russ Korth agrees: "If you allow the group to go on and on, sharing only their opinions, you will be fostering frustration. People cannot base their lives on the 'authority' of an opinion. People need the truth of the Word of God."[2]

Be sensitive to the fact that many seekers are unfamiliar with the Bible and may not own one. You should have a supply of Bibles on hand for your group members to use. Ideally, it would be best to have everyone use Bibles with the same translation so participants can easily locate passages by page numbers.

Group members, of course, may not be willing to accept the Bible as reliable and credible right away, and they may adhere to completely different belief systems based on a wide variety of "truth sources." But the idea behind a seeker group is to create a safe environment for seekers to honestly share their viewpoints *and carefully compare them with what the Bible teaches.* The genius of the seeker group strategy is that, over time, most participants become remarkably open and receptive to fully examining the Scriptures — *after* they have been given an opportunity to fully disclose what they believe and why.

Rick Hove explains the concept this way, "As a leader your role is to stimulate group members to discover biblical truths for themselves. Leaders don't need to know all the answers, but they do need to know enough to guide the group to the answers. They also need to be skilled in asking good questions to draw group members into lively discussions about biblical truth. As everyone contributes, new discoveries will be made that individuals would not have thought of on their own."[3]

It's very clear in 1 Peter 3:15 that we are to be fully prepared to assist seekers in the spiritual discovery process: "Always being ready to make a defense to every one who asks you to give an account for the hope that is in you, yet with gentleness and reverence." As your group continues to meet, there will come points in your discussion where you can gently, but clearly and compellingly, defend the Christian faith and present the truth of the gospel based on the authority of the Bible. Do all you can to get yourself adequately trained and prepared for these opportunities. To get started, you may want to check out the Recommended Resources section in the back of this book. As you make the Bible the central focus of your discussions, my prayer is that through providing solid reasons for your faith, and speaking the truth in love, you will ultimately convince non-Christians that the Bible is authoritative, truth is absolute, and Jesus is the only hope of the world.

## Prepare for the Discussion

Before you can conduct the discussion, you must plan *what* you will discuss and *how* you will talk about it. Once you carefully work through these two critical factors, you can head into your seeker group meetings with confidence. And this will go a long way in determining the success of your group beyond the first meeting.

## Select Topics

Great discussions start with a plan that identifies topics to be covered in future meetings and the order in which to tackle them. The best way to do this is to base your topic selection on the issues that resonate with the seekers in your group. Do you remember the transition icebreaker recommended for your first seeker small group meeting? "If you could ask God one question you knew he would answer right away, what would it be?"

This question is designed to draw out the topics most meaningful to those in your group. During that first meeting you'll want to jot down the "questions for God" your friends raise, so the group can discuss a different one each time it meets.

In my early attempts at leading seeker groups, I made the mistake of selecting topics based on what I thought the seekers *needed* to discuss, not on what they *wanted* to discuss. This inevitably caused some seekers to lose interest in the group and drop out. Using a seeker-oriented (or seeker-driven) approach to select the topics allows the *seekers* to set the agenda. Certainly, this approach raises a significant predicament for us as seeker group leaders: We want to identify topics that will hold group members' attention, but at the same time we wish to challenge them with spiritual truths we know are ultimately in their best interest. As you may suspect, these two concerns may pull us in different directions — and therein lies the tension. It's the classic felt-needs-versus-real-needs dilemma, and it poses a constant challenge for every leader.

But an effective leader works hard to strike a balance. During the critical start-up phase (the first four to six meetings), I have found it vitally important to let seekers drive the discussion agenda. If they have pressing personal questions and concerns, they typically are not ready or willing to examine other matters. As Christians, we know that belief in Christ and receiving him into one's life is a primary issue that begs to be settled, and in due time that discussion *will* take place. Do not try to force it too much too soon, or you'll squelch the seeker-initiated discovery process. Instead the time will come when, as the leader, you will have earned the right to lay out the critical challenges from the Bible that prompt your group to consider Christ more closely. When that happens, you'll know you've turned the corner with your group. It may take several weeks to get there, but once you do, no matter what topic is being talked about, you'll be able to interject relevant questions and, in a sensitive and respectful way, bring things back around to the central message of the gospel.

So if the aim is to eventually get your group to the point where they can address their real needs, you must first begin with discussions centered on their felt needs. The "questions for God" responses you pick up in the first meeting will greatly help you figure out exactly what those felt needs are.

Soon after the initial meeting, you and your apprentice will want to sort through the questions for God and determine the best order in which to tackle them. Some questions may be similar enough to handle as one topic. Other questions may not be relevant enough to warrant an hour-long discussion; they might work better combined with another topic. Try to put the questions in a logical sequence, but give more weight to those issues you think touched a nerve with several in the group. In other words, prioritize those issues you sense are more basic, relevant, or interesting to group members, and discuss them in a systematic way. For example, questions raised about the *existence* of God will typically need to be discussed before issues about how to *know* God. Group members will naturally have to work through their struggles and doubts about God's existence before they'll be ready to analyze having a relationship with him.

On the other hand, if only one person in the group struggled with the existence of God, and most other group members were eager to wrestle with why a loving God would allow evil and suffering, it would probably be wise to go with the more popular topic. You could simply ask the group to "suspend judgment" about the existence of God for the time being so everyone can fully engage in the current issue about evil and suffering. Then later you could easily go back and facilitate a discussion about God's existence.

This approach will also work if group members express concerns about discussing biblical issues because they doubt the authenticity and reliability of the Bible (and you're not ready to go there yet). Simply request that for the sake of the discussion, they consider temporarily suspending decisions about the historical reliability and credibility of the Bible. Usually, given that disclaimer, group members are willing to agree to take the Bible at face value and simply discuss what it says without yet deciding whether they believe it to be accurate and from God. Be sure to take your group back to that critically important topic when the timing is right.

At this point your priority is to develop a plan that will cover the group's various questions over the next several meetings. Carefully consider the special interests and needs of your seeking friends as you decide the order in which to discuss their questions. A suggested sequence for discussing a wide range of topics is listed in appendix F. I have found this order to be most effective, generally speaking, unless a majority of the group members have pressing concerns that warrant otherwise. Of course, this list is only a guide to help you determine a possible sequence of topics most appropriate for your group to discuss.

### Create the Sessions

Once you've decided on the topics and the order in which to address them, the next step is to prepare the discussion questions for each session. This is probably *the* most challenging aspect of leading a seeker small group. But take courage — Jesus has given us some comforting words for times like these. When he sent his disciples out to spread the gospel, he offered them this advice: "Be as shrewd as snakes and as innocent as doves" (Matthew 10:16). Then he added, "Do not worry about what to say or how to say it. . . . You will be given what to say, for it will not be you speaking, but the Spirit of your Father speaking through you" (Matthew 10:19–20).

Prepare? Absolutely. Worry? Absolutely not. As you prayerfully put your thoughts and ideas together in preparation for each meeting, God will guide you with his wisdom, and he will inspire you with insights during your group's discussion time. So be encouraged; you can do this.

Obviously, though, you will *not* want to waltz into your group meeting and wing it. It's very important to adequately organize your plan for facilitating each interaction and put careful thought into how you want the discussion to flow and what questions to ask.

Don't just randomly ask questions. You need a game plan and you need to be prepared. Think through what you're going to discuss and how you want to discuss it.

Basically, each discussion session should consist of a series of great questions you've formulated and compiled to facilitate interaction among your group members. Refer back to chapter 5 for a description of a wide variety of questions from which to choose. Your challenge is to figure out the most appropriate set of questions to raise within your group to captivate members and engage them in a stimulating discussion. To assist you in that endeavor, follow this basic outline:

*1. Select a specific topic or biblical text to be discussed.* As already described, the interests of the seekers in your group should normally drive the subject matter to be explored.

*2. Identify "Point B" — the one or two biblical truths you hope your group will discover.* This is your group's finish line for any particular meeting. Before you go any further in your preparation, achieve a clear picture in your mind of *exactly* where you're going. Identify the main spiritual principle or concept you hope group members will begin to discover for themselves and take away from your discussion. Then develop a series of good questions that will assist seekers in discovering this biblical truth on their own. Limit your bull's-eye to no more than one or two discovery points; otherwise your discussion will become too complex.

*3. Identify "Point A" — the current basic beliefs your group has about the topic or text.* This is something you will *not* know for sure until you begin your discussion, but try to predict where group members will say they are with regard to the subject at hand. This is your starting point. Decide on some opening icebreaker questions and then develop a couple nonthreatening observation questions. These questions should encourage your seeking friends to identify and articulate where they stand on the topic being discussed. What do they believe now? Just camp here at Point A for a while, helping your friends explain — sometimes for the very first time — what it is they believe. Many seekers don't know what they believe or why; they've never stopped to think about it. So early in the discussion help them identify, and in some cases learn, what they believe.

*4. Develop a discussion outline to move seekers from Point A to Point B.* Of course, you will never want to manipulate or artificially manufacture this movement. You want any progress they make to happen authentically and in their own time, but your aim is to challenge the seekers in your group to *consider* Point B. Some of them have never stopped to seriously determine where they are now with a given spiritual issue (Point A), and even fewer have reflected much about an alternative option (Point B).

- *Explore Point A.* Start by asking everyone to identify where they currently are (Point A) and why. This exercise alone may take half your discussion time. But it is critical to spend adequate time thoroughly exploring all aspects of Point A, because without doing this no one will be ready to examine Point B. Your greatest tools for exploring Point A are the questions "What do you believe about this?" and "Why do you believe what you do?" Never grow tired of asking those two questions.

- *Interject relevant biblical truth.* A critical juncture in your group discussion, this is the place where you turn the corner from talking about what each person thinks or feels about a topic to what they understand the Bible says about the issue. As you bring these biblical perspectives to their attention (in a nonthreatening way), give your group members the freedom to wrestle with these truths without judgment or ridicule. At this point just ask people for their observations, not their conclusions — yet. For many this will be totally new information, and it should not be your objective at this early stage in the discussion to convince seekers to believe it or even agree with it. Simply ask for opinions about what they think the Bible is teaching and why. As you patiently draw out and understand your seeking friends in this way, you will eventually earn plenty of opportunities to clearly articulate biblical truths and challenge their thinking. And remember that there's never a "wrong" response when you are simply asking for opinions.

- *Explore Point B.* This is the time in your discussion when you finally invite everyone to draw some conclusions about any new discoveries they've made (Point B). This can be quite exciting, because for many this will be one of the few times they've been respectfully invited to consider the implications of these spiritual truths to their lives. And you'll start to see the lightbulbs turn on as they gradually begin to make some life-changing discoveries.

There's an important principle at work here: People are more open to considering new ideas *after* they've had an opportunity to express their current way of thinking. The best way to motivate seekers to begin taking steps toward Point B is to adequately explore *why* they believe what they do. So keep in mind that if you allow your seekers to fully express themselves about Point A, by the end of the discussion they will be walking away seriously considering (in some cases for the first time) at least one or two nuggets of spiritual truth (Point B).

Discussion of Point B should include dialogue on which conclusions appear to be most reasonable and what applications seem to make the most sense. Again, assume the attitude that there are no "right" or "wrong" answers here; you're still inviting people to explore the possibilities. Invite group members to evaluate what they've heard so far. After they've listened to a wide variety of opinions from the group and to what the Bible says, ask about what conclusions are starting to fall into place. This is a good time to briefly share your viewpoints as well.

Before you're done, you'll want to invite people to share their feelings about what they've heard and learned. Ask questions like:

"How are these things hitting you?"
"What, if anything, is striking a chord with you?"
"What are you feeling about the discussion so far?"

It's important to invite your friends to express and process not only their thoughts but also their feelings. Meanwhile, the tone you're setting is one of acceptance, love, appreciation, and respect — which sets up a wonderful learning environment. So include some discussion about how this topic will impact everybody: "What are you going to take away from this discussion?" "What changes were made in your thinking, in your life?" "How is this going to make a difference in *you*?" The responses to these questions will give you the opportunity to gauge the progress seekers are making in their spiritual journeys.

*5. Formulate discussion questions based on your outline.* This is the final stage in the process. The premise behind preparing a discussion session is that you will formulate questions that assist seekers in discovering spiritual truths for themselves. And your job as a leader is to develop a whole set of carefully prepared questions such as icebreaker questions, observation questions, interpretation questions, reflection questions, and application questions (see chapter 5). By asking your group a series of questions, you will invite everyone into the discovery process. The quality of your group's interactions rests heavily on the questions you prepare, so formulate questions that are clear, relevant, and open-ended in order to stimulate a lot of good discussion.

---

Outline Example 1

1. *Select a specific topic or biblical text to be discussed:* Luke 15 (the lost sheep, the lost coin, the lost son). God's tremendous love toward lost people.
2. *Identify a biblical truth to be discovered (Point B):* God loves us so much that he sent Jesus to bring hope and meaning into our world of hopelessness and despair. He cares about each of us so much that he searches us out individually to invite us into a relationship with him.
3. *Identify the current basic beliefs (Point A):* Many seekers have doubts about how much, if at all, God really cares about them personally.
4. *Develop a discussion outline:*

   - *Explore Point A:* Invite seekers to share stories of when they searched for something of great value that they lost. Find out what the group thinks about how much God cares for them on a personal level.
   - *Interject relevant truth:* Introduce and discuss the three stories in Luke 15. Try to draw out that Jesus is illustrating just how much God loves each of them.

---

- *Explore Point B:* Challenge the group to share how difficult it is to sense or accept God's love for them.

5. *Formulate discussion questions:* See appendix B, Sample Lesson 2.

## Outline Example 2

1. *Select a specific topic or biblical text to be discussed:* What's the big deal about sin?
2. *Identify a biblical truth to be discovered (Point B):* Sin is a really big deal. Dismissing sin as irrelevant or without consequence is spiritually fatal.
3. *Identify the current basic beliefs (Point A):* Typically, sin is not something that is viewed as significant. It is minimized as "mistakes" that usually have few, if any, consequences.
4. *Develop a discussion outline:*

   - *Explore Point A:* Give seekers an outlet to discuss extensively their views about sin. Ask them to define "sin." Get an idea as to whether they feel people are basically good or basically bad.
   - *Interject relevant truth:* Introduce specific Scripture that clearly illustrates the significance of sin and the impact it has on our relationship with God. Provide an illustration that demonstrates that when it comes to our sin problem, comparing ourselves with others is foolish.
   - *Explore Point B:* Challenge the group to share their feelings about their own sin problem. Do they see themselves the way the Bible describes? Why or why not?

5. *Formulate discussion questions:* See appendix C, Sample Lesson 3.

## Outline Example 3

1. *Select a specific topic or biblical text to be discussed:* Is Jesus really the only way to God? (This is one of seekers' most frequently asked questions.)

2.  *Identify a biblical truth to be discovered (Point B):* Jesus himself clearly claimed to be the *only* one who, through his death and resurrection, is able to forgive sinners and bring people into a relationship with God. (Note: Point B is simply discovering *what* Jesus claimed about himself.)

3.  *Identify the current basic beliefs (Point A):* Seekers typically will maintain that the Bible does not teach that there is only one way to God, and that certainly Jesus did not claim exclusivity. They are likely to maintain that many roads lead to God. A popular analogy says that God is on a mountaintop and all roads, no matter which one you take, will eventually end up at the top of the mountain.

4.  *Develop a discussion outline:*

    - *Explore Point A:* Spend a significant time asking group members to explain their positions concerning the number of ways to go to God. Explore why they hold the positions they do. Invite them to share how they feel about a one-way claim, including any specific objections. Explore what the group thinks the Bible teaches about the subject.

    - *Interject relevant truth:* Introduce specific Scripture that clearly illustrates the only-way claim. Ask group members to interpret what they think the Bible is teaching. Introduce and evaluate the three most common objections to the exclusive claims of Christianity (see appendix D, Sample Lesson 3) and invite the group to share whether they agree or disagree and why.

    - *Explore Point B:* Challenge the group to summarize what they understand the Bible teaches about Jesus being the only way to God. Share how that position, if it were to be true, would impact their lives.

5.  *Formulate discussion questions:* See appendix D, Sample Lesson 4.

## Use Existing Guides

While some leaders will enjoy the challenge of putting together their own lessons for seeker group discussions, others may want to use existing study guides designed to facilitate group interactions. The Tough Questions Series is a curriculum I've cowritten specifically to help seeker small group leaders meet this challenge. Since the primary audience for this series is spiritual seekers, Judson Poling and I wrote these guides topically to address spiritual issues from a skeptical perspective. It is our hope that seekers will discover that their questions and doubts are not only well understood and represented in each session but also highly valued. In addition, a separate *Tough Questions Leader's Guide* is available to provide background material for each session, offering brief points of clarification along with suggested answers to many of the questions.

It's interesting to note that these discussion sessions are based on real-life responses seekers have most frequently given to the question "If you could ask God one question you knew he would answer right away, what would it be?" So as you gather and organize responses to that question from seekers in your group, there's a high probability you will find discussion sessions that match them. The seven guides in this series each include six discussions, for a total of forty-two sessions. For your reference, in the back of this book you will find a list of every discussion title (appendix G), as well as samples of three discussions (appendixes B, C, and D).

As you prepare to use these guides, think through a sequence of sessions that would best serve your group. While some groups would benefit from going through the seven books in a row, for example, others may want to tailor the curriculum by selecting the one or two books that best fit their most pressing questions and issues. Since the series does not need to be discussed sequentially, the sessions can be mixed and matched in any order, based on your group members' interests and questions. I strongly recommend, however, that you link whatever you do with the Tough Questions guide *Why Become a Christian?* Always plan to eventually incorporate discussions from this particular guide because of its strong emphasis on helping participants cross the line of faith and receive Christ as forgiver and leader.

You also may want to explore other resources, including Mark Ashton's eight guides, called Reality Check, which include great seeker group discussions based on biblical passages. And two books by Lee Strobel, *The Case for Christ* and *The Case for Faith,* feature after each chapter excellent discussion questions that can very easily be adapted for seeker groups. Keep in mind that whatever resources you use, you will still want to adapt them to fit your group. Don't ever feel compelled to use every question suggested or every session listed.

## Keep The Discussions Flowing

After you've got all your questions identified and the session is planned, you're ready to lead the discussion. But how do you actually get the discussion going? Probably the greatest principle of all is to relax, be natural, and demonstrate that more than anything else, you want to give seekers an opportunity to be heard and truly understood. Continually invite your friends to share their thoughts, feelings, opinions, and ideas. When you do that, you create an open learning environment and put everyone in a position to make some awesome spiritual discoveries. The following tips and suggestions will help you develop skills to facilitate captivating discussions.

### Stay Flexible

Even though you have your game plan all figured out, don't be overly tied to it. You won't really know how the discussion will go until you're right there in the meeting. And that's the beauty of this thing. You have to fully engage your group and live in the moment to see how and where they are. Then you can respond accordingly.

I recently showed up at my seeker group prepared with what I felt was one of my best-ever set of discussion questions. But the first couple of icebreaker questions blew things wide open as my seeking friends disclosed some of the greatest disappointments in their lives. It was sobering. Tears were shed. Given the vulnerability of the moment, I knew there was no way I could brush that off and move into my prepared lesson on arguments for the existence of God. Instead we spent the entire evening supporting and encouraging one another; it was a meaningful occasion that drew the group together as no planned lesson ever could. So use good judgment and discernment about how to apply your lesson plan. Prayerfully decide what's in your group's best interests and act accordingly.

*Watch the Pace*

Keep an eye on the clock and stay aware of the progress your group is making. Try to keep a balance between moving things along at an interesting pace and camping on a relevant issue. In some cases you have to say, "Look, we're going to have to stop here, leave this question (as important as it is), and go on to the next issue." You might have to make a little joke about it, but as the facilitator, it's your responsibility to adequately manage your time together.

*Pray Without Ceasing*

If you're looking for a way to improve your prayer life, lead a seeker small group! You will quickly discover that within this exhilarating experience, the stakes are sky-high as seekers wrestle with eternal issues. Pray before, during, and after each session. Ask God to guide you as you facilitate. Invite the Holy Spirit to lead the group through you. Dedicate yourself to honoring Christ in everything you do and say in your group meeting. Without God's hand on you and your efforts, nothing of lasting value will be accomplished. Keep Jesus' words in mind: "I am the vine. You are the branches. If anyone remains joined to me, and I to him, he will bear a lot of fruit. You can't do anything without me" (John 15:5 NIRV).

*Prompt Spontaneous Interactions*

The best discussions are not restricted to those led by the facilitator. Therefore, don't regulate the interaction to a scenario in which you ask a question, someone responds to you, then you make a comment to another person, and he or she replies directly to you. That's too controlling and too limiting. The discussion needs to flow freely among every group member, so don't allow yourself to be the main focus of the group. Rather, you should fade out of the limelight and make sure your seeking friends become the central figures. Em Griffin points out, "Actions that show evaluation, control, strategy, superiority, and certainty all have a chilling effect on spontaneity.... I work hard to bring out variant views without putting anyone on the defensive. As leader, I won't argue. If I can promote a spirited interchange *between* group members, however, I've reached my aims. A bit of conflict helps people overcome their inhibitions and enter the fray."[4] Facilitate in a way that enables group members to interact freely with each other and discover spiritual truths for themselves. When you have that mind-set, you will create a safe environment that will unleash invigorating discussions.

In the diagrams below, Karen Lee-Thorp illustrates the difference between a small group that interacts only through the leader and one in which everyone participates:[5]

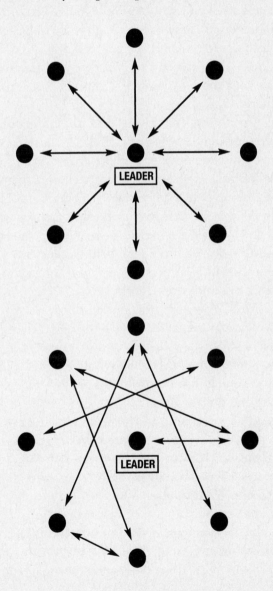

Without "permission" from you, your seeking friends will usually not feel encouraged to speak out freely to others in the group. Remember, you will be watched closely to see what the ground rules are. Group members look to you for cues as to what is and is not acceptable in "your" group, so you are the one who must create the environment and *model* exactly how you want the group to function.

From the outset you will be sending all kinds of signals (both verbal and nonverbal). And even though these indicators shouldn't be mechanically or inauthentically planned or plotted, they can and should become so ingrained into your way of thinking that they develop into your modus operandi. Consider, for example, the following scenario.

You've just tossed out a question to the group. As Laura responds, you further draw her out: "Tell me a little more what you mean, Laura, so I can better understand what you said." After she explains her response, you express heartfelt appreciation. "Great. Thanks for sharing that. I appreciate your honesty, Laura." Then you turn to the rest of the group and ask if anyone has a thought about what was just said, or anything else to add. Neil makes a comment and almost immediately Jeff, sitting across the circle, asks a clarifying question of Neil. At that most of the group glances at you for your reaction, and you eagerly give it. "Hey, hold on just a minute there, Jeff. You're running ahead of me now. Sorry, but it's not really your turn yet, and I have a slightly different follow-up question for Neil."

Okay, no one reading this book would ever react like that! But it illustrates the quickest way to kill a discussion. Talk about stifling! Let's back up and do that over.

Neil makes a comment and almost immediately Jeff, sitting across the circle, asks a clarifying question of Neil. At that most of the group glances at you for your reaction, and you eagerly give it. "Yes, Jeff, that's a very good question." You nod to Neil, indicating you'd like to hear his response.

In that split second you gave the entire group an incredibly strong signal that you want everyone to interact freely with each other. In effect you're saying, "Don't let me bog you down. This is *your* group — run with it! It's okay for group members to talk directly to each other." That's a very significant statement, and one you should make as often as you can. By doing so, you'll be witness to some pretty exciting interactions.

Other encouraging phrases you can use to prompt spontaneous interactions in your group include:

*"Tell us more."* After someone gives a response, invite more from that person. Frequently, people reserve what they really feel or think until they know for sure their input will be heard and valued, and you can affirm that by asking for more. Constantly exhibit this frame of mind: "Tell us more because we really care and want to know what you're thinking and feeling."

*"Help us understand."* Ask for clarification whenever you think there might be confusion. Do your best to truly understand what's being communicated. When in doubt, respond with something like "Help us understand exactly what you mean" or "I think what you're saying is ..." Seeking to understand the members of your group will communicate a sense of validation, which can go a long way toward creating an atmosphere of unconditional acceptance.

*"Anybody else?"* After someone shares, respond by saying enthusiastically, "Great response. What about the rest of you? Any other thoughts or comments?" A similar technique for creating good discussions is to ask for multiple responses to the same question. Again, you're setting an expectation that you don't want to go back and forth with one person but are looking for a wide range of responses. Remember to express appreciation to everyone who responds.

*"Great response. Thank you."* Russ Korth reminds us, "There are three things that people enjoy all the time. They like being right, original and appreciated."[6] Frequently express your sincere approval and gratitude toward everyone in your group — especially after they participate in the discussion. Acknowledge brave, honest comments with words of wholehearted encouragement. I rarely let someone make a comment without finding some way of honestly affirming him or her: "That's great!" "Thanks for being so open and honest." "Wow." "That's a profound insight!"[7] And don't underestimate the power to communicate through facial expressions and body language. Remember to reinforce your words with a smile and good

eye contact, and never grow weary of sharing verbal and nonverbal expressions of validation, acceptance, appreciation, and gratitude.

While expressions of judgment or condemnation should not be directed toward anyone in the group, there is of course a difference between agreement and acceptance. Learn how to model for your group that it's possible to respectfully disagree and still show total acceptance. If anyone becomes critical, remind the group that we all come from different places and that it's okay to disagree. Even saying something direct may be necessary: "Let's be careful that we don't criticize one another and that we accept everybody wherever they're coming from."

*"Hardy-har-har."* Regularly use humor in your discussions to encourage everybody to relax and have fun—and give your group members the freedom to express their sense of humor as well. If something is genuinely funny to you, lead the way in expressing hearty laughter. It's very important to let the group experience healthy doses of levity, although never, of course, at anyone's expense.

*"Way to go."* Be enthusiastic in your role as the facilitator. Be excited about what people are sharing, without being overbearing. In your voice and body posture, demonstrate an eagerness and high level of energy toward those in your group. Let everyone see that you are ready and eager to respond with wholehearted interest and gusto.

In summary, *be spontaneous.* Conduct your discussions with a healthy dose of what Em Griffin calls "planned disorder." You can't predict how your seeking friends will respond, and thus it's impossible to plan that part of the discussion. So respond in the moment to what people are saying. It's in these moments, after all, that facilitating discussions becomes so fun and exciting!

### Answer Questions with Questions

Inevitably, seekers will ask questions—when that happens, never set yourself up as the Bible answer man or woman. Avoid that at all costs. "Whenever I'm tempted to stick in my own opinion," Em Griffin explains, "I shut up. It's the height of arrogance to suppose that others are going to be more interested in hearing my views than they are in expressing their own. So whenever I feel that gnawing desire to pontificate creeping up on me, I make it a practice to wait at least sixty seconds. By that time I'm usually glad I resisted the impulse to intervene. I suspect the group is even happier."[8] You will not want the group to look to you for all the answers, solutions, and knowledge, because doing so would short-circuit their learning process. Instead you want them to learn to be good learners. And here's how you can foster their progress:

*Appreciate the questioner.* Express appreciation and gratitude to the one raising the question, with a comment like "Thanks for that good question." This will set a tone in your group that promotes inquiries. Just the act of thanking the person will send a strong signal that asking questions is not only appreciated but encouraged. Directly invite group members to raise their questions and tell them that there is no such thing as a stupid question. All questions are fair game.

*Seek clarification.* Make sure you understand exactly what is being asked. Say something like "Let me make sure I understand what you are asking. Are you saying ..." and then rephrase the question in your own words. This communicates that you were in fact really listening — and that you value both the question and the person asking it.

*Determine relevancy.* Immediately decide whether or not the question is something you think will contribute to the direction you want the discussion to go. If it's not worth pursuing at the time, treat the question as a tangent to gently avoid (see the Avoid Tangents Carefully section below).

*Invite responses.* Instead of answering the question yourself, look to the group for possible answers. Initially, this might frustrate some in your group, but in the long run seekers will appreciate having the opportunity to discover spiritual truths for themselves. One way to do this is to turn to the questioner with "Well, what do you think? How would you answer your own question?" Or you could address the rest of the group with "How would any of you answer that?" Use this as an opportunity to encourage further discussion — especially if it's in line with where the discussion was already headed.

*Plead ignorance.* When you come up against a tough question that you are unable to answer, don't fake it. It's quite appropriate (and respectable) to admit you do not know the answer. Simply say you'd like to take a little time to research the question and that you'll come back with some responses from the Bible to more intelligently discuss it. It'll be a refreshing thing for your group to hear you admit your need for further study! And you'll be greatly respected for your vulnerability and honesty.

### Show Consideration for Inaccurate Responses

Make no mistake — seekers *will* respond to your questions with inaccurate, unbiblical, off-the-wall answers. That's normal. In fact, an effective seeker small group will bring a wide range of "inaccurate" responses to the surface. So when it happens, you'll have a tremendous opportunity to show your seeking friends a lot of acceptance, patience, and grace, without judgment. Be secure enough in your own faith to patiently let most of these comments slide by. If you make it your role to "correct" seekers every time they utter something inconsistent with the Bible, not only will you quickly destroy any sense of freedom, safety, and acceptance the group members feel, but you will also be a very busy leader.

Once you determine the one or two biblical truths you'd like to see your group discover and walk away with, most everything else should go off your radar screen. Don't waste your time setting everyone straight. Many of these inaccuracies will get addressed adequately over time — especially as your group becomes more and more familiar with the Bible and seekers cross the line of faith.

The primary question seekers have on their minds is this: will they be respected and accepted no matter what — even if their beliefs are unorthodox? Inaccurate responses allow you the chance to demonstrate your unconditional regard for each one in your group. Em Griffin reminds us, "You've set up your whole discussion on the premise that there are no [bad or stupid] answers.... I'm at my best when I take a quizzical stance. 'You're not wrong, but I'm not sure you're right either.' A gentle probing works wonders — never challenging but in a friendly spirit of curiosity, exploring the depths of what another is saying."[9]

Paradoxically, when people feel the freedom to say whatever comes to their minds, they later become more open to hear what others have to say, and gain a new appreciation for the Bible's perspective. Experience teaches us that people change their minds more readily when they are first invited to express themselves. This kind of treatment puts everyone in a position to freely explore other options.

If someone says something that is really off base and you feel that if you let it go, you'll hinder the progress of your group members, then here's what to do. Address heresy, when you feel you must, by remaining positive: "Now, that's a very unique response. I've rarely come across a response like this one! How do the rest of you feel about that? Do you agree or disagree? Does anybody have another way to look at this?" When you invite others to respond, usually someone will provide a more accurate way to view the issue; if not, you could gently give the biblical perspective. You won't want to embarrass the person who made the comment or asked the question, so be sure to give your opinion or observation in a way that "saves face."

## Avoid Tangents Carefully

You must develop the skill to spot a tangent coming your way and instantly decide whether it's something to avoid or if it may possibly be helpful for the group to discuss for a while. Tangents have the potential to take your group way off the course you know is best. If a person is starting down a path you want to avoid, you will most likely need to interrupt him or her and tactfully redirect the discussion. Say something like "I can sense that we're getting a little off track here. We could discuss this at another time, but it's not going to take us where we want to go today. Would it be all right with everyone if we postpone discussing this new topic for now?"

If a tangent is raised in the form of a question, I'd suggest responding with something like "Your question raises an important issue, and I'd like to wait until we can give it the time it deserves. So let's hold off on that for now and get back on track." Do you see how you'll need to intentionally cut the tangent off at the pass? As the facilitator, you must remain in control of the overall direction the group is headed. And it's your responsibility to guide the discussion and make sure it's going where you want it to go.

Now, in some cases a tangent might be beneficial — especially if the group considers it a pressing issue. When that is the case, you'll need to make a determination to go forward with it, and communicate that to the group. That's your decision to make — just don't let it happen by accident. Stay in control.

### Balance the Participation

Part of your role as a facilitator is to make a conscious effort to keep an eye out for those who talk too much and those who don't talk enough — and then appropriately address both concerns. If you don't attempt to balance participation, you'll hinder the interaction, and your group members could easily become frustrated or discouraged.

Do your best to contain those who dominate or monopolize the group. In some cases if someone talks too much, you may need to assert yourself, interrupt, and respectfully say, "Hey, Bob, what you're saying is great, but I want to make sure there's time for others to also respond" or "I'm sorry, Bob, but we only have so much time here, so I'll have to cut you off." Your abrupt and bold move, using a little humor to bring the culprit to a halt, will be appreciated and respected by the rest of the group members. You may even have to do this several times, especially in the early stages of your group, to set a precedent for the kind of participation you expect.

If you have an ongoing problem with someone who dominates the discussion, you may need to pull the person aside and have a little conversation. Confront the person in such a way that you get him or her on your side: "Hey, Lisa, I need your help with something. Some people aren't participating as much as others, and I've noticed you're not shy in the least! You're bold, while some of the others are soft-spoken. Maybe you could assist me by making sure some of them get a chance to share. Will you help me draw them out?" "This way," Em Griffin concludes, "you've deputized the monopolizer as an associate discussion leader! Instead of concentrating solely on his own comments, he shares your concern to draw out others."[10]

Also be on the lookout for ways to pull quieter ones into the discussion — without being threatening. Usually the more soft-spoken members hesitate to participate because they refuse to interrupt others or they don't think as quickly on their feet. But you can, in a sensitive way, call on them and carve out a chance for them to participate, by directly inviting their input. Without putting them on the spot, say something like "I've noticed you haven't shared much, Sue. Don't worry. If you don't have anything to say, that's quite okay. But I want to make sure you have the opportunity whenever you're ready." Sometimes just a simple conversation afterward also will help: "I've noticed that you're not participating very much. Is everything okay?" Check in with them and ask if there's anything you can do to ease participation. They may just want to listen. Either way, a one-on-one conversation will help make them feel valued.

## Leave Loose Ends Untied

As you end the discussion, you may be tempted to extend the meeting time until you're able to tie up any remaining loose ends. Don't! Em Griffin agrees: "You'd much rather see folks walk out of the room arguing, churning with things to say, bothered by ideas they heard. The best way to accomplish this is to simply end while things are going well. 'Hey that's it. This has really been good. See you next week.' Better to leave folks agitated by quitting too soon than to miss a good stopping point."[11]

Resist the pressure to end sessions by tying up loose ends with standard answers. They don't satisfy anyway, and trying to summarize the discussion sets you up for an impossible task.[12] How could you possibly "summarize" everyone's comments and ideas completely and accurately? Why even try to do that? Leave the discussion with some unresolved issues so group members have something to wrestle with until you meet again. This forces them to remain engaged in the discovery process.

You might also notice that in some cases group members will end up with more questions after the discussion than they had before. This may be somewhat disconcerting to the members, but encourage them to maintain the process of ongoing questioning and learning. If some are interested, suggest Bible passages and books to study on their own between meetings. You may want to assure your group members at the beginning that your discussions will help them to take steps in their spiritual journeys, but they won't necessarily receive nice and tidy answers to all their questions all the time. If the discussion raises more questions than answers, that's a good sign because it opens the possibility for further discussions and more learning.

Facilitating great discussions is something *anyone* can do. And your ability to lead your group will improve with practice. It's just one of those things you have to jump in and do — sometimes by trial and error. And as your effectiveness increases, the results will be very rewarding. Few things compare with the joy of facilitating captivating interactions that assist seekers in making spiritual discoveries that will impact them for eternity. So don't ever give up!

# DICK REYNOLDS' STORY

### Associate Pastor
### Orchards Community Church
### Lewiston, Idaho

*A* few years ago my wife, Mary Etta, and I attended a Willow Creek conference with anticipation. Coming from a small but growing church, I wasn't sure how transferable things would be to my situation. But I hoped that something presented would make the conference worth my while. What God used, however, was not on my "radar screen" going in!

Once there, I found myself especially intrigued by the concept of reaching seekers through small groups. So, not knowing what to expect, I signed up for the seminar called "Seeker Small Groups."

The morning session was very enlightening and challenging, but the afternoon session brought everything to life! On the platform was a retired gentleman who led a seeker group, and three members of his group, two of whom had not yet decided to follow Jesus. The stories of their pilgrimage back to God brought me to tears. I knew right then that, God willing, I had to go home and launch such a group for spiritual seekers.

Once we returned to our residence in Idaho, my wife and I began to make plans to soon start a seeker group. However, God's timing was sooner than "soon" — he began forming the group immediately. For example, when I purchased a used vehicle from Larry, he found out I was a Christian. He began sharing some of his struggles in life — so much so that I thought perhaps it was part of his sales pitch! After I bought the car, he expressed genuine interest in spiritual things, so I invited him to the seeker group.

Before I knew it, three men had expressed interest in coming to my group. Besides Larry, there was Butch, a young man bent on suicide, and Roy, a paroled convict looking to go back to his old ways. I quickly called Mary Etta and asked, "Can we start this Friday night with three seeking men?" She enthusiastically replied, "Yes. And let's serve them dinner too!" Right after I hung up the phone, I called a friend to assist me with the group. He accepted the challenge. So that Friday evening we launched our very first seeker small group.

*Although I admit to having several concerns as to how this would work, my fears were soon laid to rest as I saw the guys' hunger for truth and belonging. We used the Bible as our text and their questions as our curriculum. Right from the beginning we set the ground rules, including the promise of confidentiality, which needed to be in place to make things safe. Because we met in our mostly unfinished basement, the guys affectionately called our meeting place "The Den of Inquiry." And they loved our discussions in that den.*

*Slowly they began to open up and take responsibility for the direction of their lives. They started to grasp the truth of who Jesus is and his great love for them. Roy, the parolee, finally felt comfortable sharing his heart's concerns. Butch, the suicidal young man, gave his life to Christ and is now growing in his newfound faith. Then it wasn't long before several of their friends, struggling with addictions, broken marriages, and other issues, began to come. Each week, six to ten men met for dinner followed by ninety minutes together exploring the Bible's answers to life's questions. A total of six men have received Christ into their lives as a result of the group.*

*Larry, the car salesman, made his decision for Christ within the first month and is now leading his own seeker group of nine men. More are being added to that number as those guys bring their seeking friends. An air traffic controller, who tragically lost his seventeen-year-old son in a drowning accident last summer, is the newest member to cross the line of faith. Others who attend include a construction worker, a computer programmer, a fishing guide, an Alaskan fishing crewman (on break), and a sawmill worker. This fascinating group of men all view Larry as their spiritual mentor. Larry and I meet together once a week for coaching, and I couldn't be more proud to see his progress!*

*From time to time I see the men from my past seeker group, and when I do, I am so amazed by the tremendous growth evidenced in them. Even though I have a seminary degree, I had to learn that head knowledge isn't what really makes a difference in the lives of seekers. Larry doesn't have that hang-up in his group. He just loves Jesus, loves those who come, and provides a safe place for seekers to discover life's answers from the Bible. For my wife and I, leading a seeker small group has been a great reminder of the faithfulness of God in using us if we are available and want what he wants. It has been such an encouragement!*

# NATHANAËL WINSTON'S STORY

### Church Planter
### Brussels, Belgium

*S*eeker small groups have become the main focus of our strategic plan as we start up our new church. There are two significant reasons we're convinced these groups are a good choice for church growth in our setting.

The first reason is that seeker-targeted services depend a lot on the quality of a program, and our church planting team simply does not have the resources to organize outstanding seeker services. But what we are good at is building solid relationships with seekers. Our strength, at the moment, is our ability to create small, casual, safe settings for seekers—so that's exactly where we are investing our energy.

The second reason is that we've determined that it's not an either-or approach. We believe that seeker small groups are complementary to seeker services. There are other churches here in Brussels that do seeker services very well. They do a good job of inviting people and preparing an excellent seeker service. But because it's hard in our culture to get people to come to anything religious, they have a difficult time getting them to return. It's our observation that it's not enough to have seeker services only.

For example, a couple of months ago a church in the city put together an amazing special outreach service with music, drama, and a powerful guest speaker. They invited dozens of seekers and many came. But those people didn't come back. They really needed to give them something else, another opportunity to follow through with the courageous step they took of coming to this one service.

Seekers need a safe place to develop relationships with other Christians, to ask their questions, talk about their frustrations about God and faith. An event is not enough—they need a process. To have both—seeker services and seeker small groups where non-Christians are invited to express their doubts and learn more in a "safe" setting—that results in seekers sticking around.

Because we're at the very beginning of our church life, we're able to choose a fresh approach. So we decided to put our energy into launching seeker small groups. We're small—but we're very *motivated. We inspire Christians to pray for the seekers in their lives, and they have invited dozens of seekers to our small groups.*

*So far, of the seekers who have participated in our seeker groups, two have made clear commitments for Christ. Our setting is very relaxed. Also, we gain a lot of trust with our seeking friends when we share a meal together.*

*Then comes a major part of the seeker small group time: They get to express their thoughts and feelings. After we've presented some of the truths of the Bible, we have a time of discussion and always start off by asking them, "What did you think of what was just said? How did you feel about it?" They honestly react to the things that were said and express what they felt. Sometimes it's positive, sometimes negative. We've discovered that seekers have twisted thoughts and feelings about God and religion, so we give them the time to share the thoughts and feelings they've held inside for years and years on the issue of faith and God. We take a lot of time showing that we understand. We don't try to convince—it's not about apologetics, debating, or defending. We really let them express themselves and sometimes, if we feel it isn't right to force an answer on them, we leave issues unresolved and move along without an answer. We patiently let the Holy Spirit do his work in them.*

*People need to feel respected and understood. When they sense we understand them, their resistance to the gospel breaks down at least a little bit. We give them space and respect. We avoid clichés and still give them the truth of the gospel. When seekers feel respected and understood, they move closer to accepting Christ.*

*Someone from our team invited a colleague, an Austrian woman. This woman decided to come and she was very, very diligent, taking notes the entire time, really thinking through everything. After the group ended, she got together with the one who invited her and started reading the gospel of John. They would read about three chapters on their own, then meet to talk about it. During one of those one-on-one sessions, this seeker became a Christian. She attends church every Sunday now, along with participating in a believer's small group. And she's growing in her faith.*

*I'm encouraged when I see someone like this woman who responded so positively to a seeker small group. It can be discouraging, but in a very difficult context like Belgium, the strategy of using seeker groups is working well.*

### Part 4

# REACHING SEEKERS THROUGH SMALL GROUPS

These final three chapters will pull together the ideas and principles outlined in this book in order to better equip you to lead seekers to Christ. Chapter 8, Maximize the Impact, examines various components of a seeker group that must be in place in order to be effective evangelistically. You will discover important ideas for building a caring community, preparing for growth, and leading seekers across the line of faith. Chapter 9, Cultivate Contagious Small Groups, explores a slightly different approach to reaching seekers through small groups. This chapter identifies ten ways believer small groups can raise their evangelistic temperature. Chapter 10, Seize the Adventure, looks at a wide variety of ideas for launching a seeker group right where you are. After all, leading a seeker group is something *anyone* can do—*anywhere!*

Chapter 8

# Maximize the Impact

*+*

*The first thing Andrew did was to find his brother
Simon. He told him, "We have found the Messiah."
And he brought Simon to Jesus.*

JOHN 1:41–42 NIRV


*I have had the privilege of preaching this Gospel in
most of the countries and all the continents of the
world. And I have found, that when the simple message of the Gospel of Jesus Christ is preached with
authority, and simplicity, quoting the very word of
God, he takes that message and drives it supernat-
urally into the human heart.*

BILLY GRAHAM


*Once to every man and nation comes the moment to
decide,
In the strife of Truth with Falsehood, for the good or
evil side.*

JAMES RUSSELL LOWELL


In his book God's Outrageous Claims, Lee Strobel tells the amazing
story of Maggie, a twenty-four-year-old neonatology nurse from a
Chicago suburb. Maggie grew up confused about Christianity. She saw
people presenting spiritually perfect facades to each other during an
hour on Sunday, and then acting quite differently the rest of the time.
What they said and what they did never coincided. And it felt to her
like she took the brunt of many of those inconsistencies. Turned off,

Maggie concluded that all Christians displayed the sort of hypocrisy she grew to hate. The discrepancies she encountered resulted in her harsh decision to never again associate herself with church.

A few years later Maggie heard about an upcoming debate, set up to be a contest between a Christian and an atheist, at a local church. Maggie's interest was piqued. *Maybe I should go if only to see the Christian get pummeled by the atheist,* she thought. Maggie tentatively ventured to the event. But to her surprise, she experienced something very different than what she had expected.

For the first time in her life, she met Christians who appeared to be open to honest dialogue and discussion. These Christians treated the atheist, as well as the skeptics in the audience, with total respect. They gave "the other side" a chance to speak and they even listened with interest. They were not afraid to let differing opinions be expressed — in fact, they encouraged it. Over the next weeks Maggie couldn't keep several of the points raised in the debate out of her mind. Eventually she wrote a letter containing a series of her most pressing questions to Lee Strobel, the debate moderator.

Never did she expect an answer. And even if she were to get a response, she certainly couldn't imagine that she would be taken seriously. The reply she received blew her away. Not only was her letter answered, but her questions seemed to have elicited a serious, thoughtful, and even accepting response! Still skeptical, but encouraged, Maggie wrote back.

The correspondence continued, and after several weeks of questions and answers, Maggie received an unusual invitation from Lee. He told her about a small group especially devoted to people like her — people with questions and doubts about Christianity. Though hesitant, Maggie took a risk and decided to try it — once. Maybe the members of this group would treat her with respect just as Lee had done through his letters. She didn't think that was likely, but she chose to take a chance because she trusted him.

Clayton and Shelley Mills were already several weeks into the start of a seeker group that met every other Sunday night. Even though it was a challenge to have newcomers join a group mid-stream, they were always excited to add another spiritual seeker into their discussions. "Shelley and I really care about seekers," Clayton explained, "and that passion is something God put deep in our hearts. So when he brings seekers our way, they don't just become a part of our group; they become a part of our lives."

As soon as they heard about Maggie's interest in the group, they began praying for her. They were especially careful to make her feel extra welcome, because they knew that walking all alone into a setting where group members have already built strong bonds often magnifies that "out-of-place" feeling. Their prayers were answered when Maggie walked through the door the very next Sunday.

Maggie was shocked. From the minute she arrived, she felt like she had always been a part of the group. Not only was she warmly welcomed and accepted, but these people seemed real. There were no pretenses here; even the leaders freely shared some of their own struggles, imperfections, and doubts. Reflecting back, Maggie wrote to Lee about her experience:

> I needed gentleness. I needed to be able to ask any question. I needed to be taken seriously. I needed to be treated with respect and authenticity. Most of all, I needed to see people whose actions match what they say. I am not looking for perfect, but I am looking for real. *Integrity* is the word that comes to mind. I need to hear people talk about real life, and I need to know if God is — or can be — a part of real life.

> Does he care about the wounds I have? Can I ever be a whole and healthy person? I have asked questions like these. And I have not been laughed at or ignored or invalidated. I have not been pushed or pressured in any way. I don't understand the caring I have received. I don't understand that the leaders seem unafraid of questions. They don't say things like, "You just have to have faith," or "You need to pray more." They don't seem to be afraid to tell who they are. *They seem genuine.*[1]

Maggie continued attending her seeker small group for several months. And out of the joy she felt from being accepted by the Christian leaders, she wrote a poem and sent copies to Clayton and Lee. "It contains the heartfelt sentiments of a spiritual seeker toward those of us who are Christians," says Lee. "Read these words carefully," he adds, "and as you do, imagine that this precious person is speaking directly to you. Because she is."

Do you know
do you understand
that you represent
Jesus to me?

Do you know
do you understand
that when you treat me with gentleness,
it raises the question in my mind
that maybe he is gentle, too.
Maybe he isn't someone
who laughs when I am hurt.

Do you know
do you understand
that when you listen to my questions
and you don't laugh
I think, "What if Jesus is interested in me, too?"

Do you know
do you understand
that when I hear you talk about arguments
and conflicts and scars from your past,
I think, "Maybe I *am* just a regular person
instead of a bad, no-good little girl
who deserves abuse."

If you care,
I think maybe he cares —
and then there's this flame of hope
that burns inside of me
and for a while I am afraid to breathe
because it might go out.

Do you know
do you understand
that your words are his words?
Your face, his face
to someone like me?

Please, *be who you say you are.*
Please, God, don't let this be another trick
Please let this be real.
*Please.*

Do you know
Do you understand
that you represent
Jesus to me?[2]

Tears welled up inside Lee as he read Maggie's poem for the first time. He reached for the telephone, to call her and ask permission to read the poem in an upcoming sermon. "Oh, Lee," Maggie responded, "haven't you heard?"

His heart sank. Now what? Someone scared her away. Maggie has been hurt once more. She's been bruised or chased away again. Sighing deeply, Lee replied, "No, Maggie, I haven't heard. Tell me what happened."

"No, you don't understand — it's good news," she said, "a couple nights ago, I gave my life to Jesus!" Lee almost leaped out of his chair.

"That's terrific! That's the best news I've heard in a long time. Tell me — what piece of evidence convinced you? What fact did you uncover that finally established for you that the Resurrection was real? What argument clinched it for you?"

"It was nothing like that," Maggie explained, "It was simply that I met a couple of people who were like Jesus to me. That's all it took."

What a lesson to learn. More than anything else, our seeking friends will be impacted by the love of Christ they see in us. We don't have to pretend to be something we're not. We don't have to appear to know all the answers. We can accept them, we can serve them, and we can be authentic with them. We can simply be like Jesus to them — and that's what will make a lasting difference.

Maggie's story might very well inspire you to dream about the amazing potential a seeker small group has to make a big impact in the lives of seekers. But more than that, I hope it reminds you of how God can use *anyone* — imperfections and all — to reach seekers for him. He is in the business of using people just like you and me — just as we are. And that should motivate you to make yourself available and take risks, because who knows all that God might do through you!

In this chapter, we will look at several ways you can take your leadership skills up a notch. The principles outlined here will give you some important ideas for making your seeker group work more smoothly and effectively. And remember — these are steps *you* can take!

## Build a Caring Community

As the seeker group leader, you will want to view your gathering as something much more than just a meeting. Think in terms of turning your group into a dynamic, caring community. Take time to hear what's going on in each other's lives and look for ways to express care and support to one another. Get intentional about creating a gathering that represents Jesus well. One of the very best ways to build a strong sense of community is to plan additional functions outside of the usual meetings. It's usually just a matter of time before someone will suggest an idea for a social outing for the group. And you should encourage it!

As people begin to open up about the difficulties and victories of their lives, I often will respond by asking for specific prayer requests that I can keep in mind throughout the week. Rarely have I encountered anyone who is offended by such an offer. After the group has been together for some time, I have found it usually appropriate to incorporate a moment of prayer at the conclusion of the meeting. Be very sensitive about this as most seekers are not familiar or comfortable with the concept of prayer. And don't necessarily ask other group members to pray out loud unless they volunteer to do so. Offering to pray is yet another way to express your concern and support for the members of your group.

### Commit to Each Individual

At a Willow Creek leadership retreat a number of years ago, Bill Hybels coined a phrase that challenged all of us. He stated that the "be with" factor best summarizes Jesus' model for making the greatest impact on others. Bill explained that Jesus influenced his disciples most by doing life with them. He invited them into his world and he got into theirs. The inspiration for life-change happened during their unplanned, spontaneous times. And this is what Bill described as the "be with" factor. "It's crucial to 'be with' the members of your groups," Bill spelled out. "Do life with them. Share yourself with them. Rub shoulders with them." But as I listened to his words, I figured that if the "be with" factor is so important in the process of influencing Christians, how much more essential it must be to influence *seekers.*

Remember Maggie's story? She was most impacted by Clayton and Shelley's willingness to share their lives with her. Clayton assured her that he and Shelley were available — and she took them up on his offer many times. Clayton and Shelley even opened their home to the group on Thanksgiving Day — and Maggie was there. She was warmly received into their world and then, in time, Maggie welcomed them into hers. As she was invited to do life together, Maggie was able to observe firsthand some of the struggles and weaknesses — and victories — Clayton and Shelley experienced. This is what God used most to reach Maggie.

It's essential to connect with your seeking friends outside of the group. Phone calls between meetings and one-on-one get-togethers will only enhance your opportunity to do life together. Due to limited time, I suggest that you focus on the two to four seekers you have the most affinity with and encourage your apprentice to concentrate on the others. Call each of them once a week to touch base and remind them of your next meeting. And try to get together with each of them individually at least once a month.

One-on-one meetings are key opportunities to influence the spiritual progress of your seeking friends. These are the times when you can devote special attention to their specific concerns, questions, and issues. You'll be able to explore further what they have said in past group interactions and where they are currently in their spiritual journey. And, as a result, you'll be able to provide specialized care and support. Your seeker small group is really a tool designed to set you up for these kinds of conversations; don't miss out on them.

Just as you create a safe environment for good interactions in your group discussions, do the same in your one-on-one meetings. Ask good questions. Focus on the responses. Listen well. Maintain two-way conversations. And when you're asked questions, answer with the same authenticity you're hoping they will exhibit. Be open and honest about the struggles you face.

As a cautionary note, be aware of your own limitations and boundaries when dealing with special needs. You will never want to get in over your head with your seeking friends and turn your one-on-one meetings into counseling sessions. (Similarly, you do not want to turn your discussions into self-help, group therapy sessions.) As the leader, you will want to exercise discernment to recognize when to suggest counseling before a conversation continues beyond your ability to adequately deal with it.

*Cast a Vision, Set a Goal*

After everyone has had a few weeks to form a bond through the caring community you've fostered, you may want to invite the group to consider setting a few simple goals. This activity will generate a high level of ownership and commitment from the members of your group. But in order for it to work well, the group as a whole needs to agree to the idea without any manipulation or coercion from you. Toss the goal-setting idea out by suggesting a couple of examples: from something as nonthreatening as meeting four more times or planning a couple social activities to more challenging goals like making a deliberate decision about reading the Bible or getting baptized.

That's exactly what occurred in the most recent seeker group I led. We had decided to sit together during one of our church's baptism services — everyone was keenly interested in observing what went on there. So the next time we met, I asked everyone what they thought of the baptism service. After a short discussion, I decided this was the right time to throw out a challenge: "Now, I know this might seem crazy, and this might be too much for you to envision, but — now hang with me here for a moment — there will be another baptism service here in six months. Maybe, as each of you take steps in your spiritual journey, you might think in terms of arriving at a conclusion between now and then about whether or not *you* will get baptized." I held my breath wondering if I came on too strong, then added, "But again, it could be just a crazy idea." I knew it was a risk, but thankfully the group rose to the challenge. Their responses were very positive: "That sounds good." "That seems reasonable" "Okay, I'm in!" Over the next six months, I never mentioned it again — I didn't have to! The group continually used that goal as a reference point to describe where they were in their journeys and how they were progressing. Then, on a hot Sunday in late June, our whole group walked into the lake, and I baptized six of our members.

Now, to be sure, not every seeker group would be ready to set such a challenging goal. You have to be sensitive to your own group and determine what, if anything, would be appropriate. In any case, look for ways to stretch your seeking friends with their involvement in the group. Cast a vision that motivates them to set goals outside of their comfort zones — and watch what God does.

## Fill the Open Chair

It is my contention that leaders should, except in very rare occasions, keep their groups open to include additional, interested seekers. As I have already emphasized, seekers are the best "bringers" of other seekers — the more they enjoy your group, the more eager they will be to invite their seeking friends. This creates the potential for explosive growth. I would hope that you would never want to shut off that potential flow, but as you probably realize, this growth does pose some significant obstacles (listed below) for your group. These hurdles may make it tempting to close off your group to new seekers — but don't do it! In the end, the advantages for keeping an "open chair" in your group far outweigh the disadvantages. So do whatever you can to overcome any obstacles for the sake of those seekers not yet connected to your group. A few ideas are listed here:

1. *The group dynamic will change when newcomers arrive.* As members develop a strong bond with the original group, they may feel especially threatened by the thought of adding new seekers. Explain from the outset that your group will be an ever-changing one — and that this can be a good thing. Just setting the correct expectations will have a settling effect on everyone. Even ask your group to help you make newcomers feel welcome. That's one reason I suggest you use icebreakers each time you meet — even if you've been together for several months and you know each other well. When a new person arrives, he or she can easily join in the process of getting to know others. Be creative with the introductions. For example, ask regular members to introduce each other — not themselves. That not only makes things new and fresh for the existing members, but welcoming for the new ones.

2. *New members will likely raise questions that have already been discussed.* That could be somewhat frustrating to existing members, but try to implement creative ways to address any repeat issues so they're interesting and informative to the regulars and helpful to

those who are new. For example, ask those who participated in the previous discussion to share their learning process and conclusions. Address the same question differently, so that existing members are brought into the discussion in a fresh way.

*3. Inevitably, as you add more people, your group will become too big for the discussion to be manageable.* The only way to address this issue is to form two groups. This process of "birthing" can be a very exciting thing! Just think: first there was one group, now there are two! Of course, forming a second group comes with its fair share of "birth pangs." But with clear, up-front communication, you can adequately prepare your group to handle this change.

Do your best to ease the separation anxiety your group members may feel during the "birthing" process. For example, you could bring everyone together for the opening icebreaker time before breaking down ("sub-grouping") into two smaller discussion groups. This method provides a few minutes with everyone to connect, but allows for better discussion time for the duration of the meeting. And if you have led the group with an apprentice up to this point, you are perfectly positioned to cover the two simultaneous discussions.

### Appoint Apprentices

Tim's reputation preceded him. I was constantly running into group members who expressed their appreciation for his tremendous leadership. Finally I met Tim and asked to have lunch with him so I could hear all about his small group experience. It turned out Tim had led a group each year for the past four years and had made an incredible impact in the lives of scores of people. A very busy family man, Tim made leading his group one of his top priorities. I was inspired by his commitment to Christ and his group members.

Tim spoke about each group with enthusiasm. It was clear that he poured himself into those people, and as he was speaking, it hit me: Tim had been leading dynamic groups for four years without apprentices. A little vision casting was in order here.

First, I expressed my sincere admiration and respect to Tim for his tremendous ministry contribution. But I also wanted to challenge him to maximize his full potential, so I painted this picture:

"Imagine your overall impact today if you had started four years ago with a *partner* who helped you colead your first group. Suppose you trained and coached this apprentice to someday lead a group with the same intensity and passion as you do. Then, when you started your second group the next year, you identified a different apprentice to partner with you. *But,* at the same time, your original apprentice also started another group with an apprentice. So in your second year, the number of groups launched and the number of people impacted was, in effect, doubled. The following years, the same process was repeated until now. Just think: If everything went as planned, instead of starting four groups in four years (which is *not* a bad thing), you would have launched fifteen groups in that same time period. And, with apprentices already in place, the growth each successive year would increase exponentially!"

"Tim," I concluded without slowing down, "you're a great leader. God has been using you in a powerful way. But now I'd like to challenge you to duplicate yourself and multiply your ministry!" Tim's face lit up as he considered the potential impact. "I get it," he said enthusiastically. "It's about pouring myself into future leaders as well as the people in my group."

"Exactly," I replied, "it's a two-pronged approach. I'd like to see you continue to make the impact you've been making in the lives of the members of your group—that's awesome. But now, at the same time, I'd like to see you raise up other leaders who will lead *just like you.* And they can even assist you as you lead your group. You will no longer go at it alone—you will have support."

One of the most essential elements of good leadership is the recruitment and appointment of key apprentices—Christian coleaders who join forces with you to effectively run the group. I cannot stress enough the value of *never* leading your seeker small group alone. Not only do apprentices make facilitating your group much more manageable, but the potential for growth is dramatically increased—that's the power behind having apprentices.

When I first launched seeker groups at Willow Creek over ten years ago, I required every leader under my care to have not one, not two, but *three* apprentices. Why do you think I insisted on a radical three-apprentice strategy? It was our *only* way to adequately prepare ourselves for rapid growth. Since all of our seeker groups were expected to remain open to receiving new seekers at any given time, the potential for explosive growth was always present. And if three apprentices were in place, the group would automatically be ready to subgroup. Once your group gets upwards of ten to fifteen seekers, it's no longer reasonable to expect the full participation of everyone in the group; it's too big for that to happen. Group members will most likely get frustrated about not being able to contribute as before. But if apprentices are in place, you're ready to tackle the problem right away because you can divide (or "birth") the group into two. You and one of the apprentices can lead one group. And your most experienced apprentice, along with the remaining apprentice, can lead the other. Each group now has both a leader and an apprentice because you sufficiently planned for growth.

There are additional advantages to having apprentices. Think of the support and encouragement an apprentice can provide. Because the work of evangelism has its fair share of ups and downs, it's important to be able to lean on other like-minded Christians who can empathize with your victories as well as your disappointments. Ecclesiastes 4:9–10, 12 puts it this way: "Two are better than one, because they have a good return for their work: If one falls down, his friend can help him up. But pity the man who falls and has no one to help him up! . . . Though one may be overpowered, two can defend themselves. A cord of three strands is not quickly broken." Just having partners to plan and pray with is reason alone to include them.

Beyond the benefit of support, apprentices essentially multiply the number of potential seekers who could be invited. You have only a limited number of seekers you can ask to come to your group. But if each of your apprentices also draws from their own network of seeking friends, you'll greatly improve the likelihood that you'll have a critical mass from which to launch your group. In addition, your apprentices will need to be available to assist you with calling seekers between meetings and getting together with them individually. It's unlikely that any one leader would have the time to frequently meet with each group member without the help of apprentices. Utilizing a team of coleaders will put you in a much more realistic position to better serve the seekers attending your group.

One word of caution is in order: Choose your apprentices wisely. Clearly communicate your expectations and prayerfully and carefully select apprentices with the qualities necessary to fulfill the role. You need to feel confident that your apprentices will come through for you. Here's a checklist you may want to use as a guide for your apprentice-selection process. An apprentice should:

- Be a fully devoted follower of Christ
- Pray for the group
- Invite seeking friends
- Attend every group meeting
- Call two or three seekers between meetings
- Meet with two or three seekers one-on-one outside of the group
- Get trained to lead a seeker small group
- Prepare and lead the group discussions from time to time
- Participate in regular evaluation and debriefing sessions with the other group leaders
- Intend to become a leader (with other apprentices) of a future seeker group

*Plan Transitions*

Your seeker small group will experience constant change. Over time, additional seekers will express interest in getting connected with your group, and in some cases, individuals who declined your initial invitation may later have a change of heart. Some seekers may choose to drop out, only to return at some point; others may lose interest altogether. Many will ultimately invite Christ into their lives. In any case, as their leader, be prepared for a wide variety of developments and do your best to lead your group through these changes smoothly.

Eventually, however, there may come a time when you and your apprentices determine that a planned transition is in the best interest of your group. For example, if everyone has been together for a long time, it may be wise to take a break for awhile and reconvene a couple months later. You could organize a few social events during the summer in place of your regular meetings. Or you may decide it's time to simply end the group. If that is the case, help your members achieve healthy closure by setting aside time to celebrate and process their group experience.

As seekers become followers of Christ, you will at some point want to give them the best opportunity to grow in their faith by transitioning them into new believer small groups where they can discuss the basics of the Christian life. The importance of a firm spiritual foundation cannot be overstated. It is critical that your new believers "continue to live in [Christ], rooted and built up in him, strengthening in the faith" (Colossians 2:6–7). Because strong bonds of friendship usually develop between participants, you may want to wait until most members have crossed the line of faith and then make the transition. Early on, you could designate an apprentice, who is gifted in and passionate about shepherding others, to take over the leadership of your group once the majority of the members become Christians. Or, of course, you could always continue to lead the group yourself. As you can tell, all kinds of scenarios are possible and different groups make these transitions at various times. Whatever happens, try to be upfront with your members about the expectations you have concerning any next steps or transitions.

## Invite Evaluation

Perhaps the quickest way to improve your skills as a facilitator and leader is to seek honest feedback and evaluation. Unfortunately few people are truly open to hearing honest feedback, and fewer people still will ask for or even press for an evaluation. It's just too difficult. But if you can muster up the courage to invite constructive criticism, you will be well on your way to becoming a great leader.

The safest way to get honest input about your leadership is not in the group meeting itself, but in the context of one-on-one meetings with your apprentices and seekers. During those conversations, possibly over a meal, look for an opportunity to say something like this. "Can I ask you a huge favor? I'm trying to get serious about improving my leadership and facilitation skills. One of the best ways I know to do that is to ask people I respect to give me input and feedback. Would you be willing to give me your honest thoughts? I would really like to hear what you think is working well and what needs improvement. What tips can you give me that would make me a better leader?"

Very few leaders are willing to be this vulnerable, but I cannot overemphasize the importance of doing so. When you start to ask these kinds of questions, people initially respond by testing the waters — checking to get a feel for how open you truly are and how much you really want to hear. They may begin by sharing fairly innocuous things like: "Well, it would be nice if you ended the group meeting on time." This brings you to a very crucial point. How you react here will make all the difference in the world — the difference between getting more feedback and shutting the door.

You could respond with something like: "What do you mean, 'end on time'? I'll bet that's only happened once, twice max. Come on. That's not the kind of feedback I need. Give me something else." You might as well pack it up right there.

Instead, appreciate the feedback. "Thank you, that's helpful. Tell me a little more. How many times would you say we've ended late, and how does that affect you or the others?"

"Well, I'm not sure how it affects the others, and it's only happened a couple times, but I've got kids and it makes it tough."

"Wow. I'm sorry. And it's so good that you're telling me. I wasn't even aware."

Let the person know you value their thoughts and are open to change — and do so sincerely. I'll usually write down the feedback I get so I'll remember it and can think more about it later. Most leaders would be tempted to stop right there, but a great leader will ask, "What else? Is there anything more you could tell me?" Sometimes I'll phrase it this way: "If you knew for sure it wouldn't hurt my feelings or offend me in any way, what feedback would you give me?" People will usually hold back to see how much you *really* want to know. They will watch you very closely to see how you'll react. And they'll want to see what you'll do if they say something you don't agree with.

A wise leader always asks for more and leaves the door wide open with words like, "Even if I don't ask you, I want you to know the door is always open for you to share your thoughts. I want to become a better leader, and the best way for that to happen is if I get feedback from people like you."

If you can do this, and all leaders should, you will send a strong message of vulnerability, openness, and respect. This is perhaps the most important characteristic of a great seeker small group leader — someone who models authenticity and a willingness to learn, along with asking questions and listening well. Exhibit these things for your group members and someday you'll see each of them do the same.

When you demonstrate that you are receptive to the seeker's honest thoughts and input about your leadership effectiveness, you will put yourself in a better position to elicit authentic responses to your questions about where they are in their spiritual journey. When they see you are willing to hear the truth, they'll know they can be honest about where they are spiritually.

## Lead Seekers Across the Line of Faith

Effective evangelism often necessitates a two-step process. First, we must convince those who *mistakenly* assume they are Christians that they have false perceptions and their definitions need to be revisited. These people call themselves Christians, but their faiths are not based on what the Bible says it means to be true followers of Christ. They may not really be Christians at all. Many conclude that if they are not Jews, Muslims, or atheists, then by default they *must* be Christians. However, the Bible clearly teaches that no one becomes a Christian by default. There has to be a definite acceptance of Jesus Christ before one can be called his follower. The second step is to help people understand what the Bible *does* teach about being in a right relationship with God through Christ. As a seeker small group leader, you will want to keep these two points in mind as you articulate the gospel and assist seekers across the line of faith.

These two issues are addressed in a direct, but seeker-sensitive way in the Tough Questions study guide called *Why Become a Christian?* As suggested in the previous chapter, you may want to consider incorporating discussions from this particular guide because of its emphasis on helping participants understand what it means to receive Christ in their lives. Consider using additional resources, including *He Did This Just for You* by Max Lucado and

*The Reason Why* by Robert A. Laidlaw, to assist you in explaining the gospel message. Be sure you are prepared to clearly articulate the gospel when you are given the chance. You may also want to describe and discuss the bridge illustration, which demonstrates how Jesus bridges the gap, caused by sin, between God and the human race. (A detailed outline of this tool can be found in the *Becoming a Contagious Christian* book and course). To gain a better understanding of where your seeking friends are in their spiritual journeys, ask them where they would place themselves on the bridge diagram. This information should be especially enlightening to you (and them!) as you plan future discussions.

It has been my experience that seekers generally feel more comfortable making a commitment to Christ during one-on-one times than they do during group meetings. This is another reason why it is so important to meet with them on an individual basis. When you inquire about their spiritual journeys, ask what roadblocks they are facing. And be prepared to help them take a step of faith when they're ready. This is what leading a seeker small group is all about — giving seekers a clear and direct opportunity to receive Christ without pressure or coercion.

Sometimes seekers are just one ask away from making the biggest decision of their lives. They may be simply waiting for an invitation from *you!* It can feel a little intimidating, but when the timing is right, be bold — ask for a response. Whether it's a one-on-one conversation or a group situation, you can simply ask, "What's holding you back from making a decision for Christ?" Take special note of the responses and draw out additional points of clarification with good follow-up questions. Then, when you sense that someone is ready and willing to make a commitment, ask a question like, "Would you want to wait and make that decision on your own, or would you like to solidify it with a prayer together now?"

And when someone makes a decision for Christ, celebrate! Recognize that there is rejoicing in heaven in those moments. I encourage you to invite the person to share his or her decision with the group, if appropriate. That can be one of the most memorable moments of your entire group experience.

In a rare occurrence, I had not one, but two seekers receive Christ during a group meeting. The likely reason Pat and Marty felt comfortable doing so was the fact that most of the other members of the group were absent that night. Nevertheless, toward the end of our discussion, I asked what roadblocks most prevented them from taking a step across the line of faith. Pat surprised us, when she responded, "I can't think of any good reason why I should wait." My apprentices and I looked at each other in disbelief! Imagine the look on our faces when Marty spoke up, "Same here. I've investigated all I need. I'm as ready as I'll ever be."

I recovered from the shock just in time to challenge their readiness. At the risk of discouraging them too much, I said, "Let me list a couple reasons why you might *not* be ready." I told them that this was a serious decision that shouldn't be made lightly. It means not only receiving God's forgiveness through Christ, but also accepting his leadership in their lives. They both remained convinced that they were ready to make a sincere commitment to Christ. I then prompted them to pray in their own words about three specific things:

1. Admit that you are a sinner in need of a Savior;
2. Agree that Jesus died and rose again in order to make payment for your sins;
3. Accept God's gift of forgiveness and leadership in your life through Christ.

Finally I prayed a prayer of thanks to God for the decision these two had made. Spontaneously each of them also thanked God for his goodness in their lives. It was a beautiful moment.

The next week I asked Pat and Marty to share their story so those who missed the meeting could also celebrate. You can imagine the reaction from the rest of the group members as they listened. They remembered well, just a few months earlier, when these two were really struggling with faith issues. But now the others were seeing firsthand how God had transformed them. It was a very powerful thing for everyone to see.

## Pray Fervently

The Bible clearly teaches that we need to pray fervently for our evangelistic efforts. We know that without God's partnership, our efforts are all in vain. We need his hand on us as we seek to honor him within our groups. The following passages of Scripture really set the proper tone for the conclusion of this chapter on how to make seeker groups work. It is only by God's grace that they "work" at all.

*No one can come to me unless the Father who sent me draws him.*

JOHN 6:44

*Pray also for me, that whenever I open my mouth, words may be given me so that I will fearlessly make known the mystery of the gospel, for which I am an ambassador in chains. Pray that I may declare it fearlessly, as I should.*

EPHESIANS 6:19–20

*Devote yourselves to prayer, being watchful and thankful. And pray for us, too, that God may open a door for our message, so that we may proclaim the mystery of Christ, for which I am in chains. Pray that I may proclaim it clearly, as I should. Be wise in the way you act toward outsiders; make the most of every opportunity. Let your conversation be always full of grace, seasoned with salt, so that you may know how to answer everyone.*

COLOSSIANS 4:2–6

*We were gentle among you, like a mother caring for her little children. We loved you so much that we were delighted to share with you not only the gospel of God but our lives as well, because you had become so dear to us. . . . For what is our hope, our joy, or the crown in which we will glory in the presence of our Lord Jesus when he comes? Is it not you? Indeed, you are our glory and joy.*

1 THESSALONIANS 2:7–8, 19–20

# DAVE DEMAS AND JOHN CRILLY'S STORY

*Entrepreneur and Engineer*
*Hanover Park, Illinois*

We remember it like it was yesterday. The hotel banquet room was filled with seekers. Our special speaker for the evening, Dr. William Lane Craig, had just finished a challenging and thought-provoking question-and-answer forum. Those in the audience were asked to fill out response cards if they were interested in attending a one-time seeker small group meeting as a follow-up to the forum. All along, we had sensed the Lord leading us to start a seeker group. This was our opportunity.

From the list of seekers who signed up that night, we contacted a group of ten to twelve people who lived in our community. We arranged to meet at a local restaurant. One by one the seekers showed up, and after some initial small talk, we asked the big question of the evening: "If you could ask God one question and you knew he would answer it, what would you ask him?" We were taken aback by what happened next. The group responded with a healthy balance of enthusiasm and cynicism. The rapid-fire questions just kept coming. We barely had enough time to write them all down. We knew we had something special here. Our biggest surprise of the evening came when we asked if anyone would be interested in meeting again — everyone gladly accepted our invitation.

Our group met twice a month over the next two-and-a-half years — something we never expected. In fact, we led each meeting as though it would be our last. We never presumed the group would want to meet another time. And yet they kept coming. Our gathering was a conglomeration of people of different ages and social groups. It included married couples, dating couples, singles, individual spouses, college students, and college teachers. We met every other Friday night at the same place — the home of one of our group members. This created a safe, warm atmosphere for our new "family."

A key component of our time together was the climate we created within the group. We always had an ample supply of humor, and *our love and concern for the members was the foundation. We wanted the group to be fun and exciting, but we also sought ways to keep it fresh and interesting. As leaders, we learned to listen closely to understand the seekers' point of view and meet them there. We were also challenged to "keep the puck in play" — to keep the discussion open-ended and focused on the group members' interaction, not our lecturing — while still seizing teaching moments and following the Holy Spirit.*

*We tried to find the delicate balance between sharing seekers' heart-felt concerns and not turning our time together into a counseling session. This was particularly a challenge when the topics of pain, suffering, and loss would come up. We wanted each person to know they had the space and time to seek in a safe and welcoming environment. But we also wanted everyone to be stretched. We allowed the group to discuss and even respectfully argue their issues and beliefs. Our role was to ask powerful questions, share what God was up to in our lives, study God's Word, pique their curiosity, and encourage the seeking process.*

*At times, we were tempted to chase "rabbit trails" — topics that pulled us away from the critical discussion. Early in our leadership, we did not quickly discern this "off-roading," but in time we became more aware of it and learned how to steer the discussion back on course. We wrestled with deflating our occasional egotistical and "know-it-all" attitude in order to create an environment of acceptance, love, and truth. We stressed that we were "co-journeyers" in the quest for God's truth. We tried to be the thermostats to set the proper temperature in the group for spiritual exploration and growth. We did not want to come across as arrogant, but neither did we want to be ashamed of the truth. Christ spoke very divisive words about who he was, and a person cannot hear those words without coming to some sort of decision. Seeking culminates in a decision to take Christ up on his offer to live life to the fullest, but we often told our group to count the cost. We added that we also had counted the costs and found that living for Christ was well worth any price.*

*Slowly but surely, lights clicked on. Hearts softened. Wisdom was gained. The two of us would sometimes sit in the car afterward and marvel that the God of the universe would entrust the care of these* precious people to us. The challenge was daunting, but the rewards were great.

After each meeting the two of us would debrief on what we thought went well and what didn't. We prayed fervently that God would use both. Neither of us were "pros" at this kind of thing. We made mistakes along the way in caring for our little flock. But God nonetheless used us in mighty ways. The Holy Spirit was at work in spite of our human limitations, as evidenced by the slowly unfolding life-changes that we were witnessing. Some of the people in our group even started to bring their friends!

Along the way, God would surprise us with stunning victories in ways we could never have imagined. Roxanne was one of our regular attendees. She invited her boyfriend, Andy, once to sit in on one of the group sessions. We will not soon forget the look on his face when he entered the room. His guard was sky-high. But he stayed. He listened. He was challenged. And his heart changed. He began to take small steps in his spiritual journey. Roxanne and Andy eventually found Christ, got married, and now regularly attend Willow Creek. They have a thriving relationship with Jesus Christ, and their growth in him has been amazing. And we're convinced that God coordinated the whole process.

We learned that seekers are very precious to God and that there is nothing in life more worthwhile than to contribute to the spiritual growth of a seeker. As leaders, this experience deepened our friendship and united our souls in a rare way. We saw the power and faithfulness of God like never before. Leading this group was by far the most thrilling ministry experience of our lives.

Our group has run its two-and-a-half-year course. But for Kathy, Mike, Paul, Cheryl, Laura, Andy, and Roxanne, the adventure is really just beginning. Each has since given their lives to the one who redeemed them. When we run into them from time to time, the warmth of gratitude on their faces is the priceless payment for the effort we extended. And it all started when the two of us simply took a risk to believe that the one who is much greater than us could accomplish something beyond anything we could ever have imagined.

# KAREN SISTARE'S STORY

Training and Development Consultant
Jacksonville, Florida

*A few years ago, I volunteered to assist in leading a seeker small group. I had never been a part of anything like this before, and I had absolutely no concept of how it would work. Nevertheless, I knew without a shadow of a doubt that this was what God wanted me to do. I sensed that this was part of God's great adventure for me — to undertake a new and exciting way to share my faith. This was just one more step outside of my comfort zone, and I do mean way outside.*

*I joined forces with two other coleaders, John and Jan, to lead the group on Sunday nights. Each of us had our own unique strengths: John, with a tremendous ability to relate to the needs and issues of others; Jan, with an in-depth knowledge of Scripture and a wealth of personal experience to share; and me, as facilitator within the group and a bent toward building solid relationships outside the group.*

*Our next step was to find and motivate seekers to attend. We prayed that God would send us the people. While I knew in my heart that there were seekers all around us, I had no idea where these people would come from or how to connect with them. But once God led us to people who were indeed seeking answers and were looking for something just like our group, it was easy to convince them to come! Beyond inviting our personal friends, we ran an announcement in the church bulletin and had several responses. Others came our way by word of mouth from church members who knew we were starting a discussion group for seekers. We began with a group of eight, including the three of us.*

*I initially invited a close friend of mine who is a long-time skeptic, yet very open to hearing about my Christian faith. She said, "No thanks," but gave me the name of her friend, Andrea, who was struggling with some tough spiritual questions about God. Andrea went on to become an integral part of our seeker group and has grown so much in her faith. God used my skeptic friend to point us toward a seeker!*

At our first meeting, we posed the question, "If you could ask God any question, what would it be?" This prompted some interesting and lively discussion, which set the tone for the weeks to follow. We used these questions to select our topics from the Tough Questions Series. The further we got into these discussions, the more we broke beneath the surface and learned what significant issues and beliefs our group members had. Some were free to share their issues openly with the group. With others, one-on-one conversation was the best way to discern where they were spiritually.

As leaders, Jan, John, and I were committed to asking lots of questions, without trying to provide all the answers. This was not easy! Nor was it clear to us about whether we should "correct" an "inaccurate" opinion or let it slide. This was so different from the way we were all programmed to "do evangelism." When do you speak and when do you just listen? We found that even when we fell short and talked when we should not have (or vice versa), God was still at work in the hearts of those in our group. What a blessing and a relief to know that God is not limited by our inadequacies.

One of our most rewarding discussions happened two weeks before Easter. Jenifer, one of our seekers, was facing many questions about God and his role in her life. That night she asked somewhat apologetically, "Why did Jesus have to die on the cross? It's really important that I know and understand that." At that point, we knew she was on the verge of a spiritual breakthrough. The discussion that followed was rich and powerful. And eventually, Jenifer committed her life to Jesus Christ and now enjoys a deep and vital relationship with God.

I first met Sue, another seeker in our group, several years ago through my business. I prayed for her and for an opportunity to share Christ with her. Nothing came of it, and we went our separate ways. Two years later, I learned that after the tragic events of September 11, Sue was actively seeking answers to her spiritual questions. After an invitation to attend the seeker discussion group, she accepted! Sue asked many questions and often challenged what the others said. But she always came back for more! Eventually she reached the point where she knew intellectually that everything pointed to Jesus as the answer. After almost eight months of participating in the group, and a lot of prayer and support from another good friend, Sue asked Jesus

Christ into her life. Shortly after that, John baptized Sue in the ocean at our church's first beach baptism. It was a spiritual milestone for many in the crowd, and especially for Sue!

Sue credits the seeker small group as the vehicle God used to draw her to Christ. She was given a safe, nonthreatening way to wrestle with some serious concerns and ask candid questions about Christianity. According to Sue, the personal interest that each of the leaders showed in her also made a huge difference. Sue is growing daily in her walk with Jesus, taking one step at a time as she learns what it means to be a Christian. She has since joined another small group with an emphasis on spiritual growth.

There is one more story of a changed life. And that is my story. My life has been changed dramatically by my involvement in the seeker small group. Before this time, I had regretfully passed up too many opportunities to talk about Christ, my Lord and Savior. My desire was strong, but my confidence was woefully lacking. Over the course of leading the group, God has opened so many doors for me, and it has been so easy to walk through them. God continues to amaze me by putting people who are without Christ in my life. A year ago I did not know any non-Christians who were genuinely seeking answers, and I could not even fathom leading a seeker group. Now I have so many opportunities to talk with people candidly and directly about their beliefs and invite them to the group. My experience has prepared me to befriend more non-Christians, some of whom are not yet coming to the seekers group. There's no other way to describe it but to say, what a great adventure!

# Chapter 9

# Cultivate Contagious Small Groups

*All I have seen teaches me to trust the Creator for all I have not seen.*

RALPH WALDO EMERSON

*Were the whole realm of nature mine, that were a present far too small*

*Love so amazing so divine, deserves my strength, my soul, my all.*

ISAAC WATTS, "WHEN I SURVEY THE WONDROUS CROSS"

*He is no fool who gives what he cannot keep to gain what he cannot lose.*

JIM ELLIOT

During my senior year at Indiana University, I became involved with the college ministry at Evangelical Community Church. The weekly gatherings were geared toward Christians and included a time of worship and deep Bible teaching. It proved to be quite beneficial to all of us.

But when some of us within that ministry thought about the possibility of inviting spiritual seekers to our meetings, we cringed. We knew that non-Christians would feel completely out of place. So along with my friends Quinten Stieff and Terry Wallace, I met with Kenneth Cuffey, the college pastor, to brainstorm ways to make our meetings more seeker-sensitive. We brought a lot of passion and energy to the discussion, because we had a certain seeker in mind — our friend Doug Martin. We knew Doug was searching spiritually, and we wanted to be confident that if we brought him along to our gatherings, he would fit in and benefit.

We ended up adding contemporary songs to our worship times and adjusting the teaching focus slightly to reach both the Christian and seeker audience. The results were fantastic — seekers were warmly welcomed, and many, including Doug, made decisions for Christ!

A few years later, after working for InterVarsity Christian Fellowship as an evangelism specialist in Indiana, I ended up serving as the college pastor of the same ministry I took part in as a student. When I was hired, church leaders Pastor David Faris and Jim Eschenbrenner gave me the freedom to align the ministry with the way I was wired — with seekers in mind. I carefully and radically shifted the focus by offering the Christians in the group a compelling vision for reaching out to their lost friends for Christ. They quickly jumped on board, and we pulled together an action plan to launch PRIMETIME every Tuesday night. We organized a contemporary band and developed drama sketches and messages relevant to non-Christian college students. We even decided to give the traditional sanctuary a makeover, equipping the stage with special lighting and sound equipment. Everyone was fired up to see what God would do through us.

The students spread the word among their friends and took out large advertisements in the student newspaper. Each Monday night, they gathered for a time of prayer and then scattered for something they called a "blackboard blitz." This was a cool scheme to pop into every classroom on campus and write an invitation to PRIMETIME on the chalkboards. That way, the next morning, students in every first period class would get the message — even the professors took special notice of the advertisement they erased!

Our ministry became a vibrant, thriving outreach to college students. It was thrilling to observe our seeker friends — many of whom would not have been as comfortable in a more traditional setting — pour into those meetings. And the greatest part was watching many of them come to know Christ. That ministry carried on for four years, after which several of the students and I left to plant a church in Indianapolis. We followed the same seeker-driven strategy for our weekend services, and on Wednesday nights, we held worship services with deeper teaching designed for believers.

The ministry philosophy I adapted for both settings was patterned after Willow Creek's seeker-driven emphasis. From its beginnings, Willow Creek designed its weekend services with non-Christians in mind. Leaders programmed and evaluated those services through the eyes of seekers. What would challenge seekers and yet be comfortable for them? What would be relevant and appropriate for them? Then, for midweek services, the church's focus was to edify the core of believers.

The idea was — and is — that Christians and non-Christians come from two very different places. Willow Creek recognized that the needs of each group are dissimilar enough that by not specifically targeting one or the other, the church would miss the mark for both audiences. That clarity of purpose and direction has served Willow Creek — and thousands of other churches all over the world — very well through the years.

This is not to say that traditional church cannot reach lost people. Of course it can! In my view, though, seeker-focused events and services are a more effective approach to attract and reach non-Christians. And that's exactly my position regarding small group evangelism: The best way to reach seekers through small groups is to specifically design those gatherings, from beginning to end, for non-Christians. Lost people are in the forefront of a seeker small group leader's mind as he or she addresses questions such as, What format would be most sensitive to my seeking friends' needs? What forum would be most helpful in serving seekers? What approach would be most effective in assisting seekers to take steps toward Christ?

Again, I'm not stating that other types of small groups cannot be evangelistic. In fact, all kinds of believer small groups have developed some very creative and effective ways to reach out to lost people, and in so doing have made a big impact for Christ and his kingdom. In my way of thinking, *every* small group should be outreach-oriented to some extent — not just seeker small groups.

In the past eleven years as the evangelism director at Willow Creek, I've had a front-row seat to our church's evangelistic potential and impact. But at one point a few years ago, we were concerned to learn that many of our believer small groups had allowed their evangelism focus to fade. They had lowered their evangelism bar so low that they were leaving outreach almost exclusively to our seeker groups. (At the time, we were supporting about 1,200 believer groups and 60 seeker groups.) In an attempt to halt this trend, I painted a candid picture for our leadership team. I explained that, on average, a seeker small group could make an evangelistic impact on 10 seekers in a given year. So, in theory, our 60 seeker groups could reach a total of 600 seekers. On the other hand, if our 1,200 believer small groups could catch a vision for reaching lost people, and if each group were able to reach out to just *one* seeker in a year, those small groups could collectively reach 1,200 seekers—or twice as many lost people as the seeker groups alone.

This example illustrated the need for *every* small group in our church to get off the bench and out onto the field to reach our seeking friends. In any given church, there are typically many more believer small groups than seeker-oriented ones. So if we can mobilize believer small groups to be outreach-focused and seeker sensitive, we will drastically increase our evangelistic potential.

With that purpose in mind, I will devote the rest of this chapter to summarizing a list of ten ideas to raise the evangelistic temperature within believer small groups. These suggestions can be implemented in two ways:

*1. As an assessment tool.* Utilize the ten points as an assessment tool to determine your small group's level of evangelistic intensity or activity. You can employ it as a checklist either apart from or within your group discussions. In any case, take this as an opportunity to evaluate evangelistic effectiveness as well as to measure strengths and weaknesses.

*2. As an activity guide.* Implement the list as a step-by-step guide to move your believer small group into highly strategic evangelistic activities. Each step presents an increasingly greater challenge, but the potential evangelistic payoff will be worth the effort. You will notice that the final step describes a plan to launch a seeker small group. So if you are considering starting a seeker group and are already involved in a believer small group, you may want to invite your group members to follow the steps outlined here to support you in that endeavor.

These ten steps fall within one of three different levels. Level One includes the basic minimum requirements for any believer small group. Every small group should prioritize the time it takes to reach this level of evangelistic activity. Level Two identifies ways that individuals within the group can make evangelism a way of life. You and your group members will want to regularly encourage each other to put these suggestions into practice. To further explore the components of this intermediate level as a group, consider using the small group discussion guide *The Three Habits of Highly Contagious Christians.* This book takes the steps in Level Two to a deeper degree of assessment and implementation. Level Three provides guidelines that can inspire your whole group to actively participate together in evangelism. This level may move your members beyond their comfort zones, but I challenge you to seriously consider taking them to this place sometime during the life of the group.

For illustrative purposes, I've included excerpts of one group's story. It's one of the best examples I've come across of a contagious small group. John Hudson and Cathy Stedman have done an outstanding job leading a contagious small group of believers within Axis, Willow Creek's "20-something" ministry. I've included John's own account of his group's evangelistic activity after the description of each step. As you read through the following list, consider these questions: At which level is your believer group? Where would you like your group to be? What steps have you and your group already put into practice? What steps will you and your group members take in order to move to the next level?

## Ten Signs of a Contagious Small Group

*Level One (Basic)*

*1. Vision Cast.* A small group leader has the opportunity to set the evangelistic pace. He or she needs to be the one to hold the value of evangelism high by modeling it, because "as the leader goes, so goes the group." If evangelism is important to the leader, it will eventually become important to the rest of the group members.

Talk with your group about the critical importance of evangelism. Inspire and motivate one another to make the idea of reaching out to seekers a priority. Lead Bible studies on how much lost people matter to God and the significance of reaching out to them. Spend time examining how group members feel about evangelism and how they can overcome any barriers that exist. Discuss the specific fears and obstacles your group members face when it comes to sharing their faith. Make an assessment of each group member's evangelistic temperature and brainstorm ways to raise it.

As group members identify how they are doing in evangelism, group leaders can tailor future meetings to address specific weaknesses or barriers. For example, if some members lack confidence to adequately articulate the gospel, the group could take turns explaining it to one another and make plans to attend an evangelism training course together.

## John Hudson's Story

*I understand the most important thing a leader can do is to set the pace and live out an evangelistic lifestyle, and I wish I could say that I have always been an evangelistic giant. But that simply has not been the case. Evangelism was not even a blip on my radar screen. Selfishly, my Christian commitment centered on me. But all that began to change when I happened to meet a seeker named Lindita, who was invited to join a group of my Christian friends on a rock-climbing trip. She ended up getting stuck with Jason and me when we all piled in a few cars to head out. On the road, the three of us exchanged our stories, and that's when I found out she was not a Christian. (At the time, that was not a big deal to me.) She also confided that what looked to us like freckles all over her was actually skin cancer—the same disease that took her older sister's life. In that moment, I was struck with an urgency to share my faith with her. She was an Albanian who grew up in a traditional Muslim family, but I was determined to help her learn about Jesus. It seemed like I was constantly praying that God would reveal himself to her in a very real way.*

*The truth is that life could end at any time for any one of us, but for me, it took meeting someone like Lindita to see the reality of how important it is to share my faith. The next chance I got, I shared my eye-opening experience with my small group. Little did I know how much my group would respond to my story about meeting Lindita. Reaching out to Lindita — and other seekers like her — soon became a top priority to us.*

*2. List and Pray.* Kevin Dyer, the founder of Bright Hope Ministries, tells the story of the time he was first inspired to pray specifically for seekers. While attending a Billy Graham-sponsored evangelism training course in 1971, he was challenged to write down on a card the names of friends and family members he hoped would someday come to Christ. "We were encouraged to identify seekers with whom we could actually develop meaningful friendships," Kevin explains. "So I listed six neighbors by name and began praying for each of them consistently." He and his wife began joining these neighbors in social activities, and over time they all became very close friends. The Dyers even opened up their home to host Bible study discussions, and most of their neighbors participated. "To this day, I still have that card as a reminder to pray for my seeking friends," Kevin says. "And so far, four of the original six have made commitments to follow Christ. One of those was a man named Ray, and as a result, his wife, all of his kids, and all of his ten grandchildren are Christ followers today! The big lesson I learned is to pray specifically and deliberately."

As a group, regularly spend time praying for seekers specifically by name. Just the act of identifying seekers in each other's lives will bring about an awareness and sensitivity to evangelistic opportunities. Pray that seekers would be open and receptive to the tugs of the Holy Spirit. Pray also that God would open doors for group members to share their faith, and that they would do so boldly. Paul set this example when he wrote, "Pray also for me, that whenever I open my mouth, words may be given me so that I will fearlessly make known the mystery of the gospel, for which I am an ambassador in chains. Pray that I may declare it fearlessly, as I should" (Ephesians 6:19–20).

## John Hudson's Story

*I suppose the first practical step our group took toward greater evangelistic awareness was the keeping of a prayer journal. I purchased a notebook and asked everyone to share the*

*3. Get Equipped.* A practical way to build confidence in the area of evangelism is to get adequately trained. As previously mentioned, *The Three Habits of Highly Contagious Christians* is a discussion guide specifically designed to help believer groups raise their evangelistic temperature. At Willow Creek, we first released this book a couple years ago during a Vision Night mid-week service. At that time, Bill Hybels asked every small group in our church to take the time to go through the *Three Habits* guide. He challenged the congregation to "push the pause button on whatever it is your small group is doing now and follow this guide — study it, discuss it, digest it, and apply it to your everyday life." Your group may want to do the same thing. Take a break from the study you're working through now and use this guide for a few weeks to better prepare your group members to reach out to the seekers all around them. Also as a group, you should consider taking an evangelism class such as Becoming a Contagious Christian. It's a great way to sharpen skills in evangelism and to support one another in the process.

### John Hudson's Story

*When it came time for our group to select our next discussion topic, I made evangelism one of the choices. But I included other options such as relationships and spiritual gifts. We were very divided on what everyone wanted to do, so we finally agreed to cover a different topic each week — including evangelism — for five meetings in a row. After our discussion on outreach, we agreed that we needed additional training. But this left us with a dilemma. Most of us were not available at the times the Becoming a Contagious Christian course was being offered. So I purchased the leadership manual and tailored the material to fit our group's needs. I led our group through the course in three weeks, asking everyone to do some preparation prior to our discussions. For example, they came to our meetings with their impact lists, personal stories, and evangelism style tests already done. Then we spent considerable time role-playing and completing the interactive parts. After this three-week run, I was amazed to watch the group members become so much more intentional in their evangelistic efforts. I did as well. We took evangelism up a notch — and it was beginning to become a real priority.*

4. *Swap Stories.* One of the best ways to encourage and inspire ongoing efforts in evangelism is to share stories. Take time to listen to your group members' various experiences interacting with seekers. As individuals open up about their roadblocks and breakthroughs, group members can offer insights, constructive feedback, and prayer support. And nothing is more motivating than to hear someone in the group tell the story of a seeking friend who has crossed the line of faith. Never neglect celebrating such occasions.

## John Hudson's Story

*Our group members love to share stories. Of course the most thrilling and inspiring stories are the ones about people coming to faith. Like the time Cathy filled us in on how two friends from her volleyball team came to know Christ. Or when Lindita accepted Christ — which was extra special to me because that was the first occasion I had ever led someone across the line of faith. And that was the first person for whom our whole group had the privilege to, in some way, play a role in a conversion. It was incredible to see all our prayers for her answered. We had been links in the chain of her transformation, and that was very special. Everyone's passion for reaching seekers was fueled by the experience of having Lindita share her story at one of our group meetings. As a group, we celebrated her first Communion together, and later, we were all there for her when she was baptized. Her decision to trust*

*Christ did more for our group than words can describe. Walking alongside Lindita in her spiritual journey deepened our relationship with God and each other. Now, we regularly set aside time in our group meetings to celebrate and console one another in our evangelistic efforts — and that takes our spiritual growth to the next level.*

## Level Two (Intermediate)

5. *Hang Out Together.* This step involves challenging the individuals in your group to build and develop friendships with seekers. This means encouraging them to break out of their "holy huddle" and look for ways in which they can build bridges with neighbors, friends, coworkers, classmates, or family members who don't know Christ. As was covered in chapter 2, one of the most effective ways to grow authentic friendships with seekers is to identify areas of common ground or interest, and then spend time doing those things. Explore with your group what activities members want to participate in with seekers, what makes relationships with seekers "safe," and how to authentically express care and respect for those who are spiritually seeking.

### John Hudson's Story

*Our group decided to set a goal for ourselves in the area of evangelism. We agreed to identify at least two seekers with whom we would each intentionally build relationships, eventually share the gospel, and prayerfully invite to visit our seeker services. This goal gave our members a clear vision and purpose for what we wanted to be about. And it became something worth striving for.*

6. *Look for Open Windows.* This step is about initiating spiritual conversations with lost people. Often, we go about our day unaware of opportunities to share our faith. Talk with your group about how members can keep their awareness level up in order to engage in spiritual conversations. Sometimes dropping clues or hints about one's faith is enough to launch significant dialogues. Discuss examples of appropriate spiritual clues to use with seekers. Pray for one another to have wisdom in boldly starting these spiritual interactions.

### John Hudson's Story

*There are probably three main reasons why our group members have been actively initiating spiritual conversations. First, we pray that God would give us opportunities and that we would not be shy about taking advantage of them. Second, the training class in evangelism gave all of us a renewed level of confidence. And third, everybody knows that I'm going to personally ask about it — I hold the group accountable!*

*7. Make the Invitation.* This last step in Level Two is to challenge group members to maximize outreach events by inviting seekers to attend — especially with the entire group. Members can encourage each other to invite their lost friends to join the group for church services or other types of seeker-sensitive events (such as Christian concerts). These kinds of special events can easily spark spiritual conversations, so whenever possible, it's important to spend quality time together with seekers before or after the events.

Because there is always the risk that seekers will decline these invitations, this step can become a tough challenge for some members. But stretching the group to move beyond their comfort zones will draw them closer together as they rise to the occasion and meet this challenge head on. They'll easily relate to one another's struggles in becoming more outreach-oriented, so be sure to invite group members to open up to each other about their fears, disappointments, and successes. Offer to spend time in prayer and then adequately discuss the best approaches to use in extending invitations. Brainstorm how your group can be seeker-friendly and safe during the events — and talk about how to avoid turning seekers into "projects."

### John Hudson's Story

*On weekends, our group usually sits together during the AXIS services and then goes out afterward. And there probably isn't a week that goes by that someone in our group doesn't have a seeker on his or her arm. We make a point to warmly greet and welcome newcomers — it's become second nature for us now — in fact, that's how Lindita got connected with the other members of our group. She came with us to AXIS and absolutely loved it.*

## Level Three (Advanced)

8. *Party with a Purpose.* In this step, the group organizes social gatherings for the purpose of inviting non-Christian friends. Around Willow Creek, we call these events "Matthew" parties, based on Luke 5:27–32. This passage describes a scene where a tax collector named Matthew, or Levi, threw a big party soon after he became a Christ-follower. Many of his non-Christian coworkers attended the gathering, but he invited Jesus to also come and mingle with everybody. Can you just picture Matthew at this party, introducing friends to Jesus; hoping and praying they would discover the source of the life-change he had found? Imagine Matthew whispering and gesturing to Jesus, "Go over and talk to him." "Make sure you meet that one over there." His plan was to host a nonthreatening environment where all his friends could rub shoulders with Jesus.

Your small group of believers could do something similar. Brainstorm ideas of seeker-friendly get-togethers your group could host for non-Christian friends. These could include anything from holiday parties, movie nights, and dinners to sporting events, service projects, and spiritual discussions. Be creative. Consider the kinds of things your group already enjoys doing — and instead of doing them exclusively as a group of Christians, make it an open invitation for members to bring their seeking friends. Help one another determine which seekers would most enjoy your event. For example, your group may want to focus on inviting those with whom members have already had a few significant spiritual conversations. Spend time as a group specifically praying for the event and the people you're inviting.

If your group decides to organize a social gathering with a considerable spiritual component, such as a discussion about spiritual things (see chapter 4 for a sample discussion plan), you'll want to carefully walk everyone in your group through the game plan, covering any guidelines they should follow. Advise everyone to be upfront with seekers about exactly what the agenda is — so there are no surprises. Don't ever pull a "bait and switch" on seekers. For example, when inviting them to someone's home for a time of coffee and dessert, be straightforward and very clear about your group's plan that the gathering will also include a short, nonthreatening discussion about spiritual things. Emphasize that this is just a one-time kind of thing, without any obligation.

Organizing a Matthew party with a spiritual discussion will take your group into a new and exciting level of evangelistic impact. It's not uncommon for some members to express fears, so be sure to take the time to openly talk things through. And make extra certain that your event is carefully planned to be fun, relaxed, and appropriate for seekers. (For starters, your group may wish to review together the section in chapter 3 called Seekers' Fears Matter.)

Your believer group may want to make hosting Matthew parties a common occurrence. For example, you could meet three times a month for your regular group times and then plan social events for your seeking friends on a monthly basis. (Leaders sometimes refer to this schedule as "three inside/one outside.")

The purpose behind organizing these kinds of events is to provide a safe place for your seeking friends to meet and build significant friendships with the other members of your group. As you begin to interact with each other's seeker friends, you will, over time, create opportunities to make a lasting spiritual impact.

### John Hudson's Story

*It may sound strange, but I think one of our best evangelism tools is our social activities, because our seeking friends love to join us for them. As a result, it seems we are always planning fun, seeker-friendly get-togethers. You name it, we've planned it: ice-skating, skiing, camping weekends, birthday dinners, and rock climbing. Lindita thoroughly enjoys coming to our events — especially the service-oriented ones like feeding the hungry or helping the poor. And to top it off, she not only comes to our gatherings, but she often brings seekers along with her. Our group greatly values these opportunities to spend time with our seeking friends. It's something that we talk and pray about frequently.*

*9. Fill the Open Chair.* This step is about inviting seekers to visit your small group a few times or, in some cases, with the hope that they might eventually become a regular part of your group. This is what it means to "fill the open chair" — newcomers are welcome. In some cases, it's not in the seeker's best interest to become a regular member of a believers' small group, because the format is not sufficiently seeker-sensitive. But other groups would do well to include seekers — especially if group members can adjust their expectations accordingly.

Be careful about taking this step. Because believers have different needs than seekers, conflicts of interest may arise. In other words, the believers in the group may not want to give up having a deeper time of prayer and Bible study, while the seekers may not be ready for anything too spiritually intense. Believers may have to suspend getting their needs met temporarily for the sake of meeting the needs of the seekers. Of course, Christians meeting together for the purpose of spiritual formation is a critically important value and may not be worth putting on the back burner. A possible compromise would be to plan a series of four to six discussion sessions in which seekers could be invited to join your group. That way, the believers can turn their full attention to meeting the needs of the seekers, knowing their own needs will once again be the focus at the conclusion of the series. In any case, the leader will need to effectively facilitate group discussions appropriate for both seekers and believers.

As with other events, it is important to understand and decide which seekers would be most appropriate to invite. Usually, the best candidates to visit a believer's group are the seekers who are furthest along in their spiritual journeys and who have expressed real interest in spiritual issues. In addition, your group may need some coaching on how to show support and encouragement to these not-yet-convinced guests.

## John Hudson's Story

*Some of the seekers who participated in our social events ended up practically inviting themselves to our small group meetings. We couldn't keep them away! They were obviously drawn there by the friendships they made with our group members. My apprentice and I supplemented their group visits with one-on-one meetings to make sure they did not feel left behind by our discussions. Lindita has not missed a single Tuesday night small group meeting in eight months! Corey said he would visit our group if I taught him how to kayak. He's been coming now for about six months — and I still owe him the lesson! A highlight about Corey that stands out in my mind came late one night after our small group meeting. Corey called me at home to ask if he could serve as our small group service coordinator even though he wasn't yet a Christian. I told him that he absolutely could. In that moment, something inside told me it was only a matter of time before he would cross the line of faith.*

*10. Sponsor a Seeker Group.* This final step is a challenge I want to issue every believer small group: expand your territory by launching a seeker small group! The most common response to this challenge is, "But where would we start?" And the answer is, "Start with *you!*" Yes, *you* could be the one to lead a seeker group. And here's how to go about it: Identify one other person from your group to join you in becoming the future leaders of a seeker group. Ask your group to pray and commission you. Do all you can to learn how to go about launching and leading a seeker small group. When your group hosts Matthew parties, introduce yourself to the seekers in attendance in order to start building some bridges of trust. Invite them, as well as those seekers with whom you've already built friendships, to visit your group. Ask your group to support your efforts by inviting their seeking friends to come with them to your seeker group. (Once their friends make a connection to your new group, they will no longer need to continue to attend the seeker group.) Keep your believer group informed of your progress and let them celebrate all that God does through you. They will certainly have a high level of ownership and support because they will have been the ones who "birthed" your seeker group.

Before becoming the associate evangelism director at Willow Creek, Mark Ashton served on the staff of InterVarsity Christian Fellowship at the University of Illinois. During his time there, he led the charge in starting a seeker small group revolution throughout the campus. He began by transforming sixty ordinary believer small groups into contagious ones. In one year, these groups took up the challenge and launched fifty-seven seeker small groups! The very next year, sixty believer small groups went through the process of birthing (or sponsoring) sixty-five seeker groups. That year the InterVarsity chapter formed more seeker small groups than believer small groups and they saw scores of students place their faith in Christ. And it all started with a vision for how believer groups could become contagious.

## John Hudson's Story

*We had so many seekers coming to our group that we recently decided to spin off a group just for them. We all agreed that the seekers' needs would be better met if they had their own group to address their specific issues. The seekers were thrilled! And now this group is growing with new seekers joining all the time.*

*There is no telling what will happen in the next couple of months now that we've got this seeker group up and running. Sponsoring the seeker group has taken the evangelistic temperature in our group up several more notches. And it's been a life-changing adventure.*

As you read through these ten descriptions, where did you and your group land? What level best represents how contagious your group is right now? Which steps could your group most easily begin to implement? Which steps would be the most difficult? Is there an endeavor that your group attempted to make in the past but found it to be too challenging? What steps will you and your group members take to move to the next level? Just the act of asking and addressing these questions will point your group in the direction of becoming more contagious. And taking one or two of these steps will set your group in motion. The stakes are much too high to settle for anything less.

# COREY CLINE'S STORY

### Accountant
### Wheeling, Illinois

*T*hree years ago, I found myself questioning everything I believed. I had earned a degree in college and thought that once I was making money in the "real world," all of life's problems would be solved. When the summer came around, I was earning enough to take care of all my needs and had some good friends who I spent almost all of my time with. Everything seemed to be in place, but something was missing. Even though I knew quite a few people in town, I wasn't developing any significant relationships. I remember thinking I could probably find some good friends if I went to church, but I figured that was the wrong reason to start attending. So I just continued on my path.

A couple years later, I found myself at a party where I met a Christian guy named John Hudson. John and I talked about some outdoor activities that we enjoyed, and we made a deal. If I checked out his small group the following week, he would teach me how to kayak. The next week, I visited John's small group and determined I could fit in there.

As I attended the Bible study over the next few weeks, I realized that most of the people in the group were already Christians. I started to feel like I didn't fit in anymore. I remember thinking that if I let these people see who I really was, they would kick me out of the group. I intended to leave John's group. At about that time, though, our group went out to celebrate a member's birthday, and I got to talk to one of the Christian guys named Mark. He shared parts of his spiritual story with me, and to my surprise, I discovered that he hadn't lived a perfect life either. This gave me the courage to hang in there. In fact, it was then that I decided to call John to volunteer my time to coordinate the group's service projects.

John and I began to meet one-on-one a few times a month to discuss spiritual matters. John would talk with me and ask simple questions about what was holding me back from becoming a Christian. During our meetings, I figured out what that was: I thought I needed to live more of a Christian lifestyle and eliminate all of the sin in my life before I could accept Jesus. John helped me realize that this wasn't true. But he did it in a nonthreatening way. He simply helped me understand that all I needed to do was invite Jesus into my life and then ask Jesus for the strength to change.

Once I realized that everyone around me wasn't perfect and I didn't have to be either, accepting Jesus was easy. I already knew the steps to take to do it, so one day I just prayed by myself and invited Jesus into my life. Since then, I have asked John to pray with me, just to make sure I got it right and didn't leave anything out!

After receiving Christ into my life, the activities that bring me the most joy have changed. Work used to dominate my life, and accumulating money was my main focus. Now, Jesus gives me life, and the community I share with my small group brings me real meaning. Instead of searching for something meaningless to fill my spare time, I find myself serving my neighbors through the Willow Creek Food Pantry. I know that I've only just begun my spiritual walk, but I am excited about the growth I'll experience in the future.

# ANGELA MAHSEREDJIAN'S STORY

*Teacher*
*São Paulo, Brazil*

*O*ver the last thirteen years, my husband, Nazareth, and I have hosted ten different seeker groups in our home. It seems we find ourselves extending invitations to seekers wherever we go, especially if we sense a particular openness to the possibility of coming to our discussion that week. Sometimes we will call or drop by our friends' homes to tell them about our group meetings. Other times, like when we meet someone at a restaurant or even the waiting room of a doctor's office, we'll make the invitation on the spot! The positive receptivity we've found has been very encouraging and exciting.

We usually start out our evening's seeker group with the cafezinho (small coffee) and cake. This is a very important time for our group members because we have discovered that, in our culture, something like this is needed to break the ice and ease anxiety. After the cafezinho, we engage our friends in lively discussions about God and the Bible. At the close of every meeting, we emphasize the concept of the "open chair," which means we encourage group members to bring others they know who also might benefit from the time of interaction. There are many wonderful stories I could tell about people who have come to know the Lord in our home over these years, but I will share just two of them.

Anna came to our home one evening, determined she would not agree with anything anyone would say. But she came back a second and a third time — and by the fourth meeting, Anna was ready to embrace Christ as her Lord and Savior. She was a very good veterinarian at the time, but a few years after her conversion, she left her practice and became involved in the children's ministry at our church. Through Anna's life, her own father and mother, as well as her husband and three children, came to know Christ. To watch these events unfold right before our eyes has been absolutely amazing.

The other story is about Maria. One day, as my husband was walking in the park, he met Maria walking the same path. He invited her right then and there to come to our group and church. She enthusiastically accepted! Later that same week she prayed and asked Christ to be her one and only savior! But then tragedy struck right in front of their residence — a thief killed her husband. And in one week, this woman met Christ and became a widow. When Maria tells her story, she shares how her decision to invite Christ into her life prepared her for what was to come. At that terrible moment when she suddenly lost her husband, God was right there with her, giving her strength and comfort. Maria has attended our seeker group faithfully ever since and is a witness for Jesus wherever she goes.

We have a general knowledge of at least eighty people who have made decisions for Christ over these past years. In writing this story, it has been incredible to think over the names of those who have come to our home and to remember their faces. Even Nazareth's own brother, along with his wife and son, came to know Christ in our home. It is overwhelming to recall.

Opening up our home for these groups is not always easy, but it is what gives us the most joy. We love to receive people in our home, serve the cafezinho, discuss the Bible in a relevant manner, and then sit back and watch to see what our great God is going to do next!

# Chapter 10

# Seize the Adventure

*I will search for the lost and bring back the strays.*

EZEKIEL 34:16

*I am compelled to preach. Woe to me if I do not preach the gospel!*

1 CORINTHIANS 9:16

*The man who will not act until he knows all will never act at all.*

JIM ELLIOT

*The Lord's power was with them. Large numbers of people believed and turned to the Lord.*

ACTS 11:21 NIRV

Do you have questions about God and the meaning of life? Do you ever wonder about who you are and where you're headed? Do you know who Jesus was and the difference he makes 2000 years later? Do you want a safe place to ask your questions, raise your doubts, and search for answers?" These words struck a chord deep in the heart of Franki Anglin. She had been attending church services for a couple months and was looking for reasons *not* to believe. "I seriously thought something was wrong with Christians," Frank admits, "and I figured that going to church would be the fastest way to prove Christians were nuts." This particular Sunday, though, she grew very interested as she listened to the speaker explain the concept of a seeker small group. Franki accepted the challenge — and it was the beginning of an unexpected, yet incredible, adventure.

That speaker, Russ Martin, is a man who is "wired up" to point spiritually lost people toward God. The founding pastor of New Life Bible Church in Norman, Oklahoma, Russ built his church completely around the idea of reaching non-Christians for Christ, making seeker small groups an integral part of that strategy. He and his wife, Janna, led their church's first seeker group several years ago, and now groups for spiritual seekers are a way of life at New Life. Incredibly, many who became Christians through their original group are now leading their own seeker groups.

While the congregation of over nine hundred people learns about seeker groups through the usual means such as announcements and special inserts, the most effective way to get the word out is through Russ' sermons. He regularly talks positively about the seeking process and invites people to check out one of the church's many seeker groups. "We disarm seekers' fears by letting them see that we are genuine and nonthreatening and present a high level of care and acceptance," he explains.

"We offer seeker groups that meet on different days and times and at a variety of locations. Once a seeker starts attending our services, the next step is to invite him or her to visit a seeker group. We want to make it as easy as possible for every seeker who walks through our doors to visit a group — it's just not an option for us to do anything less than that! A seeker group is the bridge that takes people from where they are to where they need to go."

Over the years, Russ and Janna, along with their apprentices, have led six seeker groups, and the results have been incredible. "Seventy-five percent of those who participate in our seeker groups on a consistent basis eventually cross the line of faith," Russ reports. Of course, the time it takes for that to occur varies greatly, from as little as a couple months to a year or even longer. But he's convinced that if non-Christians will simply visit a seeker group once, they are highly likely to return for future meetings and, eventually, become Christians. Russ and Janna have seen people from all ages, all backgrounds, and just about every circumstance in life come to Christ through seeker groups. Even atheists have shown up to engage in the discussions — only to discover a personal relationship with Christ and become devoted followers.

While not everyone becomes convinced through a seeker group, Russ knows the experience plants a seed. "And that's why we're training more and more leaders to launch seeker groups — we know the potential harvest is great. But the outcome of these seeker groups is more than just numbers to us. It's about reaching out to people we care about very much with a message that really matters."

Russ feels strongly that a seeker group makes a dual impact. Not only are spiritual seekers transformed, but the hearts of the leaders are also marked forever. "I have found that being around and interacting up close with lost people keeps my heart spiritually recharged and prevents vision-drift in my life," Russ says, "and that greatly impacts the way I lead and teach the church. That's why I'm convinced every pastor in every church should lead a seeker small group."

## Seeker Group Options

The possibilities for creatively launching and leading a seeker small group are limitless. As you finalize the details of starting your own seeker small group, consider the ideas and suggestions listed in this chapter. This is hardly an exhaustive list, but perhaps it will start you thinking about where to begin, given your circumstances. At Willow Creek, we've been developing a wide spectrum of seeker small group strategies for more than a decade. By sharing what we've learned and what has worked well for us, I hope you will be inspired to explore options and develop plans that will function best in your situation.

### Church Seeker Groups

Over ten years ago, I formed the first seeker group at Willow Creek from among those who attended one of our baptism information meetings. Shortly after I started working there, I was asked to assist Bill Hybels with sessions designed to help people determine whether they were ready to be baptized. I was instructed to sit in the front row and make myself available to answer participants' questions after the meeting.

That night, Bill spoke compellingly to a large crowd in the chapel about the significance of baptism. He concluded by explaining that no one should be baptized unless he or she had made a personal commitment to Christ. "And that's a decision you can make right where you're sitting now," he stressed. "But whatever you decide, don't make a mockery out of baptism. Make sure you're getting baptized for the right reasons. If you're not ready to be baptized, do whatever you can to get your questions answered. Maybe you'd like to talk with someone tonight." Bill paused to motion to me to stand up. "If so, Garry is willing to stay here all night if he has to in order to help each of you figure this out."

For hours after the meeting, I talked with people about their spiritual condition. Some prayed with me to receive Christ. Others needed further clarification and words of encouragement. But about fifteen seekers admitted they had too many doubts and concerns to go forward with baptism. And *they* were the ones I invited to a one-time discussion about spiritual issues. The following week, eleven of those seekers joined me, along with two apprentices I had recruited. We met at the church for a fascinating time of interaction. Remarkably, our seeker group continued to meet weekly for the rest of that year, and each member of the group eventually crossed the line of faith and was baptized. My apprentices went on to lead their own groups, and we've been launching seeker groups ever since.

Up until that point, there really hadn't been a next step in place for seekers who attended our services. Now, however, seeker groups provide that missing link for those who want to take their search to the next level. Either through special announcements or application points in their messages, our teaching pastors frequently encourage non-Christians at our weekend services to explore seeker groups. They invite seekers to make their interest known by calling the church or completing the tear-off portion of the bulletin. Once someone gives us contact information expressing interest in a seeker group, we get in touch with the person immediately to help find a group that best meets his or her needs.

Using both weekend services *and* seeker groups, we're now in a position to reach non-Christians more effectively than ever before. For us, that's "the genius of the BOTH AND."[1] Designed to inspire seekers to take steps forward in their spiritual journeys, the following is an overview of our current weekend evangelism strategy:

*Relational Evangelism.* Willow Creek's evangelism approach is based on relationships and processes rather than events. Therefore, we continually encourage Christians to develop ongoing, authentic friendships with seekers. As bridges of trust are established, our believers look for opportunities to interact with seekers about spiritual matters and to invite them to attend weekend services and other seeker-oriented events. We provide evangelism training workshops and resources, such as the *Becoming a Contagious Christian* course and *The Three Habits of Highly Contagious Christians* study guide, to support these efforts.

*Buzz Weekends.* Last year, thousands of NFL fans fought their way through a Chicago winter blizzard to attend weekend services featuring special guest Kurt Warner, quarterback of the St. Louis Rams. During the interview, Senior Pastor Bill Hybels asked Kurt questions about his football career, including his exciting Super Bowl appearances. The highlight, though, was Kurt's stirring declaration of his faith in Christ. A few months later, weekend guests were in awe of Lisa Beamer's amazing faith and poise, as the widow of 9/11-hero Todd Beamer openly and honestly described the details of her story. On another weekend, Bill interviewed a panel of five experts representing Hinduism, Buddhism, Islam, Judaism, and Christianity about their religious differences. Our guests hung on every word. With over 23,000 people in attendance, this World Religions service drew the largest crowd in the history of our church.

Scheduled on a regular basis, these special interest services, called "buzz weekends" are designed to attract people who might not ordinarily be willing to walk through the doors of a church. The central idea behind these events is to provide a positive, intriguing experience for seekers, so they may be more open to attend future services and seeker groups, and further explore Christianity.

*Weekend Services.* Every weekend, year in and year out, we strive to produce the highest quality seeker services possible. We incorporate contemporary music and drama sketches, as well as relevant messages, to create a safe environment where Christians can confidently invite seeking friends and family members to explore, at their own pace, the claims of Christ.

*Decision Weekends.* Pastor Bill Hybels recently gave one the most compelling invitations to the gospel I've heard. When he finished preaching on the wise and foolish builders described in Matthew 7:24–27, he invited anyone who wished to indicate their desire to trust Christ to walk up individually on stage and stand on a large flat rock so Bill could offer a brief prayer. That gesture symbolized each one's desire to place his or her life on the solid rock of Jesus Christ. As people walked off the stage, they were given a Bible and a card to complete if they wanted more information about next steps.

At least two or three times a year, we provide special opportunities during our services for people to respond to the gospel. During a recent Easter service, Bill invited people to walk across a bridge constructed on the stage if they wanted to symbolize their desire to receive Christ. Other times, he has encouraged people to indicate their decision one way or another on response cards (such as the ones found in appendix H).

*Next Steps.* In order to fully leverage each component of our weekend strategy, it is essential for us to make clear "next step" options available. Without them, the potential impact of each weekend element would be significantly weakened. Those who come to weekend services or respond at a "decision weekend" need to know what to do next. Therefore, we frequently utilize next step cards (see samples in appendix H) during our weekend services or distribute "New Christian's Kits" to people who indicate a decision to trust Christ. These kits include a Bible (such as Tyndale's *New Believer's Bible*), booklets that further explain the gospel (such as *He Did This Just for You* by Max Lucado, *The Reason Why* by Robert Laidlaw, or *My Heart, Christ's Home* by Robert Munger), and "next steps" cards that outline the importance of baptism, new believer groups, and other spiritual growth opportunities.

Those who are not yet ready to receive Christ should be given relevant next-step options as well. And that's where seeker groups step in. At decision weekends, one of our teaching pastors will suggest something like, "If you're not ready to make a decision for Christ because you still have questions and doubts, that's okay. We have seeker small groups designed for people just like you. Come one time, and check it out."

Seeker groups that meet at the church before or after services (similar to when traditional Sunday school classes meet) can be a powerful arrangement for those seekers already coming to weekend services — it's the most convenient and logical next step for them to take. At Willow Creek, these seeker groups gather around tables for refreshments and discussion in a comfortable setting, either before or after attending church together. It's a powerful one-two punch as seekers experience the service and debrief it — which personalizes things for them in a helpful way. These two complimentary sources of input greatly aid seekers in their spiritual journeys.

To create additional seeker interest, throughout the year we offer a series of larger classes that cover relevant topics such as the problem of evil or the existence of God. Sometimes we complement the subject taught during the weekend services or ask seekers to bring their most pressing questions and issues. These classes, called Investigating Christianity, Tough Questions, or For Seekers Only, meet before or after services for six to eight consecutive weeks and are designed to attract those seekers already attending our services. This approach can be a less threatening step for some to take before joining a seeker group. Existing seeker groups are invited to attend and typically make up the nucleus of the class. In addition, we also invite leaders who are interested in beginning a seeker group to come and welcome newcomers to their tables. As we promote the class, we do so in such a way that seekers feel the freedom to attend any of the sessions in any order — and with no attendance or advanced preparation requirements.

The class format centers on interaction with a speaker who combines a brief talk (five to ten minutes) with a time of questions and answers (ten to twenty minutes). The remaining time is allotted for small group discussion at individual tables. The order and duration of these three elements (lecture, question and answer, and small group discussion) varies from week to week. For example, one week may include this arrangement:

- Small group discussion (icebreaker question, 5 minutes)
- Lecture (5 minutes)
- Q & A (10 minutes)
- Small group discussion (15 minutes)
- Lecture (5 minutes)

- Small group discussion (20 minutes)
- Q & A (10 minutes)
- Small group discussion (wrap-up, 5 minutes)

This forum helps to jump-start our seeker groups at the church. By the time the series of classes end, seekers have had a good taste of what a seeker group is like, and the leaders simply invite the seekers to continue coming for the group discussions. Many of our seeker groups begin this way.

If you've never led a seeker group, the most straightforward approach is to form one for non-Christians who already attend your church. That's what Kate Maver did — at a very critical juncture in the life of her church. She wasn't sure her little urban church in the heart of Chicago would survive. The people were barely coming to worship services on Sundays and they knew almost nothing about the Bible. To make matters worse, the pastor decided that God didn't actually exist and that he wanted out of the ministry. But because he didn't want the church to die on his watch, he asked Kate, a seminary student at the time, to help him. She agreed to do her best.

The very next week, the pastor got a job in the marketplace and left. The church board voted to close its doors unless Kate would step in as their interim pastor. "I couldn't believe what I had gotten myself into," Kate recalls, "Out of the thirty-two regular worshipers, only one woman in the entire congregation was a committed Christ-follower."

"Right from the start, I decided to treat the whole church as one big seeker group," she says. Kate prepared her sermons based on the tough questions she solicited from the congregation. In every church meeting or function she attended, she applied principles she had learned about leading seeker groups. She started viewing teams of people who volunteered to do things like fixing patches in the church roof or making coffee on Sunday mornings as seeker groups. "I met with these teams and gradually inserted spiritual truths into our discussions, while at the same time I always welcomed and encouraged any and all questions. Slowly at first, and then eventually more rapidly, honest vulnerable questions and concerns about the Christian faith came up in these groups. People actually wanted to *know* the God they were serving. To my amazement, people began crossing the line of faith and receiving Jesus as their one and only savior. Initially, church members told me about their decisions to follow Christ off to the side. But later, they were more open and talked about receiving Christ within their groups — and even in front of the entire congregation!"

What about you? How could you best utilize your church services to reach out to non-Christians? What plans will you make to identify and impact seekers *already* within the walls of your church? What steps could you take to attract them to a seeker small group that you will lead?

*Outreach Events*

The evangelism ministry at Willow Creek frequently sponsors outreach events for the primary purpose of reaching out to non-Christians and connecting them into seeker groups. A few years ago, we held one such event called Tough Questions in a local hotel banquet room on two consecutive Tuesday nights. We selected this "neutral" venue because we knew unchurched seekers would view it as a less threatening location than our church campus. Lee Strobel served as the host, and we brought in Dr. William Lane Craig, a highly respected Christian apologetics expert, to give a twenty-minute presentation and then field questions from the audience. About 600 people showed up each night.

For weeks in advance, we heavily promoted the event within our church. We made platform announcements during weekend services inviting seekers to bring their toughest questions about Christianity. We printed and distributed hundreds of sharp-looking fliers that people used to invite their non-Christian friends, and we hinted that Christians should come *only* if they brought a seeker with them. In addition we provided extensive seeker small group training for the leaders we recruited to facilitate table discussions during the event.

Each night, the facilitators warmly welcomed guests to their tables and began making introductions. When it was time to start, Lee enthusiastically expressed his appreciation for everyone's attendance. He then directed people into a short time of group interaction at their tables. That was the cue for the facilitators to lead their groups through about ten minutes of light-hearted icebreakers. After that, Lee introduced Dr. Craig, who spoke about the problem of eveil and suffering.

At the close of Dr. Craig's talk, the facilitators led their groups in a twenty-five-minute discussion about what they just heard — agreements, disagreements, or whatever. Then, after a compelling explanation of the seeker group concept, Lee invited people to fill out response cards to indicate their interest in a group and to provide their contact information. (A sample outreach event response card is shown below.) As an added incentive, we told participants that several completed cards would be randomly selected to receive books written and autographed by Dr. Craig. The anticipation created an enthusiastic buzz in the room — and 95 percent of the participants turned in the response card!

---

## Tough Questions

Thanks for joining us tonight. To be eligible to win in tonight's drawing, please take a moment to answer the following questions!

1) How did you hear about Tough Questions?
   ❏ Friend/Family ❏ Flyer
   ❏ Announcement ❏ Other_____

2) Do you attend church services on a regular basis?
   ❏ Yes ❏ No

3) Have you ever attended a service at Willow Creek Community Church?
   ❏ Yes ❏ No

4) Where would you describe yourself on your spiritual journey?
   ❏ Curious about spiritual things
   ❏ Investigating Christianity
   ❏ Fully devoted follower of Jesus Christ

5) Would you like more information about small groups for spiritual seekers?
   ❏ Yes ❏ No

Name:_____

Email: _____

Phone (H) (_____)_____ (W) (_____)_____

---

As these cards were collected, each table discussed and identified questions they most wanted to ask the speaker. Lee and I roamed the room and invited table representatives to stand and ask their group's most intriguing question. Dr. Craig allotted about forty-five minutes for questions and answers and five minutes to give a concluding wrap-up. Before dismissing the crowd, Lee invited Dr. Craig to draw about ten response cards from a big box, call out the names, and give away his books. Lee extended a warm invitation to everyone to return the following week.

During the week, the table facilitators called those who were at their tables and encouraged them to come back for the final session. As a result, nearly everyone returned and most sat at their original tables. The format that night was the same as the previous week, but this time when the session concluded, facilitators turned to those at their tables and invited them to form an ongoing seeker small group. Scores of seekers responded positively, and we were able to jump-start many seeker groups from this outreach event.

Over the years we have sponsored many creative outreach events similar to this one. We've had great results bringing in other excellent guest speakers such as Norman Geisler and Cliffe Knechtle. Some of our events worked well at the church and others were better suited for off-site locations. And more recently, we've utilized an innovative resource to help us pull off these events for seekers. My good friends Lee Strobel and Mark Mittelberg lead what they call "Turnkey Outreach Events" with Church Communication Network (CCN). These events — which run the gamut of evangelistic talks, question-and-answer sessions for spiritual seekers, and outreach concerts — are offered several times a year via satellite broadcast into thousands of churches all over North America. This effective but inexpensive approach streamlines the process of organizing outreach events.[2]

After experimenting with a wide variety of formats, we've concluded that the best outreach events always provide next steps for seekers. And offering them a taste of a seeker group experience during the actual event is the most effective way to move them into ongoing seeker groups. How about you? What kinds of events for spiritual seekers could you organize? What plans could you develop to leverage one of these outreach events to form a seeker group?

## Neighborhood Seeker Groups

It all started with a simple prayer for one woman who formed a seeker group in her Fort Collins, Colorado, neighborhood. "Starting up a Bible study was definitely out of my comfort zone, and I feared the worst—that I would alienate myself from my neighbors," she says. "Fully anticipating that it would not work at all, I figured I'd forever be labeled the 'conservative, right-wing fanatic' of the neighborhood. But through prayer I decided to take that risk, give it a try, and hope for the best."

So she organized a brunch and extended invitations to fifteen women who lived on her street. Most attended, and to her surprise nine indicated an interest in getting together on a weekly basis to discuss spiritual matters! They rotated meeting in different homes and took turns bringing refreshments. Even though the women came from a variety of religious backgrounds, they were eager to get to know each other and talk about the Bible.

"My greatest challenge was creating an atmosphere of respect and acceptance in spite of our religious differences," the leader remembers. "I worked really hard to do more listening than talking. And I found that asking good questions and getting the group members to think through what they believed was much better than giving out answers. They responded best when I admitted I had things to learn just like everyone else.

"I was most encouraged by my sixty-five-year-old next-door neighbor. She was hesitant to get involved at first, so I tried to create a warm and loving environment where she would feel accepted. Now she finds great joy in reading the Bible for herself and participating in the discussions with us every week.

"So far, four of the nine women who attend the group have crossed the line of faith. The other five are growing in knowledge and understanding, and I pray that, in God's time, they will do the same. Leading this neighborhood seeker group is a blast! It has kept me humble, as every week I realize how much I don't know. But it's incredibly stimulating to study the Bible with people who do not think or believe as I do—and it keeps me dependent on God to do what I couldn't possibly accomplish on my own."

As this story illustrates, a tremendous evangelistic potential exists in our neighborhoods. With a little forethought and effort, every one of us has a tremendous opportunity to befriend those who live around us. And when genuine friendships develop in the neighborhood, the door to making a significant spiritual impact through a seeker small group swings wide open.

And that's exactly what happened in one neighborhood in West Dundee, Illinois. Lydia and Scott Benda were one of the first families to move into their subdivision. "As houses were being built all around us," Lydia recalls, "we prayed that somehow God would use us to be a spiritual light to our new neighbors." Through block parties, scrapbook workshops, lunches, babysitting swaps, and many other social activities, the Bendas began to build many quality friendships. "Our three children naturally and spontaneously brought us into contact with other parents throughout our neighborhood, which quickly created more opportunities for relationships to grow."

Through these strong bonds of trust and friendship, it wasn't long before Scott and Lydia felt like the time was right to launch a small group in their neighborhood. "Over time, we had invited some of our friends to church and had conversations with them about spiritual things." Lydia explains. "So, as we continued those dialogues, it seemed like the best next step would be to expand the group and deepen the discussions. To be honest, I was fearful that we might be getting in over our heads. I'm not particularly eloquent or gifted in evangelism, and the thought of leading a neighborhood group was a bit overwhelming. I was nervous that I might say something that would offend my friends and not only turn them away from me, but turn them off from pursuing God. I certainly didn't want to do more harm than good—and wreck havoc with someone's spiritual journey! But even though organizing a neighborhood discussion group felt like an incredible challenge, Scott and I concluded that if we did our best and prayed a lot, we could leave the results up to God.

"Our discussion times became a safe place for everyone to express their opinions—no matter how unusual or uncommon. Scott and I tried to ask pertinent questions, be good listeners, and direct people to the Bible. We simply let the Bible speak for itself. As we examined what the Scriptures taught, we found it vitally important to allow plenty of time for members to verbally process their beliefs within the safety of our group. I especially enjoyed those 'aha moments' when the group members would make important spiritual discoveries."

One group member named Kristen, who was raised in a traditional church but never studied the Bible, was particularly eager to learn all she could about Christianity from a biblical perspective. Kristen felt very comfortable discussing her spiritual questions in the meetings. "You mean to tell me that a dreadful criminal will go to heaven if he simply repents from his sin and places his faith in Jesus Christ for forgiveness? How unfair!" Later on, she revealed more of her thoughts to the group, "If my idea that you have to be a good person to go to heaven is really wrong — according to the Bible — then I need to find out what the Bible actually teaches about the right way to get there."

Kristen's search was intense. She frequently asked for recommendations of resources and books she could study. One day she called on the phone and said, "Lydia, I've got a whole list of new questions. Can you please come over here so I can have a 'private session' with you?" It wasn't long after that Kristen invited Jesus into her life.

Two members of the group became followers of Christ after the group completed the Tough Questions guide *Why Become a Christian?* Those discussions were particularly helpful in examining the false assurances people have about being a Christian. "It was so exciting to hold hands around my kitchen table and lead my friends in a prayer of repentance and faith," Lydia says. "We shared tears of relief and joy. What an amazing privilege to participate with the Holy Spirit's work in their lives."

But Lydia admits they almost missed out on making any spiritual impact at all. "Looking back, it just about didn't happen. Beyond our normal family obligations, our schedules were so full with running a business and participating in sports, school, and church activities that we were almost too busy to extend a hand of friendship to our neighbors. But thankfully we realized the need to take some time to slow down, pray, invite our neighbors over, and really listen to them — as well as build relationships in the midst of all our activities. We soon discovered just how much people appreciate it when someone reaches out in friendship — and those in our neighborhood group became our treasured friends."

Can you imagine leading a group like that in your neighborhood? Can you picture the neighbors you care about making life-changing spiritual discoveries? Just think what a thrill that would be. What steps will you take to build sincere and authentic friendships with some of your neighbors? What's preventing you from launching and leading a seeker small group in your neighborhood?

As I write this chapter, Willow Creek is in the middle of a construction project. Hoping to introduce as many seekers as possible to the love of Christ, we are building a much larger auditorium. So we want to do whatever we can *now* to best prepare our congregation to invite non-Christians once the new facility is open. If we can implement a strategy now to help believers build bridges of trust with people who are not yet ready to go to church, then, by the time our new auditorium is finished, they may very well be in a position to bring them to our services. So our plan is to train and mobilize our core to enfold non-Christians into neighborhood seeker groups.

We're so convinced of the potential impact of this approach that we are planning to train scores of leaders to launch neighborhood seeker groups. To better assist them to start these groups, I am in the process of developing and piloting a six-week video curriculum for neighborhood seeker groups called "Pathways." Each hour and a half session includes three or four short video clips interspersed with discussion questions. The three- to seven-minute clips consist of relevant drama sketches and past messages from our teaching team. The curriculum is designed to give both inexperienced and experienced leaders a tool to jump-start spiritual discussions in their neighborhood seeker groups. And if, as a result, we fill our auditorium with non-Christians from these groups, we will have fulfilled our dream to reach out to those who are searching for answers to life's greatest questions.

*Workplace Seeker Groups*

Maybe you're interested in facilitating a seeker group in your workplace. Leaders of these groups typically need to obtain permission from their employer, reserve a conference room, and invite seekers to discuss spiritual things over lunch. Workplace seeker groups provide unique forums to reach out to coworkers in a powerful yet nonthreatening way.

Every week, Eric Spake and Jill Peterson coled a workplace seeker group in Sioux City, Iowa. It was formed primarily of the workplace connections Jill had with coworkers at a major personal computer manufacturer. Most of the group members described themselves as somewhat spiritual but not religious. And what initially started out as a six-session study turned into an exciting four-month experience. "The seeker group was most rewarding because we were given the opportunity to see God work up close in the lives of people we cared about," Eric recalls.

The group members chose to discuss questions based on common on-the-job issues, including: How do you deal with competition at work? How do you handle job stress? If you could wake up and start a different job tomorrow, what would you do? When the group gathered, two important developments took place. First, participants built strong friendships through their group interactions. And second, those connections established a sense of security and safety so that real, lasting life-change could take place.

Eric and Jill made a great team. They developed authentic friendships by spending time with members individually outside of the regular group meeting. "It was as we got to know them that they became more interested to truly know Christ inside of us," Eric explains. "What a privilege to be a part of such an exciting enterprise."

One woman in the group caught everyone off guard with her honesty. Years ago she made a decision to walk away from organized religion for good because she had experienced injustice and lack of tolerance first-hand. But she continued to speak openly about spiritual things. "One night," Eric remembers, "She made a statement about her need for God that proved to be a watershed moment for her and others to take a next step. We met for coffee soon after that, and she had all kinds of questions. That turned out to be the day that Jesus Christ came into her life. When I asked about her spiritual journey, she marked the caring environment of the group as the single dominant factor in her coming to Christ. She said that all of the knowledge, without community, wouldn't have served her. Through discovering that we were a safe group in a safe place, she began to open up. She needed a small group where she felt encouraged, nurtured, and affirmed — the very things, thankfully, that we had set out to provide!"

What about you? What steps could you take to develop and deepen your friendships with your coworkers? Do you know seekers where you work that would be open to discussing spiritual matters in a group setting? How could you reach out to them through launching a seeker small group that would meet before or after work—or possibly during the lunch hour? What could you do to show respect toward those who decline your invitation as well as those who attend your group? Are you willing to take some risks in your workplace? Who knows what God might do through you?

### Sports Seeker Groups

Mike Young, from Palatine, Illinois, had been praying for his brother, Jason, for five years. "We got along great as brothers, but my newfound love for God and my enthusiasm for Jason to know him caused me to be somewhat 'in his face.' Unfortunately, my attempts to talk directly to him about God were increasingly frustrated because his heart just seemed to grow harder."

But one day the two ran into Vicki who mentioned that her volleyball team had recently won the playoffs in a league at Willow Creek. Jason's eyes always glazed over at the mention of church, but they lit up at the very mention of volleyball. In spite of his mixed feelings, he joined a team that played at Willow Creek on Sunday afternoons. Even though Mike was a novice, he played on the team too—so he could hang out with his brother.

Jason occasionally joined Mike and the other Christians on the team for social events. Even though he was comfortable with them, he still had no interest in pursuing God. "Over time I found myself spending more and more time with my teammates and others in the league," Jason remembers. "Something attracted me to them. I suppose it had to do with some of the differences I noticed between these Christians and myself. I was curious."

Several weeks later he called Mike to ask about going to church the next day. "After Jason's call, I remember sinking to my knees in shock, gratitude, and tears," Mike recalls. After the service they grabbed some lunch and then headed over to the gym for their volleyball game. Later, things came crashing down on Jason. "That night, I remember feeling an incredibly deep sense of disappointment over the person I had become without God. I sat up in my bed and wept, because for the first time I realized how sinful I was, and how I had been turning my back on a holy and perfect God. I cried because the guilt swelled up inside of me to the point that I thought my chest was going to burst. At that point I asked God to forgive me for all the ways I had disobeyed him. I thanked Jesus for living a perfect life and for dying on the cross—paying the penalty that I deserved for my wrongdoing. I thanked Jesus for making it so easy for me to simply trust in him for the forgiveness of my sins. Now, after being a Christian for a while, it's exciting to look back and see how God used my interest in volleyball to open my eyes to him."

The Willow Creek Sports Ministry is designed to be more than just a recreational league for Christians because every captain views his or her team as a seeker small group. As a result, each of our sports leagues (basketball, volleyball, football, softball, and golf) provides an outstanding opportunity for unchurched non-Christians to have fun playing sports as they investigate Christianity. (An overview of the sports ministry's five-step evangelism strategy is included in appendix I.)

Do you enjoy sports? Do you know any non-Christians who like playing sports? How could you leverage that mutual interest to sensitively and respectfully point them to Jesus. What steps could you take to organize a sports league that would attract spiritual seekers? Can you envision the sports teams as seeker groups? Do you see the potential impact?

## Coffeehouse/Bookstore Seeker Groups

One of Perry Marshall's favorite stomping grounds is a coffee shop in an Oak Park, Illinois, bookstore. That's precisely where he obtained permission to host a few attention-getting events that helped launch a seeker group. For example, a couple weeks before April 15, he sponsored a forum called, "Former IRS Agent Tells All." To promote the event, he plastered posters around the area and even faxed an announcement to a local newspaper. Thirteen curious people showed up, including a reporter! Perry arranged to have a friend from the IRS talk about how to avoid audits and other tax problems. Then, toward the end of the discourse, the IRS worker explained what tax collectors were like in the first century. He talked briefly about the widespread corruption in those days and why Jesus still hung out with them. "We had a great meeting and, as a result, a couple people actually joined my seeker group," Perry says.

Another event he planned was called "Atheist Becomes Christian/Christian Becomes Atheist." For this one, he invited two friends who fit those descriptions to tell the stories of the process they went through that changed their beliefs. "Twenty-five people turned out for that one — it was very fascinating — and a few returned for follow-up discussions," Perry recalls.

Once Perry's seeker group got underway, it wasn't uncommon for people sitting nearby to get involved in the discussions. "They couldn't resist offering their opinions, so we'd happily invite them to pull up a chair and join in," he explains.

What do you think? Could this be an option for you? Or maybe this innovative approach has sparked another idea in you. What could you do to creatively combine an interest you have with reaching seekers for Christ through a small group? What will you do?

### Grief Support Seeker Groups

Leo Modica, a computer software engineer from Wheaton, Illinois, led a group that gathered in Willow Creek's atrium every other Sunday morning. His group members shared a common experience — grief. Many had recently lost loved ones, and three other members were battling cancer. Many joined the group out of desperation. "They felt like their lives were out of control and they had nowhere else to turn," Leo reflects. "Little did we know at the time that God was going to use these feelings of helplessness to bring about healing and salvation."

A couple of his members were also involved with other grief and cancer support groups, so they invited people from those gatherings to the seeker small group. Many invited friends and neighbors. They discussed topics driven by group members' issues and needs. Given their shared experiences, the first topic was "Why does God allow suffering?" The group spent several weeks on this topic, but Leo made it a practice to end each meeting with a short discussion on God's redemptive plan of salvation.

"During the first two years, we grew from six members to twelve. And everyone in the group had become believers," Leo reports. "Our work was complete, or so we thought. But now we were faced with a dilemma. Should the group transition into a new believer's small group exclusively or should it remain open to include additional seekers? As we prayed about it and discussed it, the answer became obvious — we needed to keep our emphasis on reaching seekers. The culture of the group had always been inclusive. Closing the doors to seeking friends was simply unthinkable. We never lost our seeker focus, and the gospel message was woven into each discussion for the sake of those seekers attending. As a result we saw God do some amazing things. Our group members experienced God's hand — his healing hand, his loving hand of comfort and peace, and his saving hand."

Do you know seekers who are encountering special hardships or grieving loss? How could God use you to offer love and support through a seeker group designed especially to meet their needs? Have your life experiences uniquely prepared you to help seekers going through similar circumstances? Maybe your friendship will make all the difference. Will you make yourself available? Will you explore the options?

## More Seeker Group Options

While mixed seeker groups — ones without a specific affinity starting point — can be quite effective, some of the most engaging groups are centered around a particular niche. You may want to identify a narrow focus based on an affinity or common interest that easily lends itself to the formation of a group. Besides those already described, here's a short list of what seems to be an unlimited number of avenues to connect seekers into life-changing groups:

- Junior high/senior high student seeker groups
- College student seeker groups (sometimes called "GIGs"–"Groups Investigating God")
- Singles' seeker groups
- Men's seeker groups
- Women's seeker groups
- Couple's seeker groups
- Parenting seeker groups
- Divorce recovery seeker groups

- International seeker groups (groups spoken in other languages)
- Religious seeker groups (groups based on similar religious backgrounds)
- Apologetics seeker groups (groups focused on tough questions and deep theological issues)

## A Final Challenge

As a kid growing up in Chicago, and later Rockford, Illinois, I always wanted to be a doctor. I'm not exactly sure where the idea originated, but I developed an increasing interest in some day becoming a heart surgeon. But after majoring in mathematics and psychology in college, I began a career in computer science. And not in a million years did I ever think I'd wind up in full-time ministry. When I left the marketplace to pursue a ministry opportunity, what I thought would be a temporary experiment turned into a twenty-year stint. So far.

The more I lead seeker small groups, the more I'm convinced it's somewhat similar to performing surgery on the heart. The operation is, of course, a spiritual one. It's a critical procedure. The process is very delicate — always dependent on the guidance from the steady hand of the Great Physician. The stakes are sky high. And the rewards are great. I suppose, in a way, I *have* become a heart surgeon after all. And I can't imagine a higher calling. Any interest? You're invited to join our growing team of heart specialists!

On behalf of the spiritual seekers in your world, I challenge you to start up a discussion group. Do it for the sake of those facing a Christ-less eternity. Invite them into the discovery process. Draw them out with some good questions. Lend them a listening ear. Let them see Christ in you. Show them a supernatural love from above. Give them your best shot.

Throughout this book I've included scores of stories of people who found Christ through seeker small groups. I received so many incredible accounts that I didn't have nearly enough room for them all. I never grow tired of reading or hearing these unique and amazing stories of life-change. But I must confess that even though I'm truly grateful for the many seekers who have crossed the line of faith through seeker groups, I find myself wondering about those *still* searching.

What about those who are still lost? They still need to be found. And we *can* do something about these missing ones. Our calling is clear. Our mission is before us. For Christ's love compels us to proclaim what we know to be true. Let's not forget those who will respond to our outstretched hands of friendship. Let's not neglect those who will accept our invitations to visit our seeker groups. Reach out and see what God will do through you. Take some risks and make the effort. Even if only one seeker responds, it'll be worth it all.

One of the greatest allegories ever written is *Pilgrim's Progress.* It has been printed, translated, and read more than any other book outside of the Bible. This world classic, written by John Bunyan, describes the spiritual quest of a pilgrim — an "ordinary everyman" — a seeker. Its broad appeal spans across cultural, generational, and intellectual lines. Perhaps the reason for the book's sweeping interest is that in some sense we are *all* spiritual pilgrims. All of us are at different points along the way. Some are further along the journey than others. Some have placed their trust in Christ, but many others have yet to cross the line of faith. It's these pilgrims — the ones just starting out on their spiritual journey — who have my special attention. They are the ones who have my concern. An old song, written by Chuck Girard, captures my heart's cry for these spiritual pilgrims. Maybe it will resonate with you too.

## Little Pilgrim

Little Pilgrim, walkin' down the road of life
I know that deep down in your heart that you are just
    like me
What you're seekin' is a better way
And you're reaching out for temporary resting places
And you're glad to find a little peace of mind here and
    there
But it won't last no, no, 'cause you'll have to move
    along someday

'Til you're resting in the arms of the only One who can
   help you
'Til you give your heart and your soul and your body
   and your mind and your life to the Lord
And it's a glad thing to realize
That you're not alone no more
That you found your way back home
Back home.[3]

Seeker small groups are all about providing a safe place to show pilgrims the way home. As Romans 10:13–15 reminds us, it's our unspeakable privilege. I am hoping and praying with everything in me that God will call *you* to form a small group for those yet to find Christ.

> Everyone who calls on the name of the Lord will be saved. How, then, can they call on the one they have not believed in? And how can they believe in the one of whom they have not heard? And how can they hear without someone preaching to them? And how can they preach unless they are sent? As it is written, "How beautiful are the feet of those who bring good news!"

# FRANKI ANGLIN'S STORY

### Auto Mechanic
### Norman, Oklahoma

*I* *remember going to my very first seeker group meeting. Driving a beat up black '74 Chevy pick-up straight from my job at an auto body shop, I was dirty and sweaty. I imagined they'd think twice about opening up their home to me. Once I arrived, I sat in my truck for what seemed like forever, trying to get up the courage to go inside.*

*I sat there thinking about my years growing up far from God. My family didn't go to church, and we never talked about anything religious. We celebrated Christmas and Easter without ever considering the meaning behind those holidays. For us, it was all about presents and family gatherings, not about Jesus. I'd had a few "run-ins" with angry, judgmental Christians — a complete turn off — so I wondered what kinds of Christians were waiting for me inside.*

*Recently, my children started asking me questions about God, heaven and hell, and death. I didn't know what to tell them, so I assumed the answers could be found in church. Unfortunately, after visiting several churches, I realized that most Christians don't welcome questions from skeptics like me. So I decided to stop looking. What was the point? I was ready to give up when I decided to give it one last chance at one more church. This one was different. We were accepted just as we were, without judgment. So we kept coming back.*

*The idea of attending a seeker group made me a little nervous. I was worried about being rejected for what I did or did not believe. I was absolutely certain it would be boring and a waste of time. And most of all, I feared fighting off Christians intent on pushing their beliefs down my throat. Certainly they didn't want to hear my opinions or understand my questions, did they?*

*By this time, I was sure everyone inside had been watching me sit outside. And just when I had convinced myself to turn around and head home, I found myself getting out of my truck and walking up to the front door. "Okay," I thought, "I guess I can handle anything once."*

The group was nothing like what I expected. Russ and Janna live in a small duplex, and they created a warm, laid-back atmosphere. We sat in chairs or on the floor. That night Russ made it very clear he was not going to force his beliefs on us; he just wanted to make himself available to guide us in our search to find answers to our questions. He invited us to anonymously write down any spiritual questions or issues we had, and he told us that they would form the basis of any upcoming discussions. Russ was genuinely interested in each of us. He really cared about what we thought about God, the Bible, and Christianity. He even gave us Bibles to use and take home. Somehow I knew I would love being in this group.

For me, the best part of the group was exploring our questions together, without any fear of judgment. Russ was never slow in admitting he didn't know something, and even when we discussed stuff he did know, he still managed to let us draw our own conclusions. It was refreshing to meet Christians who were real people with real fears and issues — and who even wrestled with unanswered questions. One of the greatest lessons I learned was that God is a big God and he's not afraid of our tough questions. Eventually things came together for me through this seeker small group, and I gave my life to Christ. More than anything else, that small group motivated me to find my way home to the Father — right where I belong.

# MICHELLE SUTHERLIN'S STORY

### Journalist
### Norman, Oklahoma

*I*'m not sure exactly when I began my journey toward God. I do know I was constantly looking for something to bring me meaning and fulfillment, but I wasn't sure what I was really looking for. This left me wandering aimlessly.

I never went to church growing up. My parents were agnostic; we didn't talk much about the Bible or God, and we certainly never prayed. My first real church-related experience was in high school when I church-hopped with my friends to youth group meetings, mostly because of a cute guy or some cool event they were getting to do. But none of those experiences made a lasting impact on me.

Fast forward to April 19, 1995. I was twenty and completing my sophomore year at the University of Oklahoma. Just twenty minutes north of my house, the Oklahoma City federal building had been blown up. At the time, I was a reporter for our college newspaper, so I went to the scene. It was complete chaos. Something changed in me that day, and looking back, I think that's where my spiritual questions started. Why us? Why here? Why the children? Why me?

After I graduated from college, I went to work for an organization I had first learned about during the Oklahoma City bombing—the American Red Cross. Five weeks and one day into my role as the Director of Emergency Services, I faced another defining moment in my life. It was May 3, 1999, and the largest and most destructive tornado to ever hit land ripped a path through my homeland and sent me spinning into confusion. For months, I had been declining invitations from my boss and friend, Kristin, to attend church. Desperate and confused, I decided this was the time to go with her.

To my surprise, I loved the church services, but I still felt somewhat out of place. I had zero Bible knowledge and it seemed like everyone knew way more than I did. One Sunday, a church leader named Russ talked to me about the seeker group he was leading. He said it was for people who had questions about God and the Bible—and that it would be nonthreatening. He assured me that there would be lots of people there just like me.

Taking yet another step in my spiritual journey, I went to the seeker small group. I decided to open up, and God's reward was a room full of loving people who never made me feel inferior. During our discussions, I began to make discoveries and started to get my questions answered. Each time we met, I never wanted the group to end. And lots of times, I hung out afterward and talked with the apprentice leaders, Donna and David, about my thoughts. I also spent the week between meetings reading the Bible — and actually understanding it. Much to my surprise, I even began to pray on a regular basis.

While I was learning about God and the Bible, I also got to know some Christians — and I watched them carefully. My perception had always been that Christians were pushy, arrogant, and hypocritical. But the Christians in my group were so — human. They never claimed to be perfect. In fact, they were open and honest about their flaws and, as a result, earned my respect and admiration.

Even though I thought about it a lot, I never felt like it was the right time for me to cross the line of faith. But finally, after three months with the group, I decided to give my heart and life to Christ. I let go and prayed for forgiveness with Donna and Kristin. It was only then that I realized I had found what I had been looking for all this time. My search had finally come to an end — and it was wonderful!

A lot has happened since taking that life-changing step. My deepest passion in life now is to see lost souls find what I found — a true relationship with God through Christ. I believe God is calling me to help others who find themselves in a similar situation. I want to show seekers how incredible he is and the difference he's made in my life. I am a member of our evangelism ministry and I'm coleading my very own seeker small group. One of the greatest joys about that is that I'm leading it with one of the apprentices who led me to Christ!

The group interactions have been a strong spiritual boost for me. Initially, before going to the meetings, I would fear that I wouldn't know how to respond to a tough question or that I would say something that would push a spiritual seeker farther away. I spent time praying that God would take control of the group and have it go just the way he wanted.

Recently, I brought my one-year-old son, Ryan, to the group until Brad, my husband of five years, could come and get him. Brad, still a seeker himself, wasn't interested in going to my seeker group; he'd told me so more than once. But, that night my coleader invited him to stay. I knew he wouldn't. No way. But God's plan was much different from mine. Brad accepted! And not only that, he participated! And he really opened up. Right before my eyes, he took a step closer toward Christ.

It's moments like these, when I see things begin to click for seekers, that my fire keeps burning bright. I know not everyone crosses the line of faith when we want it to happen — it's in God's time. But I've been amazed to come across so many others who, just like me, eventually found Christ through a seeker small group. I don't know where I would be today if it were not for my seeker group. I guess I'd still be wandering.

# KIM AND TODD BOWEN'S STORY

*Teacher and Contractor*
*Lake in the Hills, Illinois*

*E*ven though I grew up in a religious home, deep in my spirit I sensed that something was missing in my life and was determined to find out what it was. So when our next-door neighbor offered to lead an informal Bible study twice a month, my husband, Todd, and I jumped at the chance to participate. We even agreed to host the meetings in our home.

Our group sessions were always informative and interesting. We all felt comfortable to be ourselves without any pretenses. And every opinion counted. That was probably the one thing that made the biggest impact on us — we felt heard and understood, without any judgment or coercion. It wasn't long after we launched our neighborhood Bible study that I knew that what I had been really looking for was Jesus; but I couldn't quite figure out how to settle things and make him my own personal savior.

Over a period of weeks I diligently read the Bible. I looked up every reference I could possibly find about being saved or born again. Between what I read on my own and what I learned from our group discussions, I finally realized that Jesus died on my behalf and all I needed to do was to simply accept the gift of forgiveness and new life from him. It was the hardest easiest decision I have ever made. It was just amazing.

The small group discussions were a real eye-opener for me because I discovered for the first time that the things I had previously believed had nothing to do with the reality of the Bible. But now I realize that the truths in the Bible provide me with a powerful guidebook for everyday living. Accepting Jesus as my personal savior has given me the internal fulfillment I had long been looking for. And I know that no matter what happens in my life, I just need to look to Jesus because he is all I need.

Todd's journey has been a little different than mine. He's got a few more questions and needs more time to figure things out for himself. I admire him for not just blindly believing in things without exploring them carefully. While he's very supportive of my spiritual journey and the decisions I've made, he's just not there yet. Todd explains it this way, "Our small group discussions got me to think about spiritual issues in ways I've never done before. They were interesting and helpful, but I'm still really just starting out. The one thing that most motivates me to keep searching, though, is my deep love for my wife and daughters. When this life is all over, I just want to make sure I wind up spending eternity in the same place with them!"

When our group decided to draw to a close, I wasn't ready for it to end. I was still hungry for more! So I asked a few women in the neighborhood if they would be interested in joining me for a summer Bible study. Even though I had never led a small group before, I was motivated to learn the ropes as I went. And besides, I was hoping and praying my friends would discover the joy and fulfillment that I had found in Jesus!

What I thought was going to be a few short weeks of meetings turned into a wonderful five-month journey into a deeper understanding of who we are and how we fit into God's plan. Through our combined efforts, we explored the Bible. Together we studied and together we grew. Our discussions were open and honest without any fear or embarrassment. And we looked for ways to apply what we learned to our own lives. The four women who started the Bible study in July were not the same women when the Bible study ended in December — our lives have been forever changed.

# Epilogue

*I pray that you may be active in sharing your faith, so that you will have a full understanding of every good thing we have in Christ.*

PHILEMON 6

*These young people are about their Father's business. They are carving a tunnel of hope through the great mountain of despair. Keep this movement going. Keep this movement rolling. In spite of the difficulties, keep climbing, keep moving. If you can't fly, run; if you can't run, walk; if you can't walk, crawl; but by all means, keep moving.*

THE REVEREND
MARTIN LUTHER KING JR.

*I consider my life worth nothing to me, if only I may finish the race and complete the task the Lord Jesus has given me—the task of testifying to the gospel of God's grace.*

ACTS 20:24

It was over ten years ago, but I remember the encounter as though it happened yesterday. Walking briskly through the crowded Willow Creek atrium, I was running late for a meeting before the start of a New Community service. Out of the corner of my eye I caught a glimpse of an older-looking man who was making a beeline for me. If I stopped, I'd be late, so my immediate reaction was to dodge him.

But he was on a mission — that was apparent from his steady stride — and in spite of my rush, I found myself slowing down for him. "Hey, you're Garry, right?" I turned to face him and resisted the urge to look at my watch. I nodded. "Yes, that's right. What's up?"

"Let me introduce myself. I'm Paul Mylander." He shook my hand and I was surprised that after demonstrating such resolve to track me down, he suddenly seemed more reserved. "I, um, read in the bulletin that you're teaching a workshop on how to lead a seeker small group, and I was wondering if maybe my wife and I could come — that is, if it's not too late."

Paul went on to explain that he and his wife, Nancy, had become Christians fairly recently and had tried unsuccessfully to find a small group in the Niles, Illinois, area — about a 30-minute drive from the church. They already came for weekend and midweek services, so they were hoping they wouldn't have to make the trip a third time each week just to be a part of a group. "I was thinking I could just go ahead and start one up myself," he continued. "Since your training class is designed to help people lead *seeker* groups, it's only fair that I tell you up front that's not an option for us — we will only lead a *believer* group. But I figure your training will prepare me just in case a seeker comes by mistake."

Hesitantly, Paul was considering leadership more out of necessity than giftedness. He wasn't a born leader, but I sensed even in that brief interaction that he had a teachable heart and a humble spirit — essential ingredients for someone wanting to lead. And even though Paul didn't have the gift of evangelism — and wasn't even intent on pursuing seekers — he did express a concern for lost people.

"Paul, it's no problem at all," I assured him. "It's not too late and you're welcome to come, so why don't you and your wife start the training this week and we'll see what happens!"

They showed up early for the first training session, but Nancy was intimidated and fearful about this whole seeker business. I remember her words well: "The only reason I'm here is because Paul dragged me. I'm not wired for evangelism and can't ever imagine doing this, so I'll support him and no more. Besides, he's my ride home."

She worried that she wouldn't have any idea how to interact with non-Christians — let alone answer their questions. "Oh and one more thing," she added, "I'm not interested in going through the class — I won't be needing it — so I'll just wait for Paul outside in the hallway." I did my best to persuade her otherwise, but sure enough, she sat patiently on a couch outside the door of our training room, determined never to set foot in our sessions.

The next week I welcomed them back to the class and reminded Nancy, "Seriously, you don't have to sit outside the room. Why don't you come in? I promise I won't make you say one word. You can just sit quietly and listen." She surprised me the third week when she dragged a chair to the back of the room. "The couch out there is occupied tonight, so I guess I'll *have* to sit in here," she explained. She declined my offer to join the rest of us in our circle — but at least she was in the room!

The following week the group had convinced her to pull her chair closer to the rest of us. Gradually, she took part in the discussions, and by the sixth week, she and Paul were actually showing some excitement about the possibility of including seekers in their group! Once reluctant participants, Paul and Nancy now had an enthusiastic *spark* in their eyes — the same one I've seen in others many times before and since — and they were well on their way to becoming passionate seeker group leaders.

Once the training sessions concluded, Paul began identifying seekers in the Niles area. He compiled a list of about thirty names — mostly from interest forms people had filled out at the church. Paul called each one, and twelve said they were interested in coming to the group.

"I scheduled our first meeting at our home on a Friday night to coincide with one of the Chicago Bulls championship games," Paul admits. "I figured that if the Bulls won, that would give our group a good start! Nancy prepared all kinds of refreshments and then we waited. And waited. Finally, the phone rang. It was my apprentice. He explained that his dog bit him and he was on the way to the hospital. Undeterred, we went back to waiting. Surely the others would come. It was a long wait — nobody showed up. We snacked alone. We were so disappointed that we barely had the courage to pray about whether to give it one more shot. We decided to swallow our pride and call everyone back to ask about the best time to meet — based on *their* availability, not ours. We set it up for a night when the Bulls were *not* playing — and people showed up — all twelve of them!"

Paul laughs whenever he thinks back to that first meeting. "In spite of the training sessions, Nancy and I made several mistakes," he recalls. "In fact, after the opening icebreakers that night, I inadvertently put everyone on the spot by asking straight out how many of them thought they were Christians (not exactly the most seeker-sensitive question!). They all raised their hands. Then, not knowing how to interpret that response, I awkwardly asked each of them to share their testimonies (another big goof!). They had no idea what in the world I was talking about. Thankfully, my apprentice came to the rescue and briefly shared his story about how he gave his life to Christ."

At that point, one young woman named Ann raised her hand and said, "After hearing his story, I have to be honest and take back what I said earlier. I can see now that I'm not really a Christian — at least not by his definition." Then one by one, the group members clarified themselves. As it turned out, except for one, *none* of them were Christians! So Paul's blunder had a bright side in that he found out the exact spiritual status of each person in the group. For better or for worse, he and Nancy were at that moment officially leaders of a *seeker* small group.

The power of Paul and Nancy's leadership, once under way, was that they were a couple that genuinely loved and nurtured seekers. They could easily relate to a wide range of people, taking anyone under their wings: younger people looked up to them as parental figures and older people trusted them as peers. Seekers were precious to them — and everyone knew it.

Whenever Paul or Nancy spotted someone sitting alone in the church atrium, one of them would go over and invite the person into their group. "We had people from all walks of life. There were motorcycle guys with long beards and people in wheelchairs. We welcomed business types and others who were out of work," explained Paul. "We didn't like seeing anyone sitting there by themselves, so we'd just say, 'Why don't you join us?' Then we'd extend a warm hand of friendship and hang out together. When they began asking spiritual questions, we'd say, 'You're raising some great issues. Well, keep them coming! You can even join our seeker group too, if you like!' And many of them did."

It's risky and even a little scary to start a seeker small group — it could be a set up for rejection. In spite of all the risks, Paul and Nancy overcame their fears and launched a group. And God honored their efforts by using them to impact lives for eternity. Everyone from that first group made decisions for Christ, and today many of them are leaders in various ministries at Willow Creek. Some are even leading their own seeker groups. But that's not all. Over the next ten years Paul and Nancy led group after group — and had the privilege of watching more than fifty seekers accept Christ.

Their passion for seekers seemed to grow with each new group they started. It seemed like every time I walked through the atrium after a service, Paul and Nancy would be there with twenty to thirty people — former or current members of their groups — crowded around them, talking, laughing, hugging, and sometimes shedding a few tears. The Mylanders were affectionately known as "seeker magnets," full of an endless supply of sincere love for all those God brought into their lives.

Recently, I sat down in the atrium with Paul to reminisce and celebrate all that God had done in and through their lives. Nancy lost a painful battle with cancer last year, but she left behind a loving legacy, with countless people paying tribute to the great things God had done through her. Nancy always claimed that she just supported Paul and supplied refreshments, but she did much, much more. She would embrace people who were hurting and listen hours on end to their problems. Once Nancy realized how her gifts of hospitality and encouragement could be used within the context of a seeker small group, she caught the vision for reaching out to lost people. "She became such a caring, loving listener," Paul explains. "And she was so much more effective than I. She knew how to draw people out and yet make them feel comfortable. She had such a big heart for seekers, and everyone was drawn to her."

My dear friends didn't start out with a lot of knowledge or experience. They had no apologetics training on how to intellectually defend the faith. Instead, they had a growing passion for pointing lost people to the Lord and simply made themselves available. Paul and Nancy are proof that *anyone* can lead a seeker small group.

Paul says, "In spite of mistakes and blunders, God uses people who are willing and available — even those who may feel hesitant and fearful — to reach seekers. I went into the original training with nothing. I wasn't qualified to lead, but we prayed to see where God would take us. And God gave us opportunities. I don't have any smarts. I think of myself as uneducated, but that's okay. God can use an ordinary, down-to-earth person like me, and he gives me all I need to serve him."

Just as I was reminding Paul of the time we first met, he stopped me with his smile. "If ever there was an unlikely pair to lead a small group of seekers, it was Nancy and me," he said with a twinkle in his eye. "Yet God did something amazing — and no one was more surprised than us."

## The Dream

The one message I most want to convey throughout the pages of this book is this: *You* can lead a seeker small group! My hope and prayer is that *every single person* who reads this book will be inspired and motivated and equipped to actually start a seeker group. That's the dream I have. It's something *anyone* can do. Are you a pastor, staff member, or volunteer within a church or ministry? *You* can do this. Do you have neighbors, classmates, coworkers, or teammates? *You* can launch a seeker group.

If you're tempted to conclude that this is a great idea for others but not something you could ever see yourself doing — stop right there! Some of the best seeker group leaders I know started out with similar doubts. They lacked experience, expertise, and evangelism gifts — and yet God chose to powerfully use them to impact seekers for eternity. What made the difference? One word: availability. They prayed, "Here am I, Lord, wholly available. Use me." And when they prayerfully took that risky step, God met them there — and that made all the difference in the world. Just think what God could do through you. Imagine the possibilities. I am.

Throughout the process of writing this book, I've prayed more than anything else that *you* would someday experience the thrill and wonderment of sharing the life-changing message of Christ in the context of a seeker small group. I know you realize the awesome privilege it is to explain the gospel to others. Paul's words in

2 Corinthians 5:20 clearly describe our mission and our message, "We are therefore Christ's ambassadors, as though God were making his appeal through us. We implore you on Christ's behalf: Be reconciled to God." It's a powerful message of love and hope — and nothing compares to it. And when you gather a small group filled with seekers, it will only be a matter of time before you'll give them a chance to discuss it, understand it, and embrace it. Don't let that opportunity slip by.

Last year, I stumbled across a song on Fernando Ortega's CD *Storm* that captures the compelling message we're called to proclaim. It's titled "Come, Ye Sinners, Poor and Needy," and I've listened to it a thousand times since. The words written by Joseph Hart, sung by Fernando Ortega and Amy Grant, rang through my mind and heart as I wrote each chapter of this book. Every time I reflect on the lyrics, my passion to engage spiritual seekers in life-changing discussions is renewed and reinforced. Who knows, it just might do the same in you.

## Come, Ye Sinners, Poor and Needy

Come, ye sinners, poor and needy.
Weak and wounded, sick and sore.
Jesus ready, stands to save you.
Full of pity, love and power.

I will arise and go to Jesus,
He will embrace me in his arms.
In the arms of my dear Savior,
O there are ten thousand charms.

Come, ye thirsty, come and welcome.
God's free bounty glorify.
True belief and true repentance.
Every grace that brings you nigh.

Come ye, weary, heavy-laden.
Lost and ruined by the fall.
If you tarry 'til you're better.
You will never come at all.

I will arise and go to Jesus,
He will embrace me in his arms.
In the arms of my dear Savior,
O there are ten thousand charms.

View him prostrate in the garden.
On the ground your maker lies.
On the bloody tree behold him
Sinner will this not suffice?

Lo! The incarnate God ascended.
Pleads the merit of his blood.
Venture on him venture wholly.
Let no other trust intrude.

I will arise and go to Jesus,
He will embrace me in his arms.
In the arms of my dear Savior,
O there are ten thousand charms.[1]

May these words reflect the loving invitation we extend to spiritual seekers everywhere to arise with us and go to Jesus.

# JOE KESSLER'S STORY

### Student
### Deerfield, Illinois

*Even though I was raised going to church, I had drifted very far from God — to the point of being hostile at the very mention of him. I was an atheist, convinced that if God existed at all then he must be distant, or even cruel. I would point out to my friends that God was only a "crutch" constructed by the weak-minded to help them get through the hardships of life they could not handle on their own.*

*Seeking to fill the emptiness in my life, I enrolled in a multitude of philosophy courses to try to bring meaning to the world around me — which seemed purposeless. I thought I could arrive at the truth through pure reason, but I didn't know where to start. My faith in reason was unquestioned, and I really believed I would find some answers there. So I studied the philosophies of many men who were long since dead, and listened to the perspectives of various professors. After awhile I became disheartened when I realized that, despite all my hopes, philosophy held none of the answers I had craved. The medieval and ancient philosophers simply chronicled their own journeys, and, like me, never found what they were seeking. I eventually came to understand that pure reason is only half the recipe, but I completely ignored the most important ingredient — faith.*

*A few years ago, my wife and I were driving by the Willow Creek campus and decided to attend a weekend service. I'm not sure why we went, but I know we were both looking for some spiritual truth. We remained skeptical, but interested. We even joined a seeker small group. We met nearly every week for a couple of years. Even though the discussions were sometimes heated, they were always sincere. The kindness and compassion of Paul and Nancy, our small group leaders, melted us. They convinced me that Christians were not as weak as I had previously assumed, but rather were strong because of the firm foundation they had in God. I wanted to have that kind of inner spiritual strength and peace. Over time, I found myself understanding the Bible, and even defended it sometimes! I'm not sure precisely the moment I became a believer, but it was clear to me that at some point a major change had occurred. I had placed my faith and trust completely in Christ. My love for the Lord has deepened to the point where his very name makes me buckle. When I remember how it used to make me so angry, I know a miracle has occurred in me. The Lord has changed me from within — and he's made my life a living testimony to his grace, mercy, and power.*

*Reflecting on my journey makes me appreciate what God has done for me. He sent his only son to pay for my sins and gave me the grace to look past my anger and accept his gift. For that reason alone, I love God with all my heart. I now pray daily that the Lord will use my life for his glory. Now I am a seminary student learning all I can to further my walk with Christ. Through the Lord, I am finding out who I really am, and with each passing day, I realize more profoundly how much he means to me. The Lord is everything to me, and in everything I now see the Lord.*

# ANNE DYER'S STORY

### Elementary School Teacher
### Niles, Illinois

*F*or me, church had almost always been an empty routine obligation. What most disturbed me was feeling "holy" for only one hour while in church, but then feeling life returning to "normal" the moment I stepped back outside the church doors. I wanted the church services to be practical so I could actually apply what I learned there to my life. I remember thinking, "There has got to be more to faith than going to church once a week, and I am going to find out what that is." I began visiting another church with a couple of close friends of mine. There, I filled out a form from the bulletin to get more information about seeker groups. I really thought I was a believer at the time, because I had grown up attending church. But I signed up for this group because I wanted to learn more about my faith.

A short time later, I got a call from a Paul and Nancy who invited me and others who had expressed interest in a small group to a party in their home. Even though I lived close by, I decided not to go. I had too many hesitations, including our age difference. They sounded a lot older than me, and I, in my mid-twenties, was more interested in hanging out with peers my own age. I just was not sure what I was getting myself into. However, they persisted, and after a second invitation to join their group, I decided to go.

I remember the very first group meeting really well. Paul and Nancy were there, along with several people I had never met. I was a little nervous as we went around the circle and told a little about ourselves, and where we were on our spiritual journeys. I expressed that I thought I was a Christian, but as I listened to each person share, it began to dawn on me that maybe I wasn't really one after all. Maybe I was really a seeker! This was kind of a frightening realization, because suddenly I had no foundation to stand on. Everything I had grown up believing began to crumble in my mind at that first meeting. I felt like crying.

Paul told me later he was impressed that I had the courage to admit that I came to the group thinking one way but quickly began to understand things differently. His words were a real comfort to me, and gave me the reassurance I needed to feel comfortable about being open and honest in the group meetings.

There were several things that kept me coming back to the group. First, I felt accepted and loved unconditionally. I felt understood and known, and that meant a lot to me. There was also the thrill and excitement of making progress in my own spiritual journey. I knew this was exactly where I wanted to be. But something that really stood out to me was the caring community I was experiencing. That was very fulfilling and was something I had never known before.

Paul and Nancy became like spiritual parents to me. I didn't realize this until later, but now I have a visual image of them taking me under their wings, showing me the way. They were very loving right from the start. The patience they demonstrated made me feel accepted for who I was and where I was in my journey at any given time. Sometimes, after the discussions were over, a few others and I would stay late into the night and talk. I always felt very comfortable expressing my doubts and questions. They were a great team: Paul often challenged me to take steps in my faith while Nancy affirmed me as I took all the time I needed.

Some days I thought I was ready to become a Christian; other days I was uncertain. During that time I was growing spiritually but had not yet made an ultimate decision for Jesus Christ. A friend once pointed out to me that "riding the fence" and not making a decision either way is the worst place to be, and looking back I'd have to say I agree. But after staying in that little group for two years, I finally decided that Jesus Christ was what I needed and wanted.

When I called Nancy and told her about my decision, I learned that Paul was in the hospital with a stroke. Although I was a little worried that it might be too much for him to handle, we decided to go and tell him the good news anyway. A few others from our group went with us. Nancy whispered to Paul, "Anne has some great news!" When I told Paul what happened, he said that it was the best news I could have ever told him. It felt like a big celebration right there in that hospital room. We all joined hands and prayed together. In that moment, I had this overwhelming sense of love and belonging; this little group had somehow become like a family to me.

*My decision to ask Jesus to be my Savior has been the most important decision in my life. No longer do I have the hopeless, empty feeling of being "holy" for only one hour each week. Instead, Christ has come into my life in a strong and very real way. I now know Jesus through a personal relationship with him on a daily basis and my life is forever changed. I am married to a godly man who leads a Christian ministry, and together we work to help the world's poor. As I look at my faith today, I cannot imagine how I ever lived my life without Jesus at its center. And it all began with a seeker small group.*

# Appendix A

# Sample Lesson 1

*

## The First Seeker Small Group Meeting

**The Setting**

The leader and apprentice leader arrive early to prepare and pray.

Comfortable chairs are arranged so everyone will be able to see each other.

Room temperature is comfortable.

Potential distractions are removed.

The leader and apprentice warmly greet people as they arrive.

**Welcome** (1 Minute)

"I'd like to welcome all of you here. It's so good to see you. Thanks for coming. You can look forward to having a relaxed and fun time getting to know each other and discussing spiritual issues together. Just so you know, I'm planning to end our discussion time in an hour and fifteen minutes, so you don't have to worry about the time getting away from us."

**Introductions** (9 Minutes)

"Besides discussing spiritual matters from the Bible, we also want to enjoy getting to know each other a little bit. So let's go around the room and take a minute or two each to share our names, where we live, our occupations, and a favorite hobby." (Leader starts.)

**Icebreaker 1** (10 Minutes)

"Tonight I brought along a book called *The Complete Book of Questions,* which is filled with lots of good basic questions to help us get to know each other. The first one hundred questions are general, lighthearted ones from the section called 'Light and Easy.' I thought it would be fun to go around and each pick a question numbered between one and one hundred to answer. So who would like to go first? Any brave persons here today?"

(Hand the book to the person who chooses a number and invite the individual to read the question aloud and answer it in a minute or less. Then pass the book to the next person, who volunteers to pick a number, read the question, and answer it. If someone prefers, let him or her select a question that was previously chosen. This continues until everyone gets a chance to answer a question.)

## Icebreaker 2 (10 Minutes)

"Now let's try some of the questions from the next section. It's called 'Personal Profile.' The questions are similar to the ones we just answered but geared more toward basic information about us. These are questions numbered one hundred and one to two hundred. So let's choose these just like we did before: The first person will select a number, read the question aloud, and answer it. Then the next person can either answer one of the questions we've already used or pick another number and answer that question. Remember to take only a minute or less for each answer."

## Transition Icebreaker (20 Minutes)

"Now here's a question I would like to throw out to everyone in the group to answer if you feel comfortable doing so. It's a question of a deeper spiritual nature, so we'll just go in random order. Don't feel like you have to answer if you don't want to share. The question goes like this: 'If you could ask God one question you knew he would answer right away, what would it be?' I'll start and someone else can take a turn after me."

(This is a good opportunity to invite people to give the reasons behind their responses. Be sure to give lots of affirmation to the people who share, and ask the group for permission to write down their responses.)

## Scripture (5 Minutes)

"Before we wrap things up, I'd like to read a short passage of Scripture from the Bible. It's found in the New Testament: 'This is how God showed his love among us: He sent his one and only Son into the world that we might live through him. This is love: not that we loved God, but that he loved us and sent his Son as an atoning sacrifice for our sins. Dear friends, since God so loved us, we also ought to love one another' (1 John 4:9–11)."

(After reading the Scripture, invite the group to quickly share their initial impressions. This gives them an opportunity to experience discussing a passage of Scripture in your group.)

"I'd like to hear your knee-jerk reaction. I'd be interested in getting your thoughts about what this passage might mean or just simply learning how you react to it."

## Conclusion (5 Minutes)

"Well, I'd like to bring things to a close by thanking all of you for your participation. It was good to hear each other's responses. Now, there are a couple of things I want to ask you. Each of you were invited to come here just one time to sort of check things out. I was wondering if this is something that you would enjoy doing again on a regular basis. Can we talk about it and decide as a group if we would like to meet again? If we choose to meet again, then we should decide when we would meet and whether we'd want to try meeting every other week for a couple of times, or once a week for a month, or what. And after we experience three or four meetings, we could evaluate again as to what we want to do from there. Something I would be willing to do, if you wanted, is to take those questions you posed for God today and prepare discussion questions and select verses from the Bible that relate, so we could then cover those issues we've all come up with. We could discuss one of our questions each time we got together. In any case let's try to decide as a group what we want to do. What do you think?"

(Give the group the freedom to choose what they want to do. If they agree to meet again, proceed in the following manner.)

"Well, I'm excited about meeting again. There are a couple of things I'd like to encourage you to do. First, feel free to invite any friends you think might enjoy participating with us in these discussions. I'd like the group to be open to newcomers anytime we meet. Is this agreeable? Second, if for some reason you're unable to make it to a meeting, could you let me know? Because these meetings tend to build on each other in terms of what we learn spiritually and in terms of getting to know each other better, it's important for everyone to be here each time we meet. So let me know if you can't attend, and I can pass the word on to everyone so we'll all know what's up."

(The leader should be sure to give his or her name and contact information to everyone.)

## Optional Closing Prayer (1 Minute)

"How about if I close now with a short prayer? Thanks again for coming. It was great to have you here." (Leader prays.)

# Appendix B

# Sample Lesson 2

✦

From the Tough Questions Series guide *How Does Anyone Know God Exists?* Discussion 5: "Does God Care What Happens to Us?"

*1. Transition Icebreaker:* Describe a situation in which you misplaced or lost something very valuable. What did you do? How did that loss make you feel? How did you react when you finally discovered the valuable for which you were looking? (If you never did find it, how did you react when you finally realized it was gone forever?)

*2. Reflection Question:* To what extent do you feel God cares about you and your life? Explain.

## The Lost Sheep

One of the ways Jesus taught was to use interesting stories (called parables) that drove home a strong point. Look at the following story:

> Now the tax collectors and "sinners" were all gathering around to hear him. But the Pharisees and the teachers of the law muttered, "This man welcomes sinners and eats with them." Then Jesus told them this parable: "Suppose one of you has a hundred sheep and loses one of them. Does he not leave the ninety-nine in the open country and go after the lost sheep until he finds it? And when he finds it, he joyfully puts it on his shoulders and goes home. Then he calls his friends and neighbors together and says, 'Rejoice with me; I have found my lost sheep.' I tell you that in the same way there will be more rejoicing in heaven over one sinner who repents than over ninety-nine righteous persons who do not need to repent."
>
> LUKE 15:1–7

*3. Observation Question:* What attitude is Jesus responding to when he begins to tell this parable?

## The Lost Coin

Jesus then told the following parable.

*Suppose a woman has ten silver coins and loses one. Does she not light a lamp, sweep the house and search carefully until she finds it? And when she finds it, she calls her friends and neighbors together and says, "Rejoice with me; I have found my lost coin." In the same way, I tell you, there is rejoicing in the presence of the angels of God over one sinner who repents.*

LUKE 15:8–10

*4. Interpretation Question:* Do you suppose this woman was greedy? What additional motive could have been behind her frantic search?

## The Lost Son

Jesus continued.

*There was a man who had two sons. The younger one said to his father, "Father, give me my share of the estate." So he divided his property between them.*

*Not long after that, the younger son got together all he had, set off for a distant country and there squandered his wealth in wild living. After he had spent everything, there was a severe famine in that whole country, and he began to be in need. So he went and hired himself out to a citizen of that country, who sent him to his fields to feed pigs. He longed to fill his stomach with the pods that the pigs were eating, but no one gave him anything.*

*When he came to his senses, he said, "How many of my father's hired men have food to spare, and here I am starving to death! I will set out and go back to my father and say to him: Father, I have sinned against heaven and against you. I am no longer worthy to be called your son; make me like one of your hired men." So he got up and went to his father.*

*But while he was still a long way off, his father saw him and was filled with compassion for him; he ran to his son, threw his arms around him and kissed him.*

*The son said to him, "Father, I have sinned against heaven and against you. I am no longer worthy to be called your son."*

*But the father said to his servants, "Quick! Bring the best robe and put it on him. Put a ring on his finger and sandals on his feet. Bring the fattened calf and kill it. Let's have a feast and celebrate. For this son of mine was dead and is alive again; he was lost and is found." So they began to celebrate.*

LUKE 15:11–24

*5. Interpretation Questions:* The two main elements in each parable symbolize the same two things. What is the common thread that binds these parables together? In other words, what do you suppose the two main elements in each parable represent?

- Parable 1 elements: shepherd and sheep
- Parable 2 elements: woman and coins
- Parable 3 elements: father and son

A. The first element (shepherd, woman, and father) represents

_____.

B. The second element (sheep, coins, and son) represents

_____.

6. *Observation Question:* Describe the reaction common to all three stories when the missing valuable was finally found.

7. *Observation Question:* According to Jesus, what do these three stories teach concerning how much God values lost people? *Interpretation Question:* How then would you suppose God reacts when lost people come to him?

8. *Interpretation Questions:* Think back to your description of how you felt when you lost something very valuable. How does your reaction in that situation compare with how God must feel toward those who are not yet part of his family?

9. *Reflection Question:* How do you feel about the idea that God hosts a heavenly celebration when a single person like you comes to him and is found?

10. *Reflection Question:* Read Matthew 6:25–26 and Matthew 10:29–31. What points in these verses are easy for you to accept? What points are difficult for you to agree with?

11. *Reflection Question:* How difficult is it for you to really sense God's love for you personally? What factors influence this ability? Describe times in your life when you have felt loved by God.

12. *Application Question:* What would God need to do in order for you to feel loved by him? What is your understanding of what he has done already?

13. *Application Question:* On a scale from one to ten, place an X near the spot and phrase that best describes you. Share your selection with the rest of the group and give reasons for placing your X where you did.

| 1 | 2 | 3 | 4 | 5 | 6 | 7 | 8 | 9 | 10 |
|---|---|---|---|---|---|---|---|---|---|

I don't think God really cares about people.     I'm uncertain about how much or little God cares about people.     I'm certain that God loves me.

# Appendix C

# Sample Lesson 3

＊

From the Tough Questions Series guide *Why Become a Christian?* Discussion 2: "What's the Big Deal About Sin?"

*1. Transition Icebreaker:* Do you think Christianity dwells too much on the negative because of its apparent emphasis on sin, hell, and judgment? Explain your answer.

*2. Observation Question:* According to your understanding of the Bible, what separates people from God: a propensity to sin, a lack of knowledge about God, or both? Explain your answer.

*3. Observation Question:* Do you believe that people are, for the most part, basically good, basically bad, or somewhere in between? Explain.

*4. Observation Question:* How would you define sin? What are the repercussions of sin, if any?

## The Sin Problem

Several verses in the Bible point to the severity of the sin problem:

> All have sinned and fall short of the glory of God.
>
> ROMANS 3:23

> The wages of sin is death, but the gift of God is eternal life in Christ Jesus our Lord.
>
> ROMANS 6:23

> As for you, you were dead in your transgressions and sins, in which you used to live when you followed the ways of this world.
>
> EPHESIANS 2:1

> Your iniquities have separated you from your God; your sins have hidden his face from you, so that he will not hear.
>
> ISAIAH 59:2

*5. Reflection Question:* How do you respond to the biblical claim above that the sin in your life is so offensive to God that it has spiritually separated you from him?

*6. Interpretation Questions:* The Bible also teaches that the penalty of sin is spiritual death. What do you suppose it means to be spiritually dead?

*7. Interpretation Questions:* Do you think it is possible to be indifferent or neutral toward God without necessarily being antagonistic or hostile toward him? Why or why not?

*8. Interpretation Question:* The Bible teaches that our sin causes us to become God's enemies (read Romans 5:10) and that we are then alienated from him (read Colossians 1:21). How might people who appear to be indifferent or neutral toward God really be his enemies?

*9. Interpretation Question:* In what sense is God the one seeking us first, before we seek after him?

## A Swim Contest

Imagine that everyone in the world lined up and down the coast of California for a contest to see who could swim all the way to the Hawaiian Islands. At the sound of the gun, everyone jumped into the ocean. Some really great swimmers would go quite far, others would get tired after only a short distance, and still others would barely make it off the shore. But one thing is for sure: the end result is the same for everyone — not one person would be able to swim the entire distance to Hawaii. Everyone would drown.

No amount of preparation or practice would make much difference in the final outcome. Swimming lessons from an expert instructor or the Swimmer's Ten Commandments would be of little value. Only a rescue operation could provide the assistance necessary to cover such a great distance. In a similar way, the distance — due to sin — between God and every one of us is very great. Some of us may appear to be better off than others, but the reality of the situation is that we all have missed the mark and no one has measured up to God's standard. No matter where we are on the "goodness" scale compared to others, we all need a rescuer.

*10. Observation Question:* How does the above illustration demonstrate that when it comes to our shortcomings before God, comparing ourselves with others seems foolish?

*11. Interpretation Questions:* Some say God rates people using a scale. He places all the good things you've done on one side of that scale, and the bad stuff on the other. Whichever side outweighs the other determines whether you are a good person or a bad person. Do you agree with this analogy? Why or why not? Evaluate the pros and cons of this rating system.

*12. Reflection Question:* Does it feel negative or scary to admit that you may have a sin problem? Why or why not?

*13. Application Question:* Do you have a tendency to minimize or maximize your sin by comparing yourself to others? Explain.

*14. Application Question:* How have you or will you deal with the sin problem that the Bible claims all of us have?

*15. Application Question:* Check the statement(s) below that best describes your position at this point. Share your selection with the rest of the group and give reasons for your response.

❏ I agree that the Bible warns about a sin problem, but I don't feel it is an issue with me.

❏ Sin is not something I want to spend my time thinking about. It is all just too negative.

❏ I think there is a difference between "sinning" and just "messing up." Sin is the big stuff. Everyone messes up.

❏ My opinion about sin and its effect on my life has changed.

❏ I think there are degrees of sin with degrees of consequences.

❏ I know that sin is something I can't overcome alone, and I would like to ask for God's help.

❏ I realize that I am a sinner, but I am unsure what I should do about it.

❏ I am overwhelmed with this lesson. How can anyone hope to ever make it if everything we do wrong separates us from God?

❏ I have a hard time believing that God views my little white lie and the terrorist attacks on September 11, 2001, the same way. It just doesn't make sense.

❏ I know that sin is a problem not only in my life but in the world also.

❏ Write your own brief phrase here:

_____

# Appendix D

# Sample Lesson 4

✦

From the Tough Questions Series guide *Don't All Religions Lead to God?* Discussion 5: "Is Jesus Really the Only Way to God?"

1. What is your immediate reaction to the claim that Jesus Christ is the only way to God? How do you suppose most people react to this claim?

2. What are some objections that come to mind concerning the claim that Jesus is the only way? Describe a path of salvation that is *not* exclusive, and that would make more sense to those troubled by the "one way" proposal.

3. Do you think the Bible specifically teaches that Jesus is the only way to God? Why? Cite a couple examples to support your answer, if you can.

4. Select one of the Bible references from the list below and put it into your own words.

> [Jesus said,] "I am the way and the truth and the life. No one comes to the Father except through me."
>
> JOHN 14:6

> Salvation is found in no one else, for there is no other name under heaven given to men by which we must be saved.
>
> ACTS 4:12

> Whoever believes in him is not condemned, but whoever does not believe stands condemned already because he has not believed in the name of God's one and only Son.
>
> JOHN 3:18

> [Jesus said,] "I told you that you would die in your sins; if you do not believe that I am the one I claim to be, you will indeed die in your sins."
>
> JOHN 8:24

*This is the testimony: God has given us eternal life, and this life is in his Son. He who has the Son has life; he who does not have the Son of God does not have the life. I write these things to you who believe in the name of the Son of God so that you may know that you have eternal life.*

1 JOHN 5:11–13

5. Based on the above list of Scripture passages, explain your reaction to the following statement: "Christianity does not claim Jesus is the only way to God."

6. Assuming Christianity does indeed assert that Jesus is the only way, what reasons might people give for viewing this claim as false?

## Three Common Objections

There are three common objections to the assertion that Jesus Christ is the only way to God:

A. About 75 percent of the world population is not Christian—how could so many people all be wrong? Far too many people do not believe in Christianity; therefore, it cannot be the only way.

B. Really nice people with good intentions do not believe in Jesus. Sincere people ought to be accepted by God on the basis of their strong convictions; therefore, Christianity cannot be the only way.

C. Christianity's claims are exclusive and narrow. Any system that's narrow-minded, limited, and bigoted is false; therefore, it cannot be the only way.

7. Each of the above objections are based on unspoken assumptions about how one determines what is true. Match each objection listed above with its corresponding assumption listed below. Explain your answer.

_____ Intensity of belief ensures truth
_____ Anything intolerant negates truth
_____ Popular opinion defines truth

## Three Assumptions Examined

Below are three assumptions commonly made about truth, each followed by a statement that directly contradicts the assumption (Ken Boa and Larry Moody, *I'm Glad You Asked*).

A. *Popular opinion defines truth.* For centuries, popular opinion stated that the earth was flat. Today, the scientific consensus is that the earth is spherical.

B. *Intensity of belief ensures truth.* Some years ago, Jim Marshall of the Minnesota Vikings picked up a fumble and fought off tacklers repeatedly until he crossed the goal line. Marshall, however, crossed the wrong goal line and scored for the wrong team.

C. *Anything intolerant negates truth.* The fact that one plus one will always equal two is very narrow, but it is also right. Landing an airplane requires some very narrow and restricted specifications. Engines that run on only unleaded fuel are very exclusive.

8. Do you think the above assumptions are still true in light of the contradicting observations? How does your answer apply to similar truths in the spiritual realm?

## Four Possible Conclusions

In his book *How to Give Away Your Faith,* Paul Little states the following challenge:

> Since you don't believe Jesus Christ was the Truth, which of the other three possibilities about Jesus Christ do you believe? There are only four possible conclusions about Jesus Christ and his claims. He was either a liar, a lunatic, a legend or the Truth. The person who doesn't believe he was the Truth must label him as a liar, a lunatic, or a legend.

9. If Jesus was not who he claimed to be (the only way to God), which of the other alternatives listed above seem most reasonable to you? Why?

10. How does concluding that there is more than one way to God make a mockery out of Christ's death?

11. If Jesus Christ really is the only way to God, what impact would wholeheartedly believing this have on our lives and relationships?

12. On a scale from 1 to 10, place an X near the spot and phrase that best describes you. Share your selection with the rest of the group and give reasons for placing your X where you did.

| 1 | 2 | 3 | 4 | 5 | 6 | 7 | 8 | 9 | 10 |
|---|---|---|---|---|---|---|---|---|---|

I believe that there are many ways to God.        I'm not sure if anyone knows if there is only one way to God.        I believe there is only one way to God.

# Appendix E

# Emotions Word List

·*·

Thrilled (delighted, excited, jubilant, ecstatic)
Glad (encouraged, happy, pleased, cheerful, joyful)
Confident (convinced, certain, hopeful, expectant, optimistic)
Enthusiastic (eager, willing, wholehearted, impassioned, energized)
Love (compassionate, adoring, fondness, passionate)
Care (sympathy, concern, protective, nurturing)
Admired (liked, applauded, appreciated, valued)
Surprised (intrigued, astonished, awed, spellbound)
Amused (pleased, silly, ridiculous)
Calm (relaxed, relieved, satisfied, peaceful, content)
Worried (tense, uneasy, nervous, panicky, distraught)
Stressed (uptight, pressured, tense, overwhelmed)
Exhausted (tired, spent, fatigued, weary, drained)
Vulnerable (defensive, exposed, helpless, threatened)
Afraid (scared, frightened, terrified, anxious)
Fear (shy, timid, hesitant, inhibited, dreading)
Ashamed (embarrassed, guilty, humiliated)
Indifferent (bored, withdrawn, isolated, apathetic, ambivalent)
Disappointed (disheartened, heartbroken)
Misled (manipulated, cheated, deceived, betrayed)
Hurt (pained, wounded, troubled, agonizing)
Sad (sorrowful, depressed, grieved, distressed, mourning)
Longing (lonely, impatient, desperate, trapped, jealous, envious)
Hopeless (helpless, resigned, despairing, depressed)
Skeptical (uncertain, doubtful, suspicious, cynical)
Dejected (discouraged, inadequate, insignificant, useless, unworthy)
Rejected (ignored, inferior, intimidated, scorned)
Offended (insulted, slighted, snubbed)
Angry (frustrated, annoyed, agitated, mad, hostile, vengeful)
Hatred (disgusted, bitter, contempt, despising, repulsed)

# Appendix F

# Sequential Recommendation for Discussion Topics

✦

Listed below is a suggested guide to help you determine the best order of topics to discuss in your seeker small group.

**1. Questions about God**
Does God exist?
What is God like?
Does God care about us?

**2. Questions about Jesus**
Who is Jesus?
Was Jesus really God?
What about the resurrection?

**3. Questions about the Bible**
Is the Bible reliable?
What about contradictions?
Is the Bible God's word?

**4. Questions about Evil and Suffering**
Where did evil come from?
Why do the innocent suffer?
Is the Devil for real?

**5. Questions about Other Religions**
Don't all religions believe the same?
How does Christianity compare?
Is Jesus the only way?

**6. Questions about Science**
Does the Bible conflict with science?
Is belief blind faith?
What about evolution?

**7. Questions about Christianity**
What's the big deal with sin?
Why is Jesus important?
How does someone become a Christian?

# Appendix G

# The Tough Questions Series

## How Does Anyone Know God Exists?

Discussion 1: Is Anybody Out There?
Discussion 2: How Can Anyone Be Sure God Exists?
Discussion 3: What Is God Really Like?
Discussion 4: How Can Rational People Believe in Miracles?
Discussion 5: Does God Care What Happens to Us?
Discussion 6: How Can a Person Get to Know God?

## What Difference Does Jesus Make?

Discussion 1: Who Was Jesus?
Discussion 2: How Is Jesus Different from Other Religious Leaders?
Discussion 3: Did Jesus Really Claim to Be God?
Discussion 4: Why Focus on Jesus' Death?
Discussion 5: Isn't the Resurrection of Jesus a Myth?
Discussion 6: What Impact Does Jesus Make Today?

## How Reliable Is the Bible?

Discussion 1: Where Did the Bible Come From?
Discussion 2: Isn't the Bible Full of Myths?
Discussion 3: What About Those Contradictions?
Discussion 4: Hasn't the Bible Changed Over Time?
Discussion 5: Why Should I Trust the Bible?
Discussion 6: Is the Bible Really God's Book?

## How Could God Allow Suffering and Evil?

Discussion 1: Where Did Evil Come From?
Discussion 2: Why Do Innocent People Suffer?
Discussion 3: Why Doesn't God Do Something?
Discussion 4: Is the Devil for Real?
Discussion 5: How Could a Loving God Send People to Hell?
Discussion 6: Is There Really a Heaven?

## Don't All Religions Lead to God?

Discussion 1: Don't All Religions Teach Basically the Same Thing?
Discussion 2: Isn't It Enough to Be Sincere?
Discussion 3: What's So Different About Christianity?
Discussion 4: Aren't Mormons and Jehovah's Witnesses Christians Too?
Discussion 5: Is Jesus Really the Only Way to God?
Discussion 6: What Happens to People Who've Never Heard of Jesus?

## Do Science and the Bible Conflict?

Discussion 1: Isn't Christianity Based on Blind Faith?
Discussion 2: Why Are So Few Scientists Christians?
Discussion 3: Doesn't the Big Bang Disprove a Creator?
Discussion 4: Doesn't Evolution Contradict Genesis?
Discussion 5: If the Bible Is True, Why Isn't It More Scientific?
Discussion 6: Won't Scientific Progress Make God Unnecessary?

## Why Become a Christian?

Discussion 1: Why Would Anyone Think I'm Not a Christian?
Discussion 2: What's the Big Deal About Sin?
Discussion 3: Why Can't I Make It On My Own?
Discussion 4: Why Is Jesus So Important?
Discussion 5: Can Someone Like Me Really Change?
Discussion 6: How Does Someone Actually Become a Christian?

# Appendix H

# Sample Response Cards

Jesus: *Up Close and Personal*
**Spiritual Journey Snapshot**

Not really seeking yet. | Open and seeking. | Received Christ today. | New Believer. | Growing Believer.

Yes, contact me with information about taking the next steps in my spiritual journey...

Name _____

Address _____

City _____ State _____ Zip _____

Phone (H) _____( )_____ (W) ( )_____

E-mail _____

Best time to reach me _____

Has this service sparked some tough questions in your mind about spiritual matters? Or are you looking to grow in the basics of your faith as a new Christian? Don't miss these upcoming opportunities to take a next step in your spiritial journey.

## Seeker

### Seeker Small Groups

Investigate a seeker small group where you can discuss answers to spiritual questions along with a few other people who are also seeking. Groups meet at a wide variety of times and locations. Just come one time and check it out! Complete the tear-off card below or just stop by the Welcome Center in the atrium on Saturdays at 5 p.m. or Sundays at 9 a.m.

## New Believers

### New Believer Small Groups

Join a new believer small group where you can more fully experience spiritual growth with others who have similar interests and questions. Groups meet at a wide variety of times and locations. Completer the tear-off card below or call (847) 765-0100 ext. 407 to sign up.

### Yes, I'm interested in finding out more:

❏ Seeker Small Groups
❏ New Believer Small Groups

Name _____

Phone (H) (      ) _____

(W) (      ) _____

email _____

# Appendix I

# Willow Creek Sports Ministry

*+*

## Evangelism Strategy Overview

### The Game

The first step in creating an effective, seeker-oriented sports ministry is to organize everything with excellence. The goal is to pull off the best quality sports league experience possible. That means the facilities and equipment must be well maintained, and the referees, scorekeepers, and volunteers must do their jobs to the very best of their abilities. As a result of this level of excellence, we have waiting lists of people who want to join these sports leagues.

### The Team

Every team captain must be a committed Christian who is totally behind our five-step strategy of reaching seekers. In order to set themselves up to do that, we ask all captains to fill their teams with at least 50 percent non-Christians. Our captains understand that the primary reason the sports ministry exists is so we can use it as a vehicle to reach lost people for Christ. Of course, we hope everyone enjoys the competition, but we want the sports ministry to be about something more than just a game. Without manipulating the situation, the seekers on our teams know they can expect to receive a spiritual component as well as a great sports experience. And our captains view their teams as seeker small groups.

### Bold Challenge

Before every game in every sport, we invite the teams to huddle up, sit down, and listen to one of our key communicators give a five-minute devotional called Bold Challenge. These talks are crafted to be creative, compelling, seeker-friendly interactions with the players. The topics are planned in advance and usually cover sports-related issues with a spiritual focus. For example, we've developed Bold Challenge talks on issues including discipline, winning in life, good character, and good sportsmanship. Usually once during the season, we schedule a "Bold Decision" and invite players to indicate on a response card their decision to cross the line of faith.

The players have expressed tremendous appreciation for this spiritual input before each game. One of the reasons for the success of the Bold Challenges is that the non-Christians in our leagues are treated with very high regard. They, in turn, respect the fact that we are church-affiliated — with a greater purpose.

## First Steps

As you might expect, our sports ministry is very interested in providing seekers with an array of specific next-step opportunities. Listed below are some of the first steps we hope and pray seekers will be open to take in their spiritual journeys.

### Spiritual Conversations

Team captains initiate spiritual conversations with team members, as appropriate. The topics discussed in the Bold Challenges easily spark future ongoing conversations among teammates.

### Weekend Services

Captains utilize the weekend church services as a supplement to their evangelistic efforts. Buzz weekends are always good opportunities for captains to bring their entire teams. For many, this will be their first visit to a service at Willow. Our Bold Challenges also point people to our services.

### Bibles

Captains provide Bibles to anyone who wants them. Our seekers enjoy the special edition Bibles with an emphasis to the athlete — which includes stories from well-known sports figures.

### One Question

Since every team is essentially a seeker small group, the captains use a simple tool to get discussions started. During the Bold Challenge, we distribute a question on a business-sized card and encourage the teams to spend about fifteen minutes after their games talking about it. The question typically relates to the topic of the Bold Challenge. While the teams do not look like typical seeker small groups, here's a summary of what their "meetings" do look like. The teams arrive early to warm up. They sit for a five-minute devotional before their game starts. This Bold Challenge provides spiritual input and next steps such as free Bibles and invitations to weekend services. The teams play their games and hang out afterwards for refreshments and a fifteen-minute discussion sparked by the question given. Captains also meet one-on-one with team members to develop friendships and give individual attention to spiritual interests and questions.

## The Adventure

Our hope is that scores of seekers would cross the line of faith through the sports ministry. Our dream is that we would also celebrate their new life in Christ through baptism services. Our evangelism strategy wouldn't be complete without expressing these goals.

# Notes

## Chapter 1: Catch the Vision
1. Norm Wakefield, *Between the Words* (Grand Rapids: Revell, 2002), 80.

## Chapter 2: Build Strong Bridges
1. Chart from *Becoming a Contagious Christian Participant's Guide* by Mark Mittelberg, Lee Strobel, and Bill Hybels. Copyright © 1995 by the Willow Creek Association. Used by permission of Zondervan.

## Chapter 4: Conduct the All-Important First Meeting
1. Garry Poole, *The Complete Book of Questions* (Grand Rapids: Zondervan, 2003).

## Chapter 5: Ask Great Questions
1. Information found at *users.libero.it/ugo.bais/just1mor.htm* and *www.columbo-site.freeuk.com* (accessed 6 June 2003).
2. Information found at *www.garlikov.com/Soc_Meth.html* (accessed 6 June 2003).
3. Karen Lee-Thorp, *How to Ask Great Questions* (Colorado Springs: NavPress, 1998), 5.
4. Becky Brodin, "Let Me Ask You Something," *Discipleship Journal* (September/October 1997), 28.
5. Robert Fisher, *Quick to Listen, Slow to Speak* (Wheaton, IL: Tyndale, 1987), 20.
6. Lee-Thorp, *How to Ask Great Questions*, 5–6.
7. Ibid., 6–14; *Lead Out* (Colorado Springs: NavPress, 1974), 48–52.
8. Lee-Thorp, *How to Ask Great Questions*, 6–7.
9. A similar example can be found in Russ Korth with Ron Wormser Jr., *Lively Discussions* (San Bernadino, CA: Churches Alive, 1988), 26.
10. Ibid., 30.
11. Similar types of questions are also described in *Lead Out*, 18–26.
12. Lee-Thorp, *How to Ask Great Questions*, 18.
13. Ibid., 26–27.
14. Ibid., 57, 60.

## Chapter 6: Listen Well

1. Stephen Covey, *The Seven Habits of Highly Effective People* (New York: Simon and Schuster, 1989), 237–38.
2. *Lead Out* (Colorado Springs: NavPress, 1974), 49.
3. Covey, *The Seven Habits of Highly Effective People,* 241; Norm Wakefield, *Between the Words* (Grand Rapids: Revell, 2002), 49.
4. Wakefield, *Between the Words,* 73, 75.
5. Robert Fisher, *Quick to Listen, Slow to Speak* (Wheaton, IL: Tyndale, 1987), 32.
6. Karen Lee-Thorp, *How to Ask Great Questions* (Colorado Springs: NavPress, 1998), 47.
7. Wakefield, *Between the Words,* 21.
8. Covey, *The Seven Habits of Highly Effective People,* 240.
9. Ibid., 241.
10. Wakefield, *Between the Words,* 79.
11. Ibid., 80–81.
12. Covey, *The Seven Habits of Highly Effective People,* 243.
13. Ibid., 245.
14. Ibid., 245–51.
15. Ibid., 249.
16. Ibid., 250.
17. Ibid., 251–52, 258.

## Chapter 7: Facilitate Captivating Interactions

1. Em Griffin, *Getting Together* (Downer's Grove, IL: InterVarsity, 1982), 89.
2. Russ Korth with Ron Wormser Jr., *Lively Discussions* (San Bernadino, CA: Churches Alive, 1988), 59.
3. Rick Hove, *Leading a Small Group* (Orlando, FL: WSN Press, 1995), 20.
4. Griffin, *Getting Together,* 89, 102.
5. Karen Lee-Thorp, *How to Ask Great Questions* (Colorado Springs: NavPress, 1998), 50–51.
6. Korth, *Lively Discussions,* 45.
7. Ibid., 46.
8. Griffin, *Getting Together,* 102.
9. Ibid., 101–2.
10. Ibid., 108.
11. Ibid., 109.
12. Ibid., 109–10.

## Chapter 8: Maximize the Impact

1. Lee Strobel, *God's Outrageous Claims* (Grand Rapids: Zondervan, 1997), 70–71.
2. The untitled poem is used with permission of the author.

## Chapter 10: Seize the Adventure

1. James C. Collins, *Built to Last* (New York: HarperCollins, 1994), 43.
2. For more information contact Church Communication Network at 1-800-321-6781 or *www.ccnonline.net.*
3. Written by Chuck Girard. Copyright © 1973 by Dunamis Music. All rights reserved. Used by permission.

## Epilogue

1. Joseph Hart, "Come, Ye Sinners, Poor and Needy," 1759.

# Recommended Resources

Ashton, Mark. Reality Check Series. Grand Rapids: Zondervan, 2002.

Benner, David G. *Care of Souls*. Grand Rapids: Baker, 1998.

Boa, Ken, and Larry Moody. *I'm Glad You Asked*. Colorado Springs: Cook, 1994.

Bunyan, John. *The Pilgrim's Progress*. New York: Signet, 2002.

Carnegie, Dale. *How to Win Friends and Influence People*. New York: Pocket, 1982.

Conway, Jim. *Friendship*. Grand Rapids: Zondervan, 1989.

Cook, Robert A. *Now That I Believe*. Chicago: Moody, 1986.

Covey, Stephen R. *The Seven Habits of Highly Effective People*. New York: Simon and Schuster, 1990.

Engstrom, Ted W., with Robert C. Larson. *The Fine Art of Friendship*. Nashville: Nelson, 1985.

Gempf, Conrad. *Jesus Asked*. Grand Rapids: Zondervan, 2003.

Griffin, Em. *Getting Together*. Downers Grove, IL: InterVarsity, 1983.

_____. *Making Friends (and Making Them Count)*. Downers Grove, IL: InterVarsity, 1987.

_____. *The Mind Changers*. Wheaton, IL: Tyndale, 1980.

*Journey, New International Version, The*. Grand Rapids: Zondervan, 1999.

Knechtle, Cliffe. *Give Me an Answer*. Downers Grove, IL: InterVarsity, 1986.

Korth, Russ, with Ron Wormser Jr. *Lively Discussions!* San Bernardino, CA: Churches Alive, 1988.

Laidlaw, Robert A. *The Reason Why*. South Plainfield, NJ: Bridge, 1994.

Laurie, Greg. *Why Believe*. Wheaton, IL: Tyndale, 2002.

*Lead Out*. Colorado Springs: NavPress, 1974.

Lee-Thorp, Karen. *How to Ask Great Questions*. Colorado Springs: NavPress, 1998.

Lewis, C. S. *Mere Christianity*. New York: HarperCollins, 2001.

Little, Paul. *The Answer to Life*. Westchester, IL: Crossway, 1987.

_____. *How to Give away Your Faith*. Downers Grove, IL: InterVarsity, 1989.

_____. *Know Why You Believe*. Downers Grove, IL: InterVarsity, 2000.

Lucado, Max. *He Did This Just For You*. Nashville: Nelson, 2001.

McBride, Neal F. *How to Have Great Small-Group Meetings*. Colorado Springs: NavPress, 1997.

McDowell, Josh. *Evidence that Demands a Verdict*. Nashville: Nelson, 1990.

_____. *More Than a Carpenter*. Wheaton, IL: Tyndale, 1987.

Mittelberg, Mark, Lee Strobel, and Bill Hybels. *Becoming a Contagious Christian Course*. Grand Rapids: Zondervan, 1995.

Moreland, J. P. *Scaling the Secular City*. Grand Rapids: Baker, 1987.

Munger, Robert. *My Heart—Christ's Home*. Downers Grove, IL: InterVarsity, 1992.

*New Believer's Bible New Testament*. Wheaton, IL: Tyndale, 1996.

Phillips, Christopher. *Socrates Café*. New York: Norton, 2002.

Poole, Garry. *The Complete Book of Questions*. Grand Rapids: Zondervan, 2003.

_____. *The Three Habits of Highly Contagious Christians*. Grand Rapids: Zondervan, 2003.

Poole, Garry, and Judson Poling. Tough Questions Series. Grand Rapids: Zondervan, 2003.

Ridenour, Fritz. *So What's the Difference*. Ventura, CA: Regal, 1979.

*Seeker's Bible, New Testament, The*. Wheaton, IL: Tyndale, 2000.

Strobel, Lee. *The Case for Christ*. Grand Rapids: Zondervan, 1998.

_____. *The Case for Faith*. Grand Rapids: Zondervan, 2000.

Wakefield, Norm. *Between the Words*. Grand Rapids: Revell, 2002.

# Acknowledgments

*I thank my God every time I remember you.*
PHILIPPIANS 1:3

This book was truly a collaborative venture—one that drew on the talents and wisdom of an unforgettable group of colleagues. I owe a huge debt of gratitude to these close friends and associates, whose insight and support served as a constant source of encouragement.

First of all, Bill Hybels, Lee Strobel, and Mark Mittelberg took a risk more than a decade ago, when they invited me to launch seeker small groups at Willow Creek Community Church. These dynamic mentors continue to open doors of opportunity that foster creativity and nurture growth; in fact, it was their persistent challenges to put all that I know about seeker groups into a book that got this project underway.

With that vision firmly in mind, I connected with the Willow Creek Association, where Jim Mellado, Joe Sherman, and Christine Anderson never failed to offer enthusiasm and wise council throughout the ongoing development of Seeker Small Groups. Along the way, John Ortberg, Doug Veenstra, Dr. Gilbert Bilezikian, Dr. Neil Wilkey, David Staal, Mike Bogue, Laura Allen, and Jim Poole offered encouragement and inspiration. Laura and Jim were especially instrumental in suggesting fresh ideas and clarity of thought on the best ways to organize and communicate this material. In addition, Judy Keene, Cara Chandler, and Ann Kroeker greatly assisted me with writing and editing, investing countless hours refining and shaping the various drafts of the manuscript—and I am indebted to them for their outstanding contributions.

Led by Evangelism Ministry volunteers fully engaged in the process of making seeker groups a reality, the people of Willow Creek Community Church enthusiastically embraced the concept of reaching seekers through small groups. And our world-class Evangelism Ministry staff provided gifted leadership to bring it all together. I cannot imagine a more dedicated team than Mark Ashton, John Angle, Len VandenBos, Kristy Rutter, Carla Potter, Kim Johnson, Peggy Kress, David Worley, and Scott Vaudrey. Peggy deserves special mention, as she handled myriad administrative details for this project with the greatest of ease.

Thanks also to everyone at Zondervan, including Jack Kuhatschek, John Raymond, Angela Scheff, Alicia Mey, and Rob Monacelli, who generously contributed their extraordinary talents. Angela's careful attention to detail and dedication to excellence was inspiring—and this book is better for it.

A special thanks goes to all those who generously gave me permission to use their real-life stories along with their real-life names. They openly shared their accounts of life-change with the hope that their experiences would inspire many others to discover the outreach potential inherent in seeker small groups. And I'm particularly grateful to all the spiritual seekers who have participated in seeker small groups over the years. They are our "glory and joy" (1 Thessalonians 2:20).

Words cannot fully express my appreciation for the immeasurable value of all the individuals and teams who supported this endeavor in prayer. And my sincere thanks to everyone who joined forces with me to accomplish something I could never have done alone. Through our collective efforts, may this book become "a fragrant offering, an acceptable sacrifice, pleasing to God" (Philippians 4:18).

*Garry Poole*
*July 1, 2003*
*South Barrington, Illinois*

We want to hear from you. Have you had a seeker small group adventure? Tell us about it. Please send your stories of life-change to seekergroups@seekerministries.org.

## Other Resources by Garry Poole

*The Complete Book of Questions*
*The Three Habits of Highly Contagious Christians*
*Experiencing the Passion of Jesus*
*Faith Under Fire*

### In the Tough Questions Series:

*Don't All Religions Lead to God?*
*How Could God Allow Suffering and Evil?*
*How Does Anyone Know God Exists?*
*Why Become a Christian?*
*Tough Questions Leader's Guide* (with Judson Poling)
*Is Jesus the Only Way?*
*Do Science and the Bible Conflict?*
*What Difference Does Jesus Make?*
*How Reliable Is the Bible?*

# Willow Creek Association
*Vision, Training, Resources for Prevailing Churches*

This resource was created to serve you and to help you in building a local church that prevails!

Since 1992, the Willow Creek Association (WCA) has been linking like-minded, action-oriented churches with each other and with strategic vision, training, and resources. Now a worldwide network of over 6,400 churches from more than ninety denominations, the WCA works to equip Member Churches and others with the tools needed to build prevailing churches. Our desire is to inspire, equip, and encourage Christian leaders to build biblically functioning churches that reach increasing numbers of unchurched people, not just with innovations from Willow Creek Community Church in South Barrington, Illinois, but from any church in the world that has experienced God-given breakthroughs.

### WILLOW CREEK CONFERENCES

Each year, thousands of local church leaders, staff and volunteers—from WCA Member Churches and others—attend one of our conferences or training events. Conferences offered on the Willow Creek campus in South Barrington, Illinois, include:

**Prevailing Church Conference:** Foundational training for staff and volunteers working to build a prevailing local church.

**Prevailing Church Workshops:** More than fifty strategic, day-long workshops covering seven topic areas that represent key characteristics of a prevailing church; offered twice each year.

**Promiseland Conference:** Children's ministries; infant through fifth grade.

**Student Ministries Conference:** Junior and senior high ministries.

**Willow Creek Arts Conference:** Vision and training for Christian artists using their gifts in the ministries of local churches.

**Leadership Summit:** Envisioning and equipping Christians with leadership gifts and responsibilities; broadcast live via satellite to eighteen cities across North America.

**Contagious Evangelism Conference:** Encouragement and training for churches and church leaders who want to be strategic in reaching lost people for Christ.

**Small Groups Conference:** Exploring how developing a church *of* small groups can play a vital role in developing authentic Christian community that leads to spiritual transformation.

### PREVAILING CHURCH REGIONAL WORKSHOPS

Each year the WCA team leads several, two-day training events in select cities across the United States. Some twenty day-long workshops are offered in topic areas including leadership, next-generation ministries, small groups, arts and worship, evangelism, spiritual gifts, financial stewardship, and spiritual formation. These events make quality training more accessible and affordable to larger groups of staff and volunteers.

To find out more about Prevailing Church Regional Workshops, visit our website at www.willowcreek.com.

### WILLOW CREEK RESOURCES™

Churches can look to Willow Creek Resources™ for a trusted channel of ministry tools in areas of leadership, evangelism, spiritual gifts, small groups, drama, contemporary music, financial stewardship, spiritual transformation, and more. For ordering information, call (800) 570-9812 or visit our website at www.willowcreek.com.

### WCA MEMBERSHIP

Membership in the Willow Creek Association as well as attendance at WCA Conferences is for churches, ministries, and leaders who hold to a historic, orthodox understanding of biblical Christianity. The annual church membership fee of $249 provides substantial discounts for your entire team on all conferences and Willow Creek Resources, networking opportunities with other outreach-oriented churches, a bimonthly newsletter, a subscription to the *Defining Moments* monthly audio journal for leaders, and more.

**Willow Creek Association**
P.O. Box 3188, Barrington, IL 60011-3188
Phone: (800) 570-9812 or (847) 765-0070
Fax: (888) 922-0035 or (847) 765-5046
Web: www.willowcreek.com